CRITICAL SOCIAL THEORY AND THE
END OF WORK

Rethinking Classical Sociology

Series Editor: David Chalcraft, University of Derby, UK

This series is designed to capture, reflect and promote the major changes that are occurring in the burgeoning field of classical sociology. The series publishes monographs, texts and reference volumes that critically engage with the established figures in classical sociology as well as encouraging examination of thinkers and texts from within the ever-widening canon of classical sociology. Engagement derives from theoretical and substantive advances within sociology and involves critical dialogue between contemporary and classical positions. The series reflects new interests and concerns including feminist perspectives, linguistic and cultural turns, the history of the discipline, the biographical and cultural milieux of texts, authors and interpreters, and the interfaces between the sociological imagination and other discourses including science, anthropology, history, theology and literature.

The series offers fresh readings and insights that will ensure the continued relevance of the classical sociological imagination in contemporary work and maintain the highest standards of scholarship and enquiry in this developing area of research.

Also in the series:

Ritual and the Sacred
A Neo-Durkheimian Analysis of Politics, Religion and the Self
Massimo Rosati
ISBN 978-0-7546-7640-9

For Durkheim
Essays in Historical and Cultural Sociology
Edward A. Tiryakian
ISBN 978-0-7546-7155-8

Max Weber Matters
Interweaving Past and Present
Edited by David Chalcraft, Fanon Howell, Marisol Lopez Menendez and
Hector Vera
ISBN 978-0-7546-7340-8

For more information on this series, please visit www.ashgate.com

Critical Social Theory and the End of Work

EDWARD GRANTER
Manchester Business School, University of Manchester, UK

ASHGATE

Published by
Ashgate Publishing Limited
Wey Court East
Union Road
Farnham
Surrey, GU9 7PT
England

Ashgate Publishing Company
Suite 420
101 Cherry Street
Burlington
VT 05401-4405
USA

www.ashgate.com

British Library Cataloguing in Publication Data
Granter, Edward.
   Critical social theory and the end of work. -- (Rethinking
   classical sociology)
   1. Work--Philosophy. 2. Technological unemployment.
   3. Employees--Effect of technological innovations on.
   4. Critical theory.
   I. Title II. Series
   306.3'6-dc22

Library of Congress Cataloging-in-Publication Data
Granter, Edward.
   Critical social theory and the end of work / by Edward Granter.
      p. cm. -- (Rethinking classical sociology)
   Includes bibliographical references and index.
   ISBN 978-0-7546-7697-3 (hardcover) -- ISBN 978-0-7546-9397-0
(ebook) 1. Automation--Social aspects. 2. Work--Social aspects. 3. Critical theory. I.
Title.
   HD6331.G79 2009
   306.3'6--dc22

2009017553

ISBN 9780754676973 (hbk)
ISBN 9780754693970 (ebk)

Mixed Sources
Product group from well-managed forests and other controlled sources
www.fsc.org Cert no. SA-COC-1565
© 1996 Forest Stewardship Council
FSC

Printed and bound in Great Britain by
MPG Books Group, UK

Contents

Acknowledgements

This book was written with the financial support of a Graduate Teaching Assistantship in the School of English, Sociology, Politics and Contemporary History at the University of Salford. I wish to thank the School and University for this provision. Sincere thanks go to those who supervised and advised on my PhD thesis, Stephen Edgell, Graeme Gilloch and Greg Smith, all of whom have been enthusiastic in their support and guidance. Their generous, thoughtful and unstintingly constructive advice has proved invaluable. I should also like to thank Paul Bellaby and Rob Flynn for their comments on the thesis as part of the Interim Assessment and the Internal Evaluation. Rob has also provided supportive mentorship during my academic career at Salford. Peter Bratsis facilitated an Interview with Stanley Aronowitz, for which I am grateful to them both. My family and my partner Jill deserve thanks for supporting me though the course of the PhD. I have been surprised how many friends have been interested in discussing the end of work.

Any deficiencies, and all views expressed, are solely the responsibility of the author.

Note

A version of Chapter 6 first appeared as 'A dream of ease: Situating the future of work and leisure' in *Futures* 40 (9) November 2008, pp. 803–811.

To my parents

Chapter 1

Introduction:
Critical Social Theory and the End of Work

Of his book *Utopia and Anti-Utopia in Modern Times*, Krishan kumar wrote: 'This is a book about books' (Kumar 1987: vii). It seems appropriate to begin with a quote from Krishan Kumar, since his work (Kumar 1978, 1987, 1988, 1997) has been something of an influence on this book, particularly in terms of approach, or, perhaps, methodology.

In fact this is a book about ideas – focused around one particular idea – just as Kumar's analytical surveys of social theory, social change, and utopian thinking are studies of ideas. It is frequently necessary, in the context of professional sociology in twenty first century Britain, to attempt to define one's methodology, but with a book such as the present one, this is rather difficult, since it operates largely in the realm of discourse, rather than empirical investigation. There is no immediately obvious reference point, no methodological template. However, by situating theories of the end of work (which we will see are more often than not critical social theories) in the context of historical, social and cultural change, and in relation to developments in social theory, I aim to evaluate their usefulness for social analysis. In this sense, this book situates itself within critical social theory in terms of approach. By looking at the effectiveness of various permutations of the end of work thesis, we will hopefully gain some useful insights about the way capitalist society, its structures, its antagonisms and injustices, and the ideological underpinnings that support it, operate. To clarify the aims of this book further, let us explain what we mean by Critical Theory and critical social theory, before outlining what is meant by the phrase 'the end of work'.

Critical Theory

The term Critical Theory is used to refer to the work of the Institute for Social Research, better known as the Frankfurt School, a group of mostly Jewish, Marxist intellectuals who left Germany for the USA following the rise of Nazism. This group included theorists such as Theodor Adorno, Max Horkheimer, Leo Lowenthal and Herbert Marcuse. Because the latter wrote most extensively and explicitly on the end of work, it is on him that our most extended analysis of one of the original Critical Theorists will focus, in Chapter 5.

Unlike positivist sociology, Critical Theory rejects the separation of facts and values, and sets out to analyse society 'from the standpoint of its emancipatory transformation' (Benhabib 1986: 2). As we shall see in our forthcoming encounter with Marcuse, Critical Theory observes that emancipatory transformation is necessary, since current society fails to satisfy the true needs of civilised individuals. Not only that, but it fails even to create civilised societies, with even the most advanced nations riven with economic injustice, alienation and violence.

Critical Theory is known for its commitment to reason, even as it is often seen as critiquing the increasingly instrumental rationality dominant in modernity. In the period when postmodernism was fashionable in sociological circles, it was common to question the very foundation of reason, and even now, statements in mainstream sociology remain tentative. Who can say what is rational and what is not, and should one section of society (the intelligentsia) propose to pass judgement for the whole? Sociologists, after all, are not philosopher kings. The Critical Theorists of the Frankfurt School were in fact steeped in the philosophical tradition, both ancient, Kantian, and Hegelian, and had no compunction about making statements about what is rational and what is not. It is possible that having narrowly escaped death in the Holocaust, and having observed fascism at first hand, the Critical Theorists had an acute sense of the irrational, since in many senses fascism demonstrated the triumph of irrationality, whilst functioning in an apparently formally rational manner. Such contradictions are at the centre of Critical Theory. Irrationality, however, inheres in modern industrial society more generally, and particularly in capitalism, of which fascism is one formation. Life in the modern democracies is equally irrational. It is irrational for individuals, and indeed nations, to annihilate each other, as they continue to do. It is irrational to condemn, structurally, whole sectors of populations to poverty, toil, unhappiness and servitude, as continues to be the case.

What is most irrational, from the standpoint of Critical Theory, is that this state of affairs is objectively avoidable. A community of free human beings, according to Critical Theory, 'is possible through technical means already at hand' (Horkheimer 1972: 217). Although we noted that only Marcuse provides an analysis that makes the end of work an explicitly extended theme, other Critical Theorists have a sense that needless toil is part of the system of domination under advanced capitalism, and therefore should be abolished. The contemporary organisation of work, for Adorno and others, should be transformed not only because it is at the centre of a particularly pathological organisation of society, but because it mutilates the individuality of identity that bourgeois society purports to value (Sünker 2007: 135). Work, for the Critical Theorists, has an individual as well as a social or economic element, and the capitalist division of labour limits the development of true individuality.

That the technical means exist for work to be abolished is one of the more obvious irrational features of advanced capitalism, according to Critical Theory. Marx had suggested that the abolition of capitalist labour as we know it was within reach many years earlier. Herein lies the essence of the analytical usefulness of Critical Theory, and its suitability for looking at the end of work: Critical Theory does not simply diagnose social injustices and irrationalities, it seeks to account for their perpetuation by proposing that capitalist (that is, all modern) societies hide their own potential from themselves, in order for the current system of economic and social domination to be perpetuated. This theory is not particularly new, of course. Marx provided an analysis that highlighted the fetishisation of commodities; that is, the tendency for impersonal economic and social structures and processes to appear to take on a life of their own. At the heart of theories that prioritise the end of work, is a conviction that people should decide for themselves how to work, produce, and live, and that there is no objective necessity for present conditions to endure.

It is clear that Critical Theory is situated in the Marxist tradition. It is equally clear, however, that Critical Theory is an attempt to adapt Marx's insights in the face of profound social and economic change. In his 1937 essay 'Traditional and Critical Theory', for example, Horkheimer pointed out that 'even the situation of the proletariat is, in this society, no guarantee of correct knowledge' (Horkheimer 1972: 213), and Marcuse saw the role of the working class as historical subject as having changed, something that will be discussed in Chapter 5. The fact that, as we shall see, the central dynamic of the end of work is set out by Marx himself, makes the task of adapting Marxism to changing socioeconomic conditions more feasible, and indeed relevant, if not necessarily easy. Not only in the case of Marxism, but more generally, Critical Theory is particularly sensitive to historical change. This makes it appropriate for analysing theories of the end of work, since these theories are intrinsically linked with change – the idea of the end of work often appears as bound up with theories about social development.

Returning to the idea of the perpetuation of domination by impersonal structures; Critical Theory seeks to identify and penetrate the ideologies that cloak this domination. Thus, Critical Theory is ideology critique. This makes it particularly useful for looking at theories of the end of work, since the ideology of work is one of the prime factors preventing its transformation or abolition. We shall see that far from evaporating in the white heat of postindustrialism, this ideology persists, and is ably assisted by the ideology of consumerism. That the theorists of the Frankfurt School were at the forefront of critical analyses of emerging consumer society further reinforces the impression of suitability of this set of theories for understanding the idea of the end of work.

Critical Theory is useful as a way of looking at the end of work because it is totalising theory. That is, it seeks to conduct social critique from the standpoint of an analysis of the social whole, including history, culture, and, as already noted, consciousness, often in the sense of false consciousness, or ideology. I think that exploring the idea of the end of work lends itself particularly well to totalising social theory because the subject of work does not only exist in the realm of economics, but extends into politics also. Work is a topic the exploration of which must also necessarily draw in existential, ontological and, indeed, quotidian concerns. As Adorno says, 'free time depends on the totality of societal conditions' (Adorno 1998: 167). Free time and work are, of course, if not dialectically, then certainly inextricably, interrelated. If we say that one of our aims is understanding the end of work in itself, as an idea referring to a dynamic of social change, in doing so we are forced to consider political, cultural, and ontological questions. Critical Theory (as we will see in Chapter 8) reminds us of the interconnectedness of society, and as such, should lend itself well to an analysis of work. At some point of course, we make a choice to embark on totalising social analysis. The history of Critical Theory shows us that this choice is not without methodological grounding in the sociological tradition.

Critical Theory is theory that attempts to be self aware. It should be pointed out that Critical Theory serves here not just as a methodology or approach, but is itself part of the subject matter of the book. This is not merely a result of the fact that the end of work is discussed within Critical Theory itself, making Critical Theory an object as well as subject, but that to some limited extent, this book will hopefully make a contribution to furthering our understanding of Critical Theory in the contemporary world. I hope to use the end of work as a way of highlighting the continued usefulness of Critical Theory, and in fact, critical social theory more widely – usefulness in the sense of understanding a social world that despite previously undreamt of technological and material advances, systematically fails to rise above barbarism and unhappiness at both a national an international level.

Critical Theory and critical social theory

Maeve Cook suggests that '[c]ritical social theory is a mode of reflection that looks critically at processes of social development from the point of view of the obstacles they pose for human flourishing' (Cook 2004: 418). Agger applies a 7 point definition of critical social theory:

1. CST [critical social theory] opposes positivism…
2. CST distinguishes between the past and present, largely characterized by domination, exploitation, and oppression, and a possible future rid of these phenomena…
3. CST argues that domination is structural…[and 4.] structures of domination are reproduced through people's false consciousness…
5. CST argues that social change begins at home, in people's everyday lives – sexuality, family roles, workplace…
6. Following Marx in this sense, CST conceptualizes the bridge between structure and agency as dialectical…
7. By connecting everyday life and large – scale social structures, CST opposes the notion that eventual progress [can only be achieved by] sacrificing people's liberties and even lives (Agger 1998: 4–5).

Clearly, critical social theory (without capitals) encompasses Critical Theory. It should be understood that while Critical Theory is a more specific term, referring to a particular group of writers – a wider range of work, encompassing a wider range of figures, can be considered critical social theory. It is the case, I believe, that theories of the end of work can be used by theorists as a keystone of critical social theory that offers insights into the development, and indeed future, of capitalist society.

One of the best known critical social theorists is, of course, Karl Marx. While much critical social theory draws inspiration from Marxism, this is not always the case. Indeed, in Chapter 3 we will examine utopian visions of a world without work, some of which were in fact constructed before Marx came to prominence. In Chapter 6, we will look at a range of theories on the future of work, many of which, like Critical Theory or Marxism, are based on the idea that social life – the economy, the polity, the individual's working life – are connected. Like Critical Theory also, some non Marxist writers on the future/end of work seek to criticise the current society from the perspective of possibility, of what could be. Similarly, many social theories focus on social change, and these dominate the discussion in Chapter 6, since it is the case that social change and changes in the sphere of work are intrinsically linked.

In Chapter 7, we examine the contribution of André Gorz, whose epistemological position illustrates the links between Critical Theory and critical social theory. As we shall see, Gorz, while not one of the Critical Theorists, develops a form of critical social theory that has, more than any other theorist, perhaps, the idea of the end of work at its centre.

The meaning of the end of work

Some readers will already have noted that *The End of Work* is used as the title for Jeremy Rifkin's 1994 book. It should be obvious that in using this phrase I am not referring to this book specifically, except when explicitly stated (such as in Chapter 6). I have attempted to think of another phrase, in order to avoid this titular clash with Rifkin, but to do so would be rather contrived. The phrase 'abolition of work', among others, is sometimes used as an alternative, as appropriate. However, the end of work is the term that most accurately sums up the various analyses that we will explore.

The end of work appears to be a fairly straightforward idea, and in some ways it is. In its essential meaning, the end of work refers to the fact that advances in production technology (automation), are increasingly eliminating the necessity for human work, and will eventually eradicate the need for human labour altogether (I am using the terms work and labour interchangeably here – see Chapter 2 for a discussion of this). Consideration of the various subtleties in the meaning(s) of the end of work will be carried out throughout the book, as one would expect. It is sufficient here to suggest that the essential definition is complicated by variations in the way work is conceptualised, and the way need (necessity) is understood also. This means that the idea of work 'ending' is somewhat more complicated that we might at first imagine. However, when one gives the matter some further consideration, it is unlikely that any social thinker would seriously propose that work, or human effort, would cease altogether. The end of work then, must be taken by the reader at this stage as a term into which many different understandings of work, technology, and humanity, are packed. The unpacking of these meanings will be part of the forward movement of this book.

Work

So far we have talked about critical social theory, the end of work, but not work. At the heart of this book, of course, is a belief that work is important. The belief in productivity or creativity as the essence of human beings can be traced back to Marx in its most explicit conception. To some extent, the value for social critique or advances in understandings of the social world (including the world of ideas and discourse) of the end of work approach depends on the extent to which one sees human productive, or creative activity, as the essence of what it means to be human, or perhaps, the 'key sociological category'. This is a question that we will deal with throughout the book.

Catherine Casey, in her book *Work, Self and Society*, sought to '[bring] critical theory back to work...' (Casey 1995: 6). Casey also seeks to return the social to critical theory, that is, to show that critical social theory can be used not only to analyse developments in the cultural sphere, but in the sphere of production and purposeful creative action. Again in common with Casey's standpoint, the present book seeks to make some small contribution against the tendency for social theory to shy away from the world of work. Casey asserts that: 'What people produce and consume, and the social relations engendered by that production, remain at the present time primary constituent elements in defining the social and cultural relations of postindustrial societies as we currently observe them' (Casey 1995: 25).

This book is an attempt to show that sociology can engage with work in a theoretical way which is totalising, and sometimes philosophical. Hopefully, the book will be sociological. Even when discussing theoretical or philosophical ideas, I hope to retain a sense of connection with actually existing society. To that end observations are made throughout the book that are based on reports, sociological investigations, and official statistics, plus literature and art. While this may not be empirical in the classic or conventional sense, I have, to repeat, attempted to maintain a commitment to social reality. In this sense the book shares much with the work not only of established figures such as Krishan Kumar or Paul Ransome (1996, 1999, 2005), but also more recent entrants onto the sociological scene such as Ernesto R. Gantman, whose 2005 book *Capitalism, Social Privilege and Managerial Ideologies* shares many characteristics, in terms of approach, with the current work.

Scope of the book

Every book has a specific scope, and in one such as this, there are going to be some omissions. I have attempted to provide a fairly comprehensive, although not exhaustive, critical survey and analysis of theories of the end of work. I have even included, if only briefly, some fairly obscure literature, such as the writings on the 'revolt against work' in Chapter 6. I have omitted extended discussions of pieces such as Lafargue's *The Right to Be Lazy* (Lafargue 1883) or Bertrand Russell's *In Praise of Idlene*ss (Russell 1932), although the former is mentioned briefly in Chapter 2. These pieces are omitted from extended discussion for the same reason as I have excluded commentary on the literary journal *The Idler*, and the book *How to Be Idle* (Hodgkinson 2004), by that journal's editor. While pieces such as these are interesting, I have made a judgement on the threshold of seriousness and engagement with sociological ideas that writers must reach in order to be discussed. The same threshold was applied to Bob Black's work (Black 1996).

Some readers may also be surprised that there is no extended discussion of unemployment. I do discuss unemployment, particularly in the latter part of the book. However, unemployment and the end of work are two quite different things. Unemployment is a (usually) temporary state within the context of a conventional labour market. The end of work is a long term tendency which has the potential to undermine the existence of this labour market, and, as we shall see, the capitalist system as a whole. The issue of unemployment in relation to globalisation is covered in Chapter 10, but as we shall see, the relationship between unemployment and the end of work remains far from straightforward.

Outline of the chapters

At the start of this introduction, I suggested that Kumar was an influence on the methodology of this book. I attempted to show how Critical Theory was influential also. I then suggested that, in fact, the present work seeks to explore and assess theories of the end of work from the standpoint of critical social theory, rather than Critical Theory, as more narrowly defined. As such, I have chosen to follow the evolution of the end of work historically, and across different intellectual contexts, just as Kumar explored and surveyed the way ideas about industrial, postindustrial and postmodern ideas evolved, and assessed their usefulness in the context of social theory.

In Chapter 2 I trace the historical development of work. This development is understood in the sense of both work as social practice, concept, and work as an ideology. This Chapter demonstrates that modern conceptions of work developed under certain social and ideological pressures, and as social constructs, practices and understandings of work (that is, the social position of work) is open to contestation and change. Chapter 3 looks at the way utopian thinkers often made the end of work part of their vision for a better future. We see in Chapter 3 many of the underlying dynamics of end of work discourse starting to develop, such as the relationship between needs, consumption and necessary work. Chapter 4 seeks to show how Marx further developed the idea of the end of work, or at least, work as understood under capitalism. Chapter 4 introduces some of the ideas, such as creative work activity as the basis of human identity, that will be important to subsequent discussions in later chapters. Chapter 5 introduces Marcuse, and attempts to place the end of work at the centre of his analysis, and show how he successfully adapted the insights of Marx to changing social conditions – and how thinking about the end of work helped facilitate this. Chapter 6 moves away from explicitly Marxist analyses to show how a broad range of commentators have incorporated thinking about the future of work into their theories about the future of human society more widely. In Chapter 6 we also begin to look more closely at the distinct lack of progress in terms of the actual reduction of working hours, let alone the end of work. Chapter 7 moves the focus back onto explicitly critical theories, and indeed, theories heavily influenced by Marx. We consider the contribution of Gorz, and compare his analysis of the relationships between technology, social change, and work, with those of earlier writers such as Marx, as well as contemporaries such as Negri and Marcuse. Continuing our focus on the way social theory mediates between changes in the social world and changes in theory itself, Chapter 8 enters the debate on whether or not work can still be considered a key sociological category, or whether we should look instead to the world of consumption for the essence of social life in late modernity. The contributions of theorists such as Offe and Habermas are also considered. In Chapter 9 we discuss the theoretical relevance of the end of work to theories to the concept of globalisation, arguing that although some sectors of the Western workforce are effected by globalisation in terms of unemployment, it is far from the case that the export of manufacturing to the developing world means the end of work in the advanced societies. The conclusion will return to some of the aims set out in this introduction, and will discuss whether or not we are right to consider theories of the end of work as a promising and insightful line of analysis within modern critical social theory.

Chapter 2

The Beginning of the End of Work

Introduction

The aim of this book as a whole is to examine the relationships between social theories, ideologies, and historical developments which have given rise to the idea that work is disappearing. The purpose of the present chapter is not necessarily to explore the historical trajectory by which we have arrived at the notion of the end of work, it is an attempt to survey the shaping of the modern idea of work itself. As we shall see, our present understanding of work[1] as an activity taking place within a specific socioeconomic and cultural setting, and to which particular ideological significance is attached, is not immemorial. Rather, it has been undergoing a process of change, evolution perhaps, since the first human societies. It is the latest stage in this evolution, the supposed end of work that is the concern of the book as a whole. It seems sensible then, to give some account of the beginning and development of work.

Definitions of work

Attempts to define work appear with disconcerting frequency in discussions both of the historical origins of contemporary concepts of work, and on the possibility of its abolition in supposedly postindustrial society. Since unearthing the former is our immediate concern, and understanding the latter our ultimate, it seems that some attempt should be made here to define what we mean by work. A basic definition of work might be 'picking something up and putting it down somewhere else because you have to' (Theriault 1995: 16). This definition is basic indeed, and as is the case with most others, fails on two fronts. Firstly, the activity it describes may in some cases not be considered work; caring for children may involve compulsory picking up and putting down, but is not usually perceived as work as such. The same might apply to shopping for food. These two examples, it is recognised, are open to debate. The activities of reproduction are considered by some to be essentially *pro*duction, i.e. work under capitalism (see for example Anonymous 2005: 20). Secondly, there are forms of activity that are conventionally understood as work, but do not fit with the above definition. Some work involves little or no physical activity, and we tend to call this intellectual work or mental labour. The

---

1 'Our' in this case can be understood as those who's cultures are shaped within a well established advanced industrial society.

status of some intellectual work, for example developing marketing strategy or doing sociological research, may be questioned in terms of its usefulness, but it is considered, formally, work when carried out for remuneration.

Another conventional view (at least in the discourses of anthropology and sociology) sees work as some kind of interaction with nature, a primal engagement through which we 'extract from nature the means of our existence' (Godelier 1980: 167). Once again it fails to satisfy. This definition seems archaic, conjuring up images of farmers, miners, craftspeople and perhaps manufacturers, but excluding once again brainworkers; intellectuals, artists, politicians, administrators etc. However, if we minimise the emphasis on 'extraction' and maximise 'interaction' with nature, we can extend this definition to cover interpersonal work, or indeed any form of activity. This is only possible, however, if we also extend the concept of nature to include everything in existence, including human society. This begs the following question;

> if by work we embrace all social activities that are in some way transformative of nature, do we end up with a set of activities too broad to be of any value; if everything is work can anything be leisure or rest? (Grint 1991: 8).

Using this definition, we might classify gardening, fly fishing or car modification as work, likewise discussing an emotional problem with a friend.

One influential commentator who used the idea of humanity transforming nature in their definition of work was Hannah Arendt. In fact, it was a distinction in the character of the product of human interaction with nature that led Arendt to distinguish in turn between work and labour. Arendt argued that the synonymous usage of the two terms masks a crucial distinction. While labour produces objects needed for the maintenance of life, which are consumed almost immediately, work produces artefacts of much greater duration that can serve as the social and cultural fabric of the human world. Cathedrals, literature, art, museums, schools, books, computer systems, these are the phenomena that make the inner, intangible world of what it is to be human, tangible; they are the product of work. Raiment and food, these are the fruits of labour, part of the human life cycle of growth and decay. Labour is portrayed in Arendt as essentially non productive. For Arendt, economic theories that privilege labour as the defining human attribute, and as the source for all value, are missing the point, and operating under a misguided productivist economic rationality. In fact, writers such as Marx and Locke, whom Arendt criticises, merely chose not to make the same idiosyncratic (and rather tenuous) semantic distinction as Arendt. There is some attempt by Arendt to draw on ancient Greek distinctions between ponein (labour) and ergazesthai (work) to explain her position, yet she simultaneously admits that 'labour and work are already treated as identical' in ancient Greece (Arendt 1958: 80). To see work and labour as distinct is an interesting conceit, but on what evidence does it rest? Is there really any useful distinction between 'the labour of our bodies' and the 'work of our hands'? It is certainly difficult, in modern society particularly, to differentiate between that which is produced for immediate consumption, and that which will form part of the objective world of humanity.

Arendt's concluding argument in *The Human Condition*, that we live in a world based on the increasingly meaningless consumption of the output of mass production, under the aegis of an ideology of capitalist expansion, is persuasive, as is her concomitant assertion that it is the ideology of *homo laborans* that is now dominant. However, it is possible to see behind Arendt's arguments specifically on the distinction between work and labour, a more prosaic divide, that between skilled and unskilled labour, the labour of the crafts-worker or the intellectual, and the manual worker.

Amidst all this confusion, Grint (1991: 8) attempts to explain (ambitiously, since most commentators simply accept) the fact that definitions of work usually fail to be sufficiently exclusive or inclusive, by referring to the indexical nature of language. That is, meanings of work do not inhere in the act itself, but are created through competing discourses. This means that whether an activity is defined as work will depend both upon the discursive understandings of those involved in the activity, and the wider universe of discourse. Thus unpaid domestic tasks, for example, may be seen as work by the individual carrying them out, as well as the commentator, if both are viewing the situation from a specific position within Marxist feminism (Anonymous 2005: 20). This argument has only limited validity in terms of definition of work within a particular culture, since it undermines the possibility of lucid social analysis by appealing to a high level of relativism. Social science, like all rational thought, rests on the possibility of attaching meanings to words within a particular society with a least some level of fixity, although this need not exclude discussion of exceptions to the rule.

Grint's analysis makes more sense in terms of differences in the understanding of the concept of work between spatial and temporal settings. Indeed, the present chapter will attempt to show how the meaning of work changes over time, and between societies. There is one sense in which Grint's argument holds true even in terms of contemporary Western definitions. The defining factor in what is and is not viewed as work in our contemporary society can be seen as the discourse of economics and economic rationality. As Gorz points out; '"Work" nowadays refers almost exclusively to activities carried out for a wage' (Gorz 1982: 1). For example; 'A market gardener "works"; a miner growing leeks in his back garden carries out a freely chosen activity' (Gorz 1982: 1). This seems to be the prevailing understanding in our society. This prevalence derives from the fact that the discourse of economics is not simply another competing discourse, but is itself dominant; it is the discourse through which human society is understood. Of course, that this is not the case in all societies, and at all points in history, is something that the present chapter will explore.

Work in nonindustrial society

Before discussing the historical origins of the modern idea of work in the capitalistically developed West, we will first examine the nature of work in what were previously called primitive, or what Godelier (1980: 167) more accurately calls pre-capitalist societies. As early as the seventeenth century, Western commentators noted differences in the cultural position of work. The following is a particularly colourful, perhaps even rather dubious, example:

> How vain the opinion is of some certain people in the East Indies, who think that apes and baboons, which are with them in great numbers, are indued with understanding, and that they can speak but will not, for fear they should be imployed and set to work (Antoine Le Grand 1694, in Thomas 1999: 5).

Of course, only a very few societies nowadays can be categorised as pre-capitalist, as even the most isolated peoples usually have some contact with the modern world of the market, coming increasingly into its orbit, often with fairly tragic consequences. Further anthropological research on the matter would be needed to comment authoritatively, but we might wonder whether there is a link between the degree of difference in traditional conceptions of work held in pre-capitalist and capitalist cultures, and the economic and social difficulties which indigenous groups often face.[2]

In his seminal article 'Work and its Representations: A Research Proposal', Godelier examines the different contexts in which work acquires its meaning. The key issue here is the wider socioeconomic context in which work takes place, as the terms capitalist and pre-capitalist suggest. Work in pre-capitalist societies does not have the abstract economic status that it does in the West. Rather than being work in general, something which can be commodified, bought, sold, and alienated, work is imbedded in familial, clan and tribal interpersonal relations; 'there are no units of production organized as separate entities distinct from the social groups, kinship system, or extended or nuclear families which make up the local group' (Godelier 1980: 167).

Certainly even 'primitive' societies must have some means of wresting the material necessary for survival from nature, so activities oriented towards this goal do take place. From this perspective then, we can say that work is carried out in pre-capitalist societies. The understanding of work in such societies will, like our own, be shaped by the socioeconomic context in which it is carried out. We might suggest then, that in a setting where work is integrated into the fabric of life in the same way as other activities, that the supposed barrier between work and life is less significant than it tends to be in the industrial world (Thompson 1982: 303). In such societies, we could possibly find that work is experienced by

---

2   Witness the dire economic and public health status, as well as the disproportionate criminalisation of many Aborigines in Australia, or American Indians in North America.

the individual quite differently, perhaps as less of an imposition, as something carried out with a greater degree of autonomy. Given the low division of labour and the clearly observable purpose of tasks carried out, there can be little cause for alienation in the sense understood by 19th and 20th century social science. Although tasks need to be completed to ensure individual and group survival, they are carried out not to the timetable set down by the rhythms of the machine or a system of industrial management, but by the more or less immediate needs of the group, and by the conditions in the local ecosystem. To the extent that compulsion, particularly in terms of time (and as we shall see in our later discussion on the European transition to capitalism, this seems to be the dimension through which early industrial discipline is primarily transmitted and experienced) exists, we might concur with Thompson that 'the compulsion is nature's own' (Thompson 1982: 302). Work discipline then, as an objective (and possibly incomprehensible) force erected and imposed heteronomously by a reified system of economic and social relations, simply does not exist.

Should it in fact be the case that necessary work or tasks are experienced as some kind of imposition in pre-capitalist societies, there is apparently little risk of individuals suffering the effects of overwork:

> Reports on hunters and gatherers of the ethnological present–specifically on those in marginal environments–suggest a mean of three to five hours per adult worker per day in food production. Hunters keep banker's hours, notably less than modern industrial workers (unionised), who would surely settle for a 21–35 hour week (Sahlins 1972: 34–35).

Writing of the Bushmen of the Kalahari, Sahlins describes a situation where the dominant sphere is that of leisure rather than work:

> One detects again that characteristic palaeolithic rhythm of a day or two on, a day or two off– the latter passed desultorily in camp. Although food collecting is the primary productive activity, Lee writes, "the majority of the people's time (four to five days per week) is spent in other pursuits, such as resting in camp or visiting other camps" (Sahlins 1972: 23).

As with English workers during the transition to industrial capitalism in the eighteenth and nineteenth centuries, a disciplined attitude to work in the commercial setting appeared lacking for the Yamana, a band of South American hunters. Sahlins here quotes Martin Gusinde, writing in 1931, and how much greater would be the despair of the twentieth century European employer, for whom the following levels of worker indiscipline would be unheard of.

> ...the Yamana are not capable of continuous, daily hard labour, much to the chagrin of European farmers and employers for whom they often work. Their work is more a matter of fits and starts, and in these occasional efforts they can

develop considerable energy for a certain time. After that, however, they show a desire for an incalculably long rest period during which they lie about doing nothing, without showing great fatigue... It is obvious that repeated irregularities of this kind make the European employer despair, but the Indian cannot help it. It is his natural disposition (Gusinde 1961[1931]: 27, cited in Sahlins 1972: 28).

Sahlins debunks the myth that non-Western pre-capitalist societies are poor[3] by pointing out that aside from none of their inhabitants considering themselves to be in poverty, and few suffering from starvation or malnutrition, they are extremely rich in terms of leisure time, that is, time spent in autonomously determined activities. This proposition rests on an understanding of wealth that we will encounter throughout our exploration of theories of the end of work; it represents a counter-current to conventional notions of wealth in market societies.

Historical conceptions of work

Many of the central ideas in modern philosophy, politics and social science can and have been traced back to their origins in ancient Greece. In terms of the idea of work however, we find that the Greek understanding, far from paralleling our own, can almost be seen as its obverse. According to Tilgher; 'To the Greeks work was a curse and nothing else' (Tilgher 1930: 3). Tilgher points out that the Greek word for work, ponos, has the same root as the Latin poena, or sorrow. Tilgher's characterisation is not necessarily inaccurate or unfair; it does, however, require some qualification. Although the ancient Greeks did use the word ponos to refer to painful activity, they used the term ergon to mean task, and this they applied to agricultural labour and the arts of warfare (Godelier 1980: 171). Broadly speaking, it seems that in the classical period, agricultural work and work relating to war were held in relatively high esteem. The bulk of the evidence suggests that the artisan was considered something of an inferior figure. Further, it is interesting to note that physical labour was not disdained, and this, again, runs quite contrary to contemporary views of work. The key to understanding Greek thought on work is to grasp that it was not the actual act of work that the Greeks despised, but rather the status of having to work out of necessity. Aristotle divided activities into praxis – work that is carried out for its own sake, and poiesis – work that has some extrinsic purpose, representing a means to an end rather than an end in itself.

The negative connotations attached to the work of the artisan, who later came to represent something of an aristocrat in the hierarchy of labour, stem from the fact that ancient Greece represented a peculiar form of consumer society. The nature of artisanal work, as well as that of its product, was in a sense read backwards from the needs of the consumer. This meant that the artisan served

---

3   Although as Sahlins and others note, in some nomadic societies rates of senilicide and infanticide may be high (Sahlins 1972: 34).

only as an intermediate functionary in supplying a product to the consumer, the latter of whom defined the essence of its form. The artisan was seen as working to supply the needs of another, to be working out of a form of necessity, and therefore deemed unfree.

Greek thought on work does continue to influence contemporary commentators, particularly critics of work. As we will discover, the Greek attitude to work, that it is the status of work as an imposition, representing unfreedom – that represents the negative nature of work – persists. Marx, for example, can be seen as drawing on the idea that true freedom begins where necessity ends. In another interesting parallel to later critics of work, and again, Marx springs to mind, the Greeks seemed to consider work as rather degrading to both mind and body. It is unclear whether this criticism was applied to all forms of work, or more narrowly, work in dark and fetid workshops, and the sedentary work of scribes.

It is impossible to mention Greek attitudes to work without commenting on slavery.[4] The institution of slavery existed in order to allow citizens to engage in more worthy pursuits than the drudgery of work, even honourable work such as farming and soldiering. As Applebaum relates;

> For Aristotle, music and contemplation were the highest ends of a cultivated man, and the pursuit of philosophy and the noblest pursuits could be mastered only by education and training which, in turn, could only be available to the man of leisure (Applebaum 1992: 64).

Slavery was, of course, the means by which the Greeks were able to secure the abundant leisure time necessary for the individual to fully participate in the intellectual and political life of the polis. It is likely that despite the existence of slavery, large numbers of free citizens *were* obliged to work; philosophers then, as now, tended to write in terms of the ideal, rather than the actual. Interestingly, in the later period of the ancient world, as the institution of slavery began to decline, and land became more scarce, the discourse of work began to change. By the time the Roman poet Virgil was writing (70–19BC), the notion of a necessity free existence was being portrayed quite differently; 'Under the reign of Saturn... the earth produced of itself what was needful so that men in their torpor were becoming as thick witted as dumb beasts...' (Virgil [*Georgics* 1: 29BC], cited in Applebaum 1992: 8). When discussing the concept of work in the ancient world, we are heavily reliant on a narrow range of evidence – that produced by the intellectual elite. Indeed, up until quite recently, the perceptions of the workers themselves leave little imprint in the discourses of history. For our purposes, and

---

4 In 1983, Margaret Thatcher's then energy Minister, Peter Walker, predicted the creation of 'Athens without the slaves, where the slaves will be the computer and the microchip and the human race can obtain a new sense of enjoyment, leisure and fulfilment' (Walker 1983, cited in *The Sunday Times* 1994).

certainly at this stage, this is not prohibitively important, as the aim of the book is not to survey public opinion on work.

If we find the ancient Greek concept of work to be expressed fairly ambivalently, the situation changes little when we examine the concept of work in early Christian and Jewish discourse. Early Judaic thought appears to have been split between those, like Rabbi Simeon, who saw work as detracting from spiritual life, and others, like Rabbi Ismael, who suggested that mere contemplation is not enough; it is also necessary to work with God towards humankind's salvation, and this means labour (Applebaum 1992: 17). For the former the second coming will occur anyway, at a predetermined time, and there is little point in pursuing earthly work; time would be better spent in religious contemplation. For the latter, reading the Torah is all well and good, but work is necessary to re-conquer our spiritual dignity through atoning for original sin. Philo, in his *De op mundi* says that 'God imposed labour on sinful man so that he was no longer supplied with unearned food and could no longer indulge in the twin evils of idleness and satiety' (Applebaum 1992: 182). This notion of labour as a curse, as an imposition, is similar not only to the Greek understanding, but to that of the early Christians.

The Fall is an important element in early Christian thought on work. The story of Adam and Eve's ejection from the Garden of Eden is well known, as is the fact that their punishment for original sin was to toil for the rest of their days. This would seem to suggest a wholly negative view about work. However, we find that like the Greeks and the Jews, early Christians held something of an ambivalent position. Jesus himself seems to hold work in some disdain. 'Consider the lilies how they grow: they toil not, they spin not; and yet I say unto you, that even Solomon in all his glory was not arrayed like one of these' (Luke 12:27, cited in Beder 2000: 14). And again; 'Behold the fowls of the air; for they sow not, neither do they reap nor gather into barns; yet your Heavenly Father feedeth them...' (Matthew 6:26, cited in Tilgher 1930: 23). There is little in the New Testament to suggest that Jesus, who in all other matters is held as exemplary, had any inclination to work, certainly not of the physical kind. Jesus can hardly be seen as idle; it is just that his work tended to involve activities, such as miracle working, that are difficult to classify.

Others, for example Saint Paul or Saint Augustine, are more positive, emphasising the supposed joyful element in work. In terms of morality, early Christian thought began to see work as an obligation; partly because it allowed successful members of the community to offer charity to the less successful, but also because it helped occupy minds that might otherwise entertain unclean thoughts.

The attitude of the Church continued to be ambivalent during the mediaeval period in what is now Britain. However, the notion that work helped distract the minds of the people from less wholesome concerns continued, as did the idea of work as conducive to a sense of charity. In something of a continuation of Greco Roman tradition, agricultural work remained prized above virtually all other forms. This perhaps reflects a form of primitive physiocracy, or materialism that sees only the production of useful, tangible goods, and not necessarily abstract value, as important. This was a society where wealth was still firmly associated with the ownership of land. The socioeconomic system and level of economic development must be taken into account when assessing attitudes to work in the mediaeval period, as in other historical periods, including our own. As P. D. Anthony has pointed out, mediaeval society was a society where social and economic relationships were based on personal obligation. However, during the 11th and 12th centuries, the ruling class of landowners began to find that villeins could be motivated better by wages than by the traditional system of obligation (Anthony 1977: 32). Catastrophic events such as the Black Death are thought by many historians to have hastened the breakdown of the system of obligations in feudal society, and to have furthered the development of a system of wage labour as peasants became detached from their land. However, society up until perhaps the 18th century was not one dominated by modern economic rationality; the rise of 'economic man', as well as the rise of the work ethic was to develop momentum alongside the process of industrialisation.

Of course modern concepts of economics, as well as the modern attitude to work, are not linked with the Industrial Revolution alone. The connection between the rise of Protestantism and the development of the modern work ethic will be familiar to many, possibly because this was the subject of one of the most significant sociological works ever written, Max Weber's *The Protestant Ethic and the Spirit of Capitalism*. The debate as to whether the system of thought and behaviour erected by Luther and Calvin gave rise to capitalism, whether the two emerged with serendipitous simultaneity, or whether Protestantism merely gave ideological support to an already emerging capitalist system, is well rehearsed. For our purposes, it is enough to accept that Protestant religious and social thought was at least partly instrumental in creating the overwhelmingly positive attitude to work that is hegemonic today.

Without wishing to reduce history to the story of great figures, it might be suggested that Protestantism began with Luther. The same cannot be said of one of the key concepts associated with the Protestant work ethic, that of the calling, at least in its original conception. The calling was first associated with the monastic life, and with the vocation of the priest. These were individuals who had chosen to withdraw from the sphere of worldly concerns in order to serve God with greater devotion and purity. Luther's teaching attacked this artificial division of worldly and divine existence. For Luther, all work was to be carried out in the service of the almighty. Monks and priests were open to criticism on the grounds of parasitism, in fact, since in many cases they depended for survival on the work of others – mendicant orders being one example. In a depiction that was to echo through the work of later writers, work was seen by Luther as the basic creative activity in society, as the base upon which the world of men, and by extension God, was built; we might express it as the activity by which God works through men. So all work, not only that devoted to meditation and contemplation, is worthy; 'The labour of the craftsman is honourable, for he serves the community in his calling; the honest smith or shoemaker is a priest' (Tawney 1961: 101). In fact, the honest Christian should earn their living 'by the sweat of their brow' (Tawney 1961: 101). As with the Greeks, agricultural work was held in high esteem in Lutheran discourse, if for different reasons. For the Greeks the farmer was honourable because they answered to no other but nature itself; the peasant was elevated by Luther because they remained untainted by the corruption of trade and mercantilism – what Tawney called the 'corroding spirit of commercial calculation' (Tawney 1961: 101). As is often the case with the discourse of the privileged and powerful, it is interesting to ponder the gulf between their perception, or perhaps depiction, of reality, and the way reality was experienced by those about whom they wrote. We might wonder how far a sense of honour and spiritual prestige filtered into the consciousness of the peasant class in mediaeval Europe, just as we might wonder how the Greek disdain for work was received by the slaves whose purpose it was to carry it out. Again, our prime purpose is not to gauge public opinion about work, even if this were possible eons later – we remain focused on tracing the emergence of an ideology of which the contemporary penetration into everyday life is all too apparent.

Although Luther was far from radical in terms of his views on social hierarchy, his proposition that the work of all members of society, even the most lowly, is worthwhile in that it is done ultimately in the service of God, is radical indeed. Luther is one of the first social theorists (we might consider many of the historical figures discussed here as the social theorists of their time) to attach an unambivalent moral and spiritual positivity to work; the traditional notion of work as a curse, as a painful and burdensome activity, began to erode, the notion of work as life's essence began to solidify.

Every positive has its negative. For Luther this meant that while those who toil were to be praised and rewarded (at least in the afterlife), those who avoided work were to be castigated. This vilification focused not only on the gilded idleness of the Catholic priesthood, but on the poor; or rather, on the dishonest poor. Luther, like many Protestants and puritans who followed him, had little sympathy for the homeless and destitute, who were seen as lazy, feckless, and open to punishment, banishment, and compulsory labour by the harshest of means. More accurately, Luther did have sympathy for some of the indigent, but only those who wished to work but for some reason were prevented from doing so. This latter group, in accordance with Christian tradition, were to be offered appropriate charity, which the work of others would provide, according the latter further value. Other Protestant writers followed suit, including the Swiss reformer Zwingli, whose programme for poor relief in 16th century Zurich rested on withdrawal of support from those who were idle or prone to iniquitous pursuits (Tawney 1961: 22). Here we apparently see the emergence of the concept of the deserving and undeserving poor, a distinction that crystallised further in Victorian discourse, and continues to

to work in modern society, and contempt for the leisure class who made up parts of the economic elite (1915). While the evangelists of work helped supply a willing labour force for the expanding industrial economy, it seems their employers were sometimes less than convinced by the moral and social value of work, at least when it might involve themselves.

D. H. Lawrence was both a critic of the crushing drudgery of work, and an observer of the hold it had on the early twentieth century imagination. For him the middle classes, the serried ranks of Edwardian clerks, appear the most willing victims of the ideology of work.

> I could not bear to understand my countryman, a man who worked for his living, as I had worked, as nearly all my countrymen work. He would not give in…I looked for his name in the book. It was written in a fair, clerkly hand. He lived at Streatham. Suddenly I hated him. The dogged fool, to keep his nose to the grindstone like that. What was all his courage but the very tip-top of cowardice? (Lawrence 1915, cited in Harvie et al 1970: 441).

Robert Tressell, author of the classic socialist fable *The Ragged Trousered Philanthropists*, clearly had little time for those who were happier to wax lyrical on the benefits of hard physical labour than actually participate in it. Writing (around 1914) of a group of decorators in turn of the century Hastings, he notes pithily that;

> Extraordinary as it may appear, none of them took any pride in their work: They did not "love" it. They had no conception of that lofty ideal of "work for work's sake", which is so popular with the people who do nothing (Tressell 1967: 92).

Conclusion

The great paradox of the nineteenth, and many would say the twentieth, centuries, was that just as work was being elevated to a position of moral and ideological prominence, its rationality was being brought into question by two countervailing logics. Firstly, while the logic of the factory meant that instilling an ethic of diligent work into the consciousness of the workers was essential, the same logic, or more accurately the logic of capital, meant that the owners of these same factories were compelled to seek ever more effective ways of eliminating labour through the substitution of dead for living labour. The ideology of work here appears in a kind of dialectical relationship with the rationality of capital: the two are in conflict because while the perpetuation of the latter depends on that of the former, it is at the same time inimical to it. More accurately, the ideology of work is not inimical to capitalism – rather, it is the worker who represents an increasingly unnecessary expense, and possibly an irritation. It is this contradictory logic that forms one of the central arguments put forward by those who advocate the abolition of work, and will be an important question throughout the rest of the book; what is to be the synthesis of this dialectical relationship? Secondly, at the same time as advancing technology and production methods helped make the formation of a suitable concept of work, and a peculiarly modern, urban way of life a necessity for continuing advances in efficiency and production, these same advances were degrading the act of work to an unprecedented degree. Further, the factories and the industrial centres that sprang up to serve them began to be seen as inimical to healthy and vital human existence. These contradictions are at the centre of the end of work debate, and have been since they were first expressed by utopian socialists such as Charles Fourier in the eighteenth century. It is to these early critics of work in the modern world that we now turn.

Chapter 3
Industrialism, Utopia, and the End of Work

As scholars of the subject have pointed out (Levitas 1990: 183) studies of utopia often ask very different questions. That is, they seek to focus on a particular role played by utopias in the development of specific ideologies or discourses. The five utopian visions that will be examined here have been chosen because they reflect the central question of the present book; what role has the end of work thesis played in modern social thought? That any vision of a world without work is a utopian vision is an assertion that can be questioned, to be sure. As we shall see later in the current book, contemporary end of work theorists would argue that their assertions on the decline and fall of labour are based on empirical investigations, and that their conclusions can be reached largely through a lucid and rational analysis of widely acknowledged economic, cultural and social changes. Our utopians from centuries past make similar claims, but their status as utopians is difficult to challenge if we define utopia as an alternative or future better society, designed to ensure the total fulfilment of all human needs. To this of course we might append the qualification; 'as defined by their author', since what these needs precisely are varies to some extent from utopian to utopian.

At the centre of most of these utopian visions is what Roger Paden has referred to as 'the greatest human need, the need for autonomous self-development' (Paden 2002: 80). End of work theory from Marx to the present, as we shall see, has this need for autonomous self-development at its heart. A key question for the present discussion will be the extent to which Western thought's utopias of the past share this concern, and its connection to the question of work. Utopias are always, by definition, critical of the society extant at the point of their composition. For the writers of some of the most radical utopias in Western intellectual history, the issue of work and its abolition formed a central element of their critique. Maeve Cook has argued that critical social theory is; 'a mode of reflection that looks critically at processes of social development from the point of view of the obstacles they pose for individual human flourishing' (Cooke 2004: 418). It will be argued here that our utopians were working very much in this tradition of critical social theory, and we shall begin to see that many of their ideas have much in common with those working within one of the most radical streams of critical social discourse today; theories of the end of work.

The utopias which form the focus of the current chapter have been chosen with two criteria in mind. Firstly, we will be restricted to utopias that are, if not always well known, at least regarded within the field of utopian studies as important. The nineteenth century, for example, produced a plethora of utopian schemes, but we will restrict ourselves to the imitated, rather than the imitators. Secondly, all the utopias examined here have something relevant to say about work and the potential for its abolition, or at least its radical reconfiguration. We begin with a brief analysis of St. Thomas More's *Utopia*, and move on to discuss the work of Charles Fourier, J. A. Etzler's *The Paradise within the Reach of All Men, Without Labour, by Powers of Nature and Machinery: An Address to All Intelligent Men*, and Edward Bellamy's *Looking Backward 2000 – 1887*. A discussion of William Morris's review of *Looking Backward* will complete our study.

More's *Utopia*

The *Utopia* of St. Thomas More might be seen as something of a prototype for later visions of an alternative world. Certainly, More's tract can hardly have failed to influence any utopian vision which succeeded it, being as it is the utopia that coined the term itself, thus sparking nearly 600 years of debate (*Utopia* was published at Louvain in 1516) on the precise meaning of the word. We discuss More here because although he wrote before the advent of the industrial society that later utopians would criticise, his work contains some of the central concerns that have echoed down the centuries until the present day. Firstly, as the Manuels (Manuel and Manuel 1979: 129–130) have pointed out, More made the link between production (work) and consumption. That is, More was aware that an adjustment to patterns of consumption, which are directed by what we might call wants and needs, might necessitate a consequential adjustment of the amount of labour performed by society, and vice versa. 'Then, as now, the key economic utopian questions revolved around the amount of labour required to fill the needs of the society, and a definition of the character and extent of those needs' (Manuel and Manuel 1979: 132).

More limited the working day of his utopians to six hours.[1] He did suggest that 'The chief and almost the only office of the Syphogrants [magistrates] is to see and take heed that no man sit idle...' (More 1962: 64). However, no-one is to work from early morning until late at night, as many almost certainly did in 16th century European society. If everyone works less, will this not lead to a scarcity of goods and services – a retrograde step in the standard of life? Not according to More: '...perchance you may think that the lack of some necessary things may hereof ensue. But this is nothing so' (More 1962: 65). How is this the case? More's analysis here prefigures those of Fourier, Bellamy, and Morris in particular, and consists of three central premises.

Firstly, in conventional society, much of the population does not work, thus increasing the necessary amount of labour to be furnished by those who do. More includes 'all rich men...also sturdy and valiant beggars...' (More 1962: 66) in this

---

1   In actual fact, this figure is rather ambiguous. At one point More writes 'For seeing they bestow but six hours in work...' (More 1962: 65) At another, he writes of six hours work before noon, and another three after dinner, taking the total to nine hours (More 1962: 64).

Etzler's vision is the fact that he does not stop at painting pictures of a mythical land, but, in the intellectual spirit of his time, provides a rational and technological means of achieving it. As Etzler himself says, 'here is no idle fancy...' (Etzler 1842: 2). Etzler's work has become even more relevant, it could be argued, as awareness of impending environmental catastrophe has increased, since what Etzler proposes is not only an end to work but an end to reliance on fossil fuels, and the harnessing of wind, solar, wave and tidal energy to fulfil all of society's power needs.

> I show here, that there are powers in nature, sufficient to effect in one year more than hitherto all men on earth could do in many thousands of years; that these powers may be applied, to do all human labour (Etzler 1842: 1).

It is extremely tempting to give a detailed account of Etzler's designs, and were we examining the (pre)history of renewable energy, this might be appropriate. We are confined here, however, to the highlights.

Firmly grasping the first law of thermodynamics, Etzler quickly dispenses with those seeking to create perpetual motion machines. Moving on to wind power, our technological utopian proposes that this be harnessed by what we would recognise today as giant wind farms, with systems of sails 200 feet high arranged around central axes. Etzler is vaguer on what form of motive power is to be produced, and confines himself to more formal discussions of physical work – that is, the movement of mass. He does, however, anticipate a system of energy storage of some kind.

Etzler then discusses the massive power producing potential of the tides. His scheme involves a system of boxes that are raised and lowered by the rising and falling water. The power produced will be used to build artificial islands along the coast, replete with cities 'consisting of the most magnificent palaces' (Etzler 1842: 15). It can also be used in what appears to be a prototype form of factory fishing. For harnessing the power of the waves, Etzler has designed a Naval Automaton, bearing some similarity to what we now know as a wave power platform. Etzler's wave powered floating islands would be propelled at dizzying speeds of up to of forty miles per hour, or be used to span the oceans with telegraph wires.

Etzler's design for utilising the power of the sun is quite striking, since it closely resembles a method of generating solar power that is actually in use today. An automatically aligning system of mirrors focuses the sun's rays on huge cylinders of water, which generate steam and via a piston, motive force. Taking all these forms of power generation together, we might well concur with Etzler that; 'We have superabundance of power – powers without limits – million times greater than all men on earth could effect hitherto...' (Etzler 1842: 25). These grand designs for a new generation of power production that equips humanity with the ability to complete huge feats of civil engineering, with virtually no effort, are but one part of Etzler's scheme. Domestic arrangements too are to be revolutionised to the point where work is eliminated. In the kitchen, for example; 'The cleaning of the vessels and all washing of utensils…is to be done by streaming water, the washing of other stuffs by steam. All this requires no work, but is done by slightly moving some crank' (Etzler 1842: 37).

In Etzler's utopia, not only are we free from work (one day a year spent slightly moving a crank excepted), we are free *in* work, since what very negligible amount of work we must do has become but an amusement. Work then, becomes play for Etzler, as it did for Fourier.

So renewable energy sources are to provide power for a new generation of construction and cultivation projects, and technologically wondrous machines are to render domestic living a veritable *Fantasia* of ease. In addition, people will live in prefabricated apartment blocks made from cast pieces of a vitrified substance, rather like reinforced concrete, that is 'indestructible for many thousands of years' (Etzler 1842: 38). Twentieth century urban planning has succeeded at least in demonstrating the literally fantastic credentials of this element of Etzler's grand design. Thus, as in More's *Utopia*, the amount of work required for survival is drastically reduced. The problem of producing the machines that will perform all this work is solved by having machines capable, once built, of creating others with negligible or no human intervention.

As work is eliminated, and the physical environment transformed, so are social relations revolutionised. Competition and profiteering become obsolete in the cooperative communities in which the citizens of the near future will live. Human identity is fully realised, existence is raised to the highest possible level. Without the necessity of daily toil, man will be able to 'enjoy life as well as possible by mutual sociality, by social arrangements, by reciprocal communications, by public pleasures and instruction' (Etzler 1842: 41).

We return again to the notion of a developmentalist utopia. The human subject is viewed, in an almost technological sense, as something that can be modified and perfected. And yet Etzler's is a typically humanistic view. Time not working, which is all the time, is to be spent in autonomously chosen activities of great variety;

> Man may rove about in the gardens, in pleasant walks of crystal, and between flowers and vegetables of infinite variety…he may amuse himself in amphitheatrical and level places, filled and bordered with every thing that art and nature can produce for the delight of man (Etzler 1842 :1).

People's talents are to be given the opportunity to develop, be they mechanical, artistic, or musical. Botanical gardens and museums, laboratories, mineralogical displays and collections of maps (to name but a few examples) provide unlimited opportunities for self enrichment and learning. Etzler even anticipates the development of information technology: 'A tachigraphy, with peculiarly-adapted characters, and lithography…and printing establishments, by which the composing of words may be affected as quick as one speaks, and the copies multiplied without labour' (Etzler 1842: 43).

This is a utopia of knowledge, learning and ideas. In a conceptualisation with similarities to Marx's ideas on automation, praxis and scientific knowledge, Etzler foresees humankind's knowledge becoming exponentially self generative. 'And knowledge begets knowledge, ideas beget new ideas, and dormant faculties of man will be roused, a spirit of enquiry will be kindled...' (Etzler 1842: 44).

With Etzler the dialectic of work time and autonomous time is taken to its limits; work time is eradicated, and the autonomy of free time is both multiplied and magnified through bringing humanity's thirst for knowledge and creativity into unrestricted play. This is, like Fourier's, a theory which elevates the human individual to a position where the social and physical world is analysed rationally and acted upon by him or her. In a world where the rationality of work seemed to be in the ascendant, Etzler asserts that work in conventional society is anything but rational. Work represents compulsion and slavery, non work represents freedom, reason and enlightenment. Etzler's view of the human individual is optimistic; were he or she not able to live without the enslavement of work, they would be a poor specimen indeed. To continue to be enslaved to work is to commit that most heinous of crimes; it is to be irrational.

The manner in which Etzler rebuts criticism of his proposals for the end of work is particularly interesting, since it represents a critical logic that continues to inform end of work discourse. If Etzler's proposals are attainable, why have they not yet been put into operation? Etzler counters that although people have boiled water for thousands of years, only recently has steam power been seen as viable. Etzler attempts to show that what at one point seems impossible and fantastic, the next is taken for granted. This is a truly modern attitude, one that recognises that all that is solid melts into air; it is a radical attitude also. In a similar fashion, later end of work theorists were to argue that it was only the inability of the collective consciousness to grasp the possibilities of a changing socioeconomic reality that prevented recognition of the fact that work has become obsolete.

Bellamy: Work in the rational society

Edward Bellamy's 1888 book *Looking Backward* can be distinguished from the work of Fourier and Etzler in the first instance, since whereas our French clerk and our German engineer composed their utopias in the form of the treatise, Bellamy's was framed as a novel. Lest the reader begin to think we have strayed into the realm of literary criticism however, Kumar assures us that 'Looking Backward is...offered primarily as a work of social theory' (Kumar 1987: 138). Perhaps it is the fact that Bellamy was attempting to express clearly sociological sentiments in the form of a novel that made Bellamy's work so 'didactic and wooden' (Manuel and Manuel 1979: 760). Didactic and wooden it may have been, but Edward Bellamy's tale of a nineteenth century gentleman who wakes from a trance to find himself in the Boston of the year 2000, was something of a sensation at the time, and became a cultural landmark in his native USA (Tichi 1986).

Like the work of Etzler, Bellamy's thinking emerges in the context of rapid technological change and social chaos. Having grown up in the heavily industrialised town of Chikopee Falls, Massachusetts, Bellamy was well aware of the squalor and inequality that industrialisation could produce, and yet his utopia is ultimately optimistic about the possibilities for a better life in a rationally organised industrial society. Much like More, Fourier, and Etzler, Bellamy gives a detailed account of the institutions, economy, citizenry and architecture of his alternative society, yet as with our other utopians we must review this scheme in outline, reserving detailed discussion for Bellamy's pronouncements on the end of work.

In the year 2000, the chaotic and rapacious capitalist economy has been replaced with a rationally planned, centralised system. This rational organisation of production and distribution has allowed for a massive advance in the standard of living, to the extent that scarcity is a thing of the past. Indeed, all citizens live in simple luxury. Inequality has been eradicated, and all workers are paid the same; a hierarchy of rank still exists, but reward is through prestige and honour, not financial remuneration. Production is organised on military lines, with an industrial army (industrial in the more conventional sense, as opposed to that used in Fourier) comprising the workforce. All citizens receive education up to the age of 21, after which they spend three years as a labourer. After these three years, workers select a specialisation and serve an apprenticeship, which allows them to become a full worker and a member of a guild. Labour is to be divided, as in the conventional industrial world, but one's specialisation is to be selected out of choice, not compulsion.

Kumar has suggested that the problem of work incentive in Bellamy is to be solved by a transition to a new consciousness where the collective understanding of the importance of individual work to the wealth of society as a whole is enough to ensure full commitment (Kumar 1987: 154). Manuel and Manuel, however, note that in Looking Backward, there were to be sanctions for those who resolutely refused to work: 'A man able to duty, and persistently refusing, is sentenced to solitary imprisonment on bread and water till he consents' (Bellamy 1888, cited in Manuel and Manuel 1979: 763). Thus Bellamy is cast in the mould of a Calvinist, for whom work was a moral imperative. Certainly, reading Bellamy's prescriptions that standard working time is to be eight hours a day, unless the job is particularly arduous, in which case the figure is reduced to four (Bellamy 1986: 124), one could easily characterise him as little more than an enlightened nineteenth century bourgeois. To do this would be somewhat unfair, however. Bellamy's nineteenth century Bostonian is informed by one of the citizens of the future that:

> ...the labour we have to render as our part in securing for the nation the means of
> a comfortable physical existence is by no means regarded as the most important,
> the most interesting, or the most dignified employment of our powers. We look
> upon it as a necessary duty to be discharged before we can fully devote ourselves

to the higher exercise of our faculties, the intellectual and spiritual enjoyments
and pursuits which alone mean life (Bellamy 1986: 148).

Work is a necessary duty, certainly, but one that for Bellamy is subordinate to self
realization through intellectually and spiritually enriching non work pursuits, or
to put it more succinctly, we should work to live, and not vice versa. It seems that
for Bellamy, like Marx, as we shall see, the realm of true freedom begins where
necessary work ends. That is not to say that work is to be irksome in the year 2000
– this is anything but the case, although Bellamy does not explain in any detail
how this is to be achieved.

Like More, Fourier, and Etzler, Bellamy employs the logic that by eliminating
those classes of people who in conventional society do little productive work;
in this analysis the judiciary, police, the military etc., much greater wealth
can be produced, and the overall amount of work required from each citizen
decreased. Bellamy extends this approach to capitalist competition, which is seen
as an irrational waste of resources. As in Fourier, laundry and cooking are done
communally, thus achieving economies of scale.

In the same vein as our other end of work utopians, Bellamy's protagonist
is asked to observe that; '...the waste of the very rich in your day on inordinate
personal luxury has ceased...' (Bellamy 1986: 167). If the wants and needs of
yesterday's leisure class are to be reigned in, however, the concept of limitation
of needs should not be overestimated. Although people will for example choose
accommodation that is of appropriate, and not palatial, dimensions, the population
will by no means live in genteel poverty.

In fitting with Bellamy's perhaps more moderate predictions, the role of
technology is not overstated. We can presume that Bellamy's rationally ordered
society will utilise advanced technology in production, although there is no
extended treatment on this theme. We are told that since now everyone must work,
all have an interest in lightening the burden, and that this has given 'a prodigious
impulse to labor-saving inventions in all sorts of industry' (Bellamy 1986: 102).
Domestic work, as already noted, is to be minimised through the use of communal
facilities, but is also to be lightened through advances in household technology.
When assessing the importance of work reduction in the domestic, as opposed to
the industrial realm, it should be remembered that, as every school history student
knows, domestic work in the nineteenth century involved inordinately more labour
than is now the case. Interestingly, Bellamy has one of his characters explain that
labour saving technology can be of little use, unless the organisation of society is
transformed also.

Bellamy has solved the familiar problem of drudgery. That is, who will perform
the menial and unpleasant jobs? The simple answer is; everyone. During their
three years as a labourer, the citizens of the year 2000 will perform a range of
what we in conventional society call menial jobs. Further, our time traveller, in
an encounter with a waiter, learns that the epithet of menial has become obsolete,

since previously low status workers are afforded the same recognition as any other.

We have outlined Bellamy's designs for a world without waste, in which all will work, but work less, and yet we have also noted a prescribed standard work-day of eight hours. How can this be the case? The answer lies in a very structured and generalised form of delayed gratification – compulsory retirement at age forty five. In Bellamy's future society, the life course is turned upside down, and people's middle age, rather than youth, represents the enviable part of life. Life after forty five represents freedom from work, for Bellamy. Work, however fulfilling, cannot compete with this period of extended leisure. Bellamy's view of non working time is in some ways similar to that of Fourier, in that it seems to distinguish between different classes. Although more enlightened people will embark on intellectually enriching pursuits, which for Bellamy seems to be the ideal, the majority do not

> have those scientific, artistic, literary, or scholarly interests which make leisure the one thing valuable to their possessors. Many men look upon the last half of life chiefly as a period for the enjoyment of other sorts; for travel, for social relaxation in the company of their lifetime friends; a time for the cultivation of all manner personal idiosyncrasies and special tastes, and the pursuit of every imaginable form of recreation... (Bellamy 1986: 149).

In his commentary on leisure in Looking Backward, Kumar seems to be edging towards a critique that is reminiscent of the Frankfurt School's culture industry approach. Kumar points out, correctly, that a prototypical, and suspiciously anodyne mass broadcasting system is to play an important role, and goes on to brand Bellamy's vision of mass culture a 'publicly arranged circus' (Kumar 1987: 163). This, it seems, is far from a developmentalist utopia, at least for the majority. Liesure is set in opposition to work in a manner that does seem to conform to what Adorno and Horkheimer were later to criticise; non work time as essentially passive, rather than active, a four decade recovery period from twenty four years of industrially regimented work. Bellamy's utopia then, is perhaps the least radical of those examined here; the world is rearranged around the human subject, who must be slotted into a new social order, however rationally organised.

On the other hand, we can evaluate Bellamy's vision as more realistic, and therefore potentially more radical. Leaving aside the question of whether his dialectic of work and non work allows for the full expression of active or creative human autonomy, Bellamy's realisation that it is unfeasible to eradicate labour altogether, and that it is better to limit it in some way, for it to at least end at some point, is a realisation that is shared by some contemporary end of work theorists, as we shall see.

The work of art and the art of work: William Morris

William Morris was far from impressed with Bellamy's work, so much so that he composed a scathing review of *Looking Backward* in what was effectively his house journal, *Commonweal*, which appeared in June 1889. Morris considers Bellamy's utopia to be 'State Socialism'. His criticisms are wide ranging, but are focused on the status of the human subject in Bellamy's 2000AD. The new world of Looking Backward is seen by Morris as an improvement on nineteenth century capitalism, for sure, but he criticises Bellamy for concentrating '...on the mere *machinery* of life: for clearly the only part of their system which the people would or could take over from the monopolists would be the machinery of organisation' (Morris 1889).

Morris views Bellamy's utopia as one dimensional, and typically bourgeois. Bellamy's pronouncements on work are singled out for the harshest of criticism. Morris is not convinced by Bellamy's vague assertions that labour will be free and fulfilling;

> ...he tells us that every man is free to chose his occupation and that work is no burden to anyone, [but] the impression which he produces is that of a huge standing army, tightly drilled, compelled by some mysterious fate to unceasing anxiety for the production of wares to satisfy every caprice however wasteful and absurd... (Morris 1889).

Thus the dark hand of compulsion, human life directed by some opaque mechanism, enters the picture. This compulsion is conceptualised most powerfully in relation to work. Morris is highly sceptical that individuals will be able to suddenly become self directing and autonomous once freed from their years of compulsory labour: 'Heavens! think of a man of forty-five changing all his habits suddenly and by compulsion!' (Morris 1889).

Morris is also dubious about the possibility of machinery reducing the need for labour, as machinery, it seems to him, merely breeds a need for more machinery, and thus more work. Morris's critique of Bellamy is useful because it contains a summary statement of the former's view of the nature of work; 'I believe that the ideal of the future does not point to the lessening of men's energy by the reduction of labour to a minimum, but rather to the reduction of *pain in labour* to a minimum' (Morris 1889).

Ultimately, for Morris, as for Fourier, the ultimate incentive to work is 'pleasure in the work itself' (Morris 1889). Whereas for Fourier work was to be combined with love, for Morris, true human freedom is to be achieved by combining work and art. That is, creativity is placed at the centre of Morris's vision of the transformation of work, just as it was in Marx:

> Thus worthy work carries with it the hope of pleasure in rest, the hope of the pleasure in our using what it makes, and the hope of pleasure in our daily creative skill (Morris 1915: 100).

Like that of Fourier, Morris's wider work proposes a return to something of a rural idyll. Manufacturing is to be done mostly by hand, thus satisfying men and women's innate creativity, and Morris's sense of the aesthetic. In *News From Nowhere*, written partly as a response to *Looking Backward*, Morris details a world where people have realised that 'only slaves and slave holders could live solely by setting machines going' (Morris 1979a: 154). However, in his essay *Useful Work Versus Useless Toil*, Morris does see some role for machinery in reducing working hours.

In this essay, as elsewhere, Morris follows a by now familiar logic; waste is to be eliminated through a reconfiguration of needs towards consumption of goods that are both durable and aesthetically worthy. The production of low quality, ersatz goods by the workers, for their own consumption, is to cease. Idle classes – the rich and their lackeys – are to be no more. On this latter point, Morris goes quite far. Understanding the aristocracy, as Marx did, as a class in relative decline (Morris 1915: 101), Morris instead emphasises the burden placed on the working portion of society by the middle classes. This group, comprising not only traders and manufacturers, but also professionals such as doctors and lawyers, are engaged in a 'private war for wealth' (Morris 1915: 102). Although, as Morris notes, the middle classes tend to work hard, their work is not directed to the production of useful commodities, but rather the competitive scramble to acquire enough wealth so that their children need not work – a kind of privatised, intergenerational end of work.

The scramble for wealth, involving, for instance, profiting from distribution, rather than actual production, apparently engages the upper middle classes so intently that their needs in the spheres of administration and reproduction, must be catered for by domestic servants and an 'army of clerks, shopassistants [sic], and so forth' (Morris 1915: 102). This interestingly prefigures late twentieth century debates over the status of service workers in the postindustrial economy (it also serves as a reminder that the novelty of this issue should not be overstated). In Chapter 7 we will explore Gorz's notion of the expansion of economic rationality; Morris's analysis anticipates, once again, the idea of the economically rich but 'time poor' being serviced by time rich, cash poor individuals in more marginal employment. As with Marx, and indeed later theorists such as Gorz, this situation is posed as one which is inherently irrational.

If Morris shares with Fourier the position of seeking freedom in work, his solution to the problem of drudgery is a synthesis of Fourier and Bellamy, with volunteers called on to perform the most unrewarding tasks (Fourier's Little Hordes?), and the performance of unpleasant work to be limited to short periods (four hours, perhaps?). And for work that is so unappealing that it simply cannot be imbued with any attraction whatsoever? 'Let us see if the heavens will fall on us if we leave it undone, for it were better that they should. The produce of such work cannot be worth the price of it' (Morris 1979b: 107). Morris's solution seems hardly to be a solution at all.

Conclusion

What emerges from our examination of the end of work in these five utopian visions? Firstly, we can begin to discern a pattern in how social thought at a relatively early stage perceives the reduction or elimination of work to be possible. In all our utopias, we encounter the following; some sort of limitation of needs which is linked to an end to the production of waste. Material goods are to be of a higher quality, with the concept of built in obsolescence, appropriately, obsolete. Work is to be shared out amongst the entire population. In all these utopias then, work time is reduced, to one degree or another. The role of technology is conceptualised differently, and yet there is always some realisation that the tools with which we produce can be used to lessen the burden of work.

The most important insight that emerges from our analysis is that in the radical social thought of previous centuries, there is a realisation that work and human identity are linked. A cleavage exists between those utopians who seek freedom in work, and those that seek freedom from it, and yet these are two solutions to the same problem. Creative activity, even in the perverted form of work in conventional society, is that which makes us truly human. Our utopians seek to provide the means for this creative activity to be truly autonomous, by freeing it from what is known as work. That the realm of freedom is ideally to be a realm of true creativity, of self enrichment through learning, a paradise of knowledge, reflects an enlightenment view of the subject that is still with us today. The individual, like society, has the potential for perpetual progress, development and improvement – activity by human individuals (conceptualised conventionally as work) is that which creates the world, and thus both individual and society must be reconfigured; they appear locked in a dialectical embrace. Work is seen not only as physical domination, but as an iron cage of irrationality, it is the embodiment of society's inability to rationally grasp the true nature of what it means to be human. Work is the result of a chaotic society where norms are the result not of rational deliberation, but of contingency and needless competition.

The remainder of this book will seek to demonstrate that theories of the end of work should be seen as critical social theories. We will see that radical alternatives to life and work in capitalist society do not end with the utopians of the nineteenth century, and that although they are thoroughly updated, many of the key concerns, freedom, autonomy, self development, and full realisation of authentic human identity, remain the same; and just as these goals endure, so does the understanding that the only way to attain them is through the abolition of work. The ideas of the utopians covered in this chapter have certainly had an influence on radical sociologists/social theorists such as Marcuse and Gorz. Their influence on mainstream sociology, including the sociology of work, is perhaps less marked, but the actual extent of utopianism's influence on sociology, both critical and mainstream, is possibly a question for further research.

Chapter 4
Marx and the End of Work

Introduction

André Gorz, whose work we will examine later in some detail, asks: 'When am I truly myself, that is, not a tool or the product of outside powers and influences, but rather the originator of my acts, thoughts, feelings, values?...' (Gorz 1986–1987: 138). It may appear strange to open a discussion of Marx with a quote from a French social theorist speaking 103 years after Marx's death. The question Gorz poses, however, is at the heart of not only Western philosophy in general, but Marx's work in particular. This is true not only of the Paris Manuscripts, the existential flavour of which is well known, but also of Marx's work as a whole. The key to answering this question, for Marx (and for Gorz, as we shall see later in this book), is the analysis of the nature of work in capitalist society. Receptivity to the notion that work is a, if not the central issue for Marx in terms of human emancipation may depend on the epistemological position of the reader. That there are many Marxisms requires little reaffirmation here. To many individuals, particularly those involved in or calling for revolutionary struggle, both now and in the past, the issue of the expropriation of private property or the means of production appears as central. This is what William Booth, after G. A. Cohen, has called the Plain Marxist Argument (Booth 1989: 207). The aim here is to approach Marx's analysis from another perspective – not in terms of ownership and exploitation, or the rule of some people by others, but in terms of 'the idea of domination by an autonomous economic process' (Booth 1989: 207). Marx himself writes that 'The abolition of private property is therefore by no means identical with communism' (Marx 1975a: 207). In fact the present account proceeds from the understanding that for Marx, it was work that held the key to the elevation of humankind from 'prehistory'.

To the observer not fully acquainted with the sometimes obscure world of Marxist discourse in the twentieth century, and indeed with Marx's own writings, it may seem incredible that Marx was in any way 'against' work, and saw its disappearance, or (almost total) radical reconfiguration as inevitable. This incredulity might spring from the fact that Marx and Marxism have always been linked to the political struggles of 'the workers', or those supposedly acting on their behalf. The erstwhile Soviet superpower that many saw as operating on Marxist principles, and liked to present itself as such through the use of Marxian hagiolatry, appeared orientated around the elevation of the (industrial) worker, and by extension (traditional heavy industrial) work. To complicate matters, even the observer fully acquainted with Marx might question the latter's dedication to ending work, since Marx does indeed seem to place work in something of a key role in the development of society, and the human subject itself. The issue may never be fully resolved, as characteristically, Marx retains a degree of ambiguity in his analysis of work that makes an unequivocal conclusion virtually impossible. Even at this early stage it is possible to conclude, with Berki, that 'Marx himself, in his dazzling synthesis, could not clearly decide if communism meant liberation from labour or the liberation of labor (as human essence)' (Berki 1979: 54). We might note that the question of whether Marx's critique was one aimed at liberation is answered in the positive without ambiguity.

Work as the human essence

Even if it remains a source of confusion, the fact that Marx saw work, or labour, as it is often referred to[1] as central both to the constitution of the human individual qua human, and the historical development of the species, is beyond debate. As Sean Sayers writes; 'labour is the main means by which human beings develop and become fully human' (Sayers 2003: 108). In a manner that reflects nineteenth century sensibilities, Marx characterises labour as something that separates the human species from those of the animal kingdom;

> We can distinguish men from animals by consciousness, religion, or whatever we like. They themselves begin to distinguish themselves from animals as soon as they begin to produce the means of life, a step which is conditioned by their bodily organization. In producing their means of life, men indirectly produce their material life itself (Marx 1959a: 8).

Certainly, non-human creatures sometimes appear to produce the means of their existence, even to the extent of building structures to support this production. However, Marx writes that:

> ...what from the very first distinguishes the most incompetent architect from the best of bees, is that the architect has built a cell in his head before he imagines it in wax (Marx 1974: 170).

Work for humans is a conscious process of self expression, not merely an instinctual impulse – although, conversely, humans do possess an almost instinctive need to create/work.

---

1   An etymological discussion of the distinction between the usage of the terms labour and work in Marx will not be entered into here. It is my conviction that the distinction between the two terms and the way they are used in Marx is often overplayed and possibly largely irrelevant. On this I am in concurrence with Cleaver (2002: 138–142). The key distinction is between labour/work, and *capitalist* labour/*capitalist* work.

From his earliest substantive writings, Marx views work as the existential bedrock of human existence, the material activity through which human beings create themselves and society; '…for socialist man the *whole of what is called world history* is nothing more than the creation of man through human labour, and the development of nature for man, so he has palpable and incontrovertible proof of his self-mediated *birth*, of his *process of emergence*' (Marx 1975b: 357). Note that Marx refers to *what is called* world history. This is a reference to the fact that although it is labour that creates both 'man' and society, this labour is not yet capable of creating the true or fully human individual, just as it is not the source of true or fully human society. The real history of humanity, as opposed to its pre-history, according to Marx, will begin when this flawed, alienated mode of labour is abolished. This issue will become clearer when Marx's critique of labour is outlined below; suffice it here to say that whatever conceptual reservations exist, Marx is clear on the basic constitutive role of work. The most well known way of characterising the essentiality of labour in Marx is for labour to be seen as constituting the 'species being' or 'species life' of humankind. Thus Marx writes:

> It is therefore in his fashioning of the objective [sic – object? E.G.] that man really proves himself to be a *species – being*. Such production is his active species – life. Through it nature appears as *his* work and his reality. The object of labour is therefore the *objectification of the species life of man*: for man reproduces himself not only intellectually, in his consciousness, but actively and actually, and he can therefore contemplate himself in a world he himself has created (Marx 1975b: 329).

This passage also serves to illustrate that for Marx, work serves the role of mediator between objective and subjective reality; between the realm of the human individual, and the objective world of nature, institutions, social reality, and indeed production at the meta-systemic level. To paraphrase C. J. Arthur, mediation in this sense is a dynamic relationship between humans and nature in which both poles are transformed (Arthur 1986: 2). The corollary of the mediating role of labour is that if this labour is somehow flawed, dysfunctional, dehumanised, or in Marxian terms, alienated, humankind's relationship with external nature and its institutions and relationships will be flawed, dehumanised, and alienated. Equally, the human individual is constituted in a flawed, alienated, and ultimately dehumanised reality. In fact when Marx is writing of the constitutive role of labour in human (pre)history, it is a flawed, and in the case of work in capitalism, alienated form of labour about which he writes. It is important to remember, however, that although these historical modes of labour have been, according to Marx, incomplete and flawed in various ways, they still bear within them a creative and constitutive function.

It would appear initially that Marx is making some quite radical statements (one might even call them assumptions) about labour/work constituting the essence of the human species' existence. Indeed, some might see this as something of a leap of logic, or an idea plucked from the ether.[2] As Kostas Axelos notes; 'The fundamental premise that allows the transcendence of alienation, namely, the essence of man (something that has never yet been empirically found), is metaphysical in nature' (Axelos 1976: 225). Metaphysical it may be, but Marx is usually seen as having based this premise, at least in part, on his reading of Hegel. It can be observed that actual, material work is absent in Hegel's analysis, with labour existing in a purely mental sense, as Geist manifesting itself in thought. Sayers, however, has asserted that '…work is a major theme in Hegel's philosophy' (Sayers 2003: 108). Berki stands diametrically opposed to this view; 'Marx's concept of labor owes nothing to the notion of labor in Hegel's own writings' (Berki 1979: 42). We leave this debate to others, whilst noting that, at least for some, Marx's 'metaphysical' view of the existential function of labour is not without precedent, or outside philosophical tradition. We should consider also the historical specificity of Marx. During the nineteenth century, social thought remained closely linked to philosophy, and it was generally acceptable for thinkers to make statements based on metaphysical, rather than empirical, observations. Interestingly, Berki subscribes to the view that Cieszkowski, Novalis and Schiller, thinkers with more aesthetic concerns, were a greater influence on Marx than was Hegel (Berki 1979: 47–49). It is to the aesthetic element of work that we now turn.

Aesthetics and affirmation in work

If work, even the alienated labour of capitalism, is both species constitutive and the motor of human social development, it is the creative, fulfilling elements of this labour (minimal or obscured though they may be), that have the most generative power. Marx proposes, throughout his oeuvre, a vision of what true or authentic work should be like. This is the ideal which he opposes to the alienated, degrading nature of work in capitalism. This vision can be seen to change as Marx's work matures, and the issue of pinning down exactly what ideal work (work in communist society) will consist of will be discussed later on. It is possible to make some assertions at this stage as to what constitutes, for Marx, the ideal – true and fully human work under non-alienated conditions. In his early writings, Marx begins to suggest what truly human work might be like. An extended quotation begins our examination of what authentic, un-alienated work meant for Marx:

> Let us suppose that we had produced as human beings. In that event each of us would have *doubly affirmed* himself and his neighbour in his production.

---

2   As John Elster notes, later Marxists have interrogated this assumption, sometimes critically. Habermas, for example, suggested that 'The development of moral competence through rational discussion is a form of self-realization that ought to be valued as highly as self-realization at the workplace' (Elster 1986: 116). We will return to Habermas in due course.

(1) In my *production* I would have objectified the *specific character* of my *individuality* and for that reason I would both have enjoyed the *expression* of my own individual *life* during my activity and also, in contemplating the object, I would experience an individual pleasure, I would experience my personality as an *objective sensuously perceptible* power *beyond all shadow of a doubt...* (Marx 1975c: 277).

From this passage, and from Marx's own emphases, we can deduce (albeit at the risk of merely translating Marx into contemporary parlance) that in truly human work, the individual experiences self affirmation, a true sense of concrete individuality, a sense of creative self expression, and a sense of personal empowerment. Not only that, but the work is pleasurable. For Marx, work should fulfil the fundamental human drive for self fulfilment and self expression.

To characterise work for Marx as containing a strong creative element is not a matter of exaggeration. Aesthetes such as Schiller and Novalis have been mentioned briefly already, but some commentators see Marx as inheriting a prioritisation of the aesthetic from Hegel. For Sayers, Marx, like Hegel, places creativity – art, in fact – at the centre of his vision of ideal work. 'For Marx too, art is the highest form of creative activity, free creative activity, the highest form of work' (Sayers 2003: 114). Marx himself comments on '[r]eally free labour' elsewhere (Marx 1972a: 124), and gives the composing of music as an example. It seems that truly free and authentic work is that which contains a definite creative, even aesthetic element. Elsewhere, Marx writes of the role of the senses, clearly expressing a concern for the aesthetic: 'Only through the objectively unfolded wealth of human nature can the wealth of subjective *human* sensibility – a musical ear, an eye for the beauty of form, in short, *senses* capable of human gratification, be either cultivated or created' (Marx 1975b: 353).

This 'objectively unfolded richness of man's essential being' corresponds to Marx's understanding of labour. The mediating function of work is again clear, with work serving to develop the individual's aesthetic and creative sensibilities, as well as being, ideally, an outlet for them. We may now be in a position to offer a suggestion as to why the aesthetic is an important element in Marx's vision of ideal human labour. Wessel suggests that the self affirmation of humans is mediated through their senses and thus aesthetically (Wessel 1978: 199). If any further evidence were needed, Wessel quotes Marx, who writes: 'Thus Man creates also according to the laws of beauty' (Marx 1967: 295 cited in Wessel 1978: 189). Going further, Wessel suggests a link with Schiller's notion of play: 'Schiller claimed that man is only free when he plays with objects, for in play he "feels" the surplus of his power [over objective material reality]. Marx similarly talks about "free physical and mental energy" generated by emancipated labour (play?)' (Wessel 1978: 199). The notion that Marx's ideal of creative, fulfilling and self expressive work constitutes play is an interesting one.

Marx's critique of work under capitalism

Having attempted to portray what, for Marx, constitutes really free, truly human productive activity, it is now necessary to examine Marx's critique of work, or more accurately, work as it exists under capitalism. It should first be briefly noted that Marx did not view pre-capitalist work as ideal, although the matter is complicated by occasional approving references to agricultural work. G. A. Cohen gives a clear account of Marx's view of the situation of the pre industrial worker: 'His contentment with, and absorption in, his own narrow trade compose what Marx deemed a "servile relationship"' (Cohen 1988: 189). The craftsperson was, however, at least connected to their work; the hand weaver, for example, usually owned their means of production. The industrial proletarian, on the other hand, is seen by Marx quite differently.

Alienation is a concept most often associated with Marx's analysis of capitalist labour. A huge body of work on the concept of alienation in Marx already exists, and there will be no extended account of it here.[3] Alienation, or estrangement, is best seen as a concept used by Marx to express the ontological distortion of the ideal role of labour, under conditions of capitalist production. Thus, instead of work constituting the self creating activity of the human individual, it becomes 'a mere means for his existence' (Marx 1975b: 328). The very essence of what makes us human becomes merely the survival tactic of a living organism. Not only are people estranged from their 'species being' as individuals, they are estranged from other individuals, and truly human society, social relations, do not exist. Marx explains the cause of this alienation with reference to capitalism's laws of economic operation, the social context in which the worker produces. The expropriation of the product of the worker's labour is a major element in alienation.

> In tearing away the object of his production from man, estranged labour therefore tears away from him his *species-life*, his true species-objectivity, and transforms his advantage over animals into the disadvantage that his inorganic body, nature, is taken from him (Marx 1975b: 329).

Lest the reader begin to think that that it was private property that Marx was in fact criticising, as opposed to labour, Marx makes it clear that private property is 'the product, result and necessary consequence of *alienated labour*, of the external relation of the worker to nature and to himself' (Marx 1975b: 331–332). Although private property may appear as a cause of alienation, it is, rather, a '*means* through which labour is alienated' (Marx 1975: 1844b, 332). Marx also views work in capitalist society as forced labour, with this forced nature a contributing factor in alienating the worker. This stands in contradistinction to the ideal, where work would be performed through natural impulse, as somehow 'for the sake of work'.

---

3   For an extended examination of the concept of alienation, see for example Ollman 1976.

It was left to researchers in the twentieth century such as Robert Blauner (Blauner 1964) to move explanations of alienation from the abstract to the empirical, whilst attempting to make the concept easier to grasp as a critique of labour. Marx's analyses of the division of labour, and his writings on the degrading nature of work in mechanised industrial capitalism are perhaps more descriptive, easier to relate to contemporary understandings of capitalist work, and clearer evidence of a call for an end to work as we know it.

Having discussed Marx's characterisation of fully human work as involving a definite aesthetic element, we can now show how Marx sees this as absent from work in capitalism:

> The man who is burdened with worries and needs has no *sense* for the finest of plays; the dealer in minerals sees only the commercial value, but not the beauty and the peculiar nature of the mineral: he lacks a mineralogical sense. Thus the objectification of the human essence, in a theoretical as well as a practical respect, is necessary both in order to make man's *senses human*, and to create an appropriate *human sense* for the whole of the wealth of humanity and nature (Marx 1975b: 353–354).

A lack of aesthetic sense is perhaps one of the less serious criticisms levelled at capitalist work, and life under capitalism more generally, by Marx. Work in capitalism is seen by Marx as degraded and degrading, fragmentary, enervating, and lacking in creativity, the polar opposite of aesthetic creation.

The division of labour is a key factor in Marx's critique of capitalist work. The division of labour represents both alienation and coercion, as Craig Conly has noted (Conly 1978: 86). Taking the former representation first, the worker is alienated from the product of their labour because they are responsible for, and have understanding of, only a fraction of the activity involved in that which is being created; they are therefore estranged from the objectification of their species being – the product of their labour. Marx phrases it thus; 'the total labour is not the achievement of individual workers, and their product is only a totality through the enforced combination of efforts that they cannot themselves coordinate' (Marx 1972a: 117).

In the first volume of the *Grundrisse*, Marx retains a strong sense of the division of labour as degrading for the worker: 'Even the division of labour in society at large entails some crippling both of mind and body' (Marx 1974: 384). The division of labour thus reduces the worker to the archetypal cog in the machine, it robs work of interest and creativity, and helps sever the connection between the worker and the objectification of their essential being – the product of their labour.

We have so far discussed what is sometimes known as the detail division of labour, a term that was introduced by the political economists whose work was such an influence on Marx. The detail division of labour, of course, involves each individual worker playing a restricted and highly specific role in the production process. Marx was also critical, however, of the division between mental and physical labour in capitalism. Not only does the division of mental and physical labour reduce the intellectual capacities of the mass of workers, and thus their ability to create themselves and objective reality as autonomous human individuals, this division helps strengthen the domination of capital. Under capitalism, scientific knowledge and technical skills are appropriated by the capitalist. Cohen writes: 'The capitalist may be personally ignorant, but he is the social repository of science, since those who know are in his hire' (Cohen 1988: 193). Further, the worker finds herself in a position of ignorance vis-à-vis the technical apparatus with which she works, confirming the worker's status as a mere appendage to the technology of industrial production.

How does the division of labour represent the coercion of the worker? Marx, among others, saw the division of labour as leading to individuals being assigned a restricted social role and being essentially trapped within it. Thus the worker is a 'hunter, a fisherman, a herdsman, or a critical critic, and must remain so if he does not want to lose his means of livelihood (Marx 1976: 47). Elsewhere Marx writes of the 'enslaving subordination of the individual to the division of labour...' (Marx 1972b: 17). The corollary of the division of labour is of course the class structure. The power of class to influence life chances, systems of meaning, and indeed personal identity is hard to overestimate. The very notion of a social structure that stands above individuals, outside their control, and constituting a force of domination, is one totally inimical to Marx. Thus the division of labour helps to reinforce the superstructure of coercion and control in capitalist society, a seemingly opaque structure apparently outside the control of individuals, yet one that influences them profoundly at every level.

The division of labour becomes most extensive as production develops from manufacture to large scale machinofacture. Marx's *Grundrisse*, and the volumes of *Capital* share the preoccupation, indeed fascination, with machinery and technology of many other works of social thought written during the rise of modern industrial society.[4] Even in the early writings, Marx's view of the role of technology in capitalist production was becoming clear: 'The machine accommodates itself to man's *weakness*, in order to turn *weak* man into a machine' (Marx 1975b: 360).

Machinery, value and the transformation of work

In the later works, Marx's criticism of the effect of machinery on labour in capitalism is similarly strident. Drawing on the work of other observers of industrial labour, Marx characterises work in the mechanised factory as almost the total opposite of the fulfilling, creative, self affirming and pleasurable work we discussed earlier:

---

4   For example, Babbage's *Economy of Machinery and Manufactures* (1832), or Ure's *Philosophy of Manufactures* (1835).

In manufacture, the workers are parts of a living mechanism. In the factory, there exists a lifeless mechanism independent of them, and they are incorporated into that mechanism as its living appendages…While labour at the machine has a most depressing effect upon the nervous system, it at the same time hinders the multiform play of the muscles, and prohibits free bodily and mental activity. Even the lightening of the labour becomes a means of torture, for the machine does not free the worker from his work, but merely deprives his work of interest (Marx 1974: 451).

Machinery, for Marx, takes on a character that is at times almost vampiric – 'Through its conversion into an automaton, the instrument of labour comes to confront the worker during the labour process as capital, as dead labour, which controls the living labour power and sucks it dry' (Marx 1974: 451) – at others diabolical;

…we now have a mechanical monster whose body fills the whole factory, and whose demon power, hidden from our sight at first because of the measured and almost ceremonious character of the movement of his giant limbs, discloses itself at length in the vast and furious whirl of his numberless working organs (Marx 1974: 403).

Marx's descriptions of the degrading and enervating effects of machinery on the worker are so unequivocally negative as to be fairly self explanatory.

What will require further analysis, however, is a seemingly typically Marxian paradox that has stood at the heart of discussions of the possibility of abolishing work since well before Marx. Possibly, the roots of this paradox extend even into antiquity;

if every tool, when called upon, or even of its own accord, could do the work that befits it, just as the inventions of Daedalus moved of themselves, or the tripods of Hephaestos went on their own initiative to their sacred work – if the weavers' shuttles were to weave of themselves – then there would be no need either of apprentices for the master craftsmen or of slaves for the lords (Marx 1974: 434).

Marx is here quoting Aristotle, whose notion of the 'good life', incidentally, is sometimes seen as inspiration for Marx's vision of communist society (Booth 1991: 8). The paradox for us is that despite Marx's description of the degrading effects of machinery on work in capitalism, it is machinery that he sees as ultimately holding the promise of freedom from toil. This can be seen as indicative of an ambivalent attitude to modernity, viewing it as both rich in potential and laden with negative implications for the individual. As we will see in the chapters that follow this, other writers on the end of work share Marx's ambivalence.

The machinery that under capitalism enslaves humankind, in fact offers the key to escaping this slavery; '…capital in this instance has quite unintentionally reduced human labour, the expenditure of energy, to a minimum. This will be to the advantage of emancipated labour, and is the condition of its emancipation' (Marx 1972a: 138). Machinery, according to Marx, is the 'most potent means for increasing the productivity of labour, that is to say for reducing the amount of labour time necessary for the production of a commodity' (Marx 1974: 428). The paradox for Marx,[5] which he saw as a contradiction at the heart of capitalism, was that the developments in the forces of production (machinery) that were precisely those most capable of reducing the necessity for human labour and degrading work, were exactly those which under capitalism extended and intensified work to an unprecedented degree. Thus his observation above, when completed, reads:

> Though machinery be the most potent means for increasing the productivity of labour, that is to say for reducing the amount of labour time necessary for the production of a commodity, in the hands of capital it becomes the most powerful means…for lengthening the working day far beyond the bounds imposed by nature (Marx 1974: 428).

Explanation for why this is the case must be given on two levels; firstly, in terms of commercial logic as it appears to the capitalist, within the context of capitalism; secondly, at the more abstract level, using Marx's concept of value.

There are four key reasons, from the point of view of the factory owner/ capitalist, why the introduction of increasingly advanced machinery should lengthen the working day, rather than shorten it. Firstly, the capitalist has spent a large amount of money on the machinery, and therefore wants it used as much as possible. When a navvy puts down his spade, he renders useless a tool of production of negligible cost, but 'When one of our people leaves the mill, he renders useless a capital that has cost £100,000' (Marx 1974: 432). Secondly, when innovative and more efficient machinery has been introduced, the capitalist wants to make use of their exclusive adoption of the new technology to maximise profits before others catch up. Thirdly, when application of machinery becomes more general, the price (social value) of the product falls. Since profit can only be made from surplus labour (people) and not machines, and the number of people has dropped, they must be made to work for longer hours in order to produce surplus labour and thus profit. Finally, the number of unemployed in society increases and so more people

---

5   Marx himself acknowledges that others had already noted the paradox of machinery failing to reduce the burden of labour: 'In his Principles of Political Economy, John Stuart Mill writes "It is questionable, if all the mechanical inventions yet made have lighted the day's toil of any human being"' (Marx 1974: 391). Marx inserts a swipe at the bourgeoisie by way of a sardonic footnote; 'Mill should have said "of any human being not fed by other people's labour"; for, beyond question, machinery has greatly increased the number of well-to-do idlers' (Marx 1974: 391n).

are subject to the dictates of capital and can be made to work for longer. Not only does machinery extend labour, it intensifies it. The speed up of machinery is one reason for this, as is the fact that the number of people tending machinery tends to decrease, even as the amount of machinery used increases.

In discussing the role of technology in Marx's analysis, it is necessary to avoid characterising him as a technological determinist. Technological determinism for Marx, meant the way in which the nature of work was determined by machinery, the way in which the capitalist organisation of production reduced the worker to an appendage of the machine. In Marx's analysis, if technology determined social change, working time would already have been greatly reduced. The use to which technology is put, according to Marx, is determined by social organisation, and not vice versa.

It is the fact that value constitutes the measure of wealth in capitalism that for Marx is the hidden cause of capitalism's fundamental contradiction. By defining wealth in terms of value, society allows itself to be held in thrall to an abstract concept, albeit one of humankind's own making. Value, Marx asserts, is not coterminous with wealth. As Moishe Postone writes; 'value does not refer to wealth in general, but is a historically specific and transitory category that purportedly grasps the foundation of capitalist society' (Postone 1993: 25). Value is extracted from the worker via surplus labour. According to Marx in the *Grundrisse*: 'Capital itself is the moving contradiction, [in] that it presses to reduce labour time to a minimum, while it posits labour time, on the other side, as sole measure and source of wealth' (Marx 1993: 706).

While under capitalism wealth is bound, through value, to human labour power, it need not be, and could be redefined (and expanded) by connecting it more directly to the massive productive potential of modern science and technology. Marx writes: 'The theft of alien labour time, on which the present wealth is based, appears a miserable foundation in face of this new one, created by large scale industry itself' (Marx 1993: 705). The new wealth of which Marx writes is both the potential material abundance, and the expanding realm of free time, that new technology (were it to operate in a productive context outside the circuit of capital) would open up. Marx argues that in conditions of large scale production, using more-or-less automated technology, the worker is no longer at the centre of the production process, but rather performs a directing and supervisory role.

> ...it is neither the direct human labour he himself performs, nor the time during which he works, but rather the appropriation of his own general productive power, his understanding of nature and his mastery over it by virtue of his presence as a social body – it is, in a word, the development of the social individual which appears as the great foundation-stone of production and of wealth (Marx 1993: 705).

If it is no longer direct labour on the part of the worker that produces wealth, but rather a system of largely automated technology under the direction of (or with the possibility to be directed by) a technologically conscious worker then, 'labour time ceases and must cease to be [value's] measure, and hence exchange value [must cease to be the measure] of use value' (Marx 1993: 705).

Value represents, for Marx, the abstract lynchpin of the alienated social (so called) reality that men and women have created for themselves. We might use the analogy of the stock market – an invention, an abstract creation, yet one that has the potential to affect the lives of billions of individuals. Lukács's theory of reification comes close to capturing the function of value as a concept for Marx– value represents the way commodities take on an illusory autonomy (Macey 2000: 336), and come to direct the lives of individuals, who appear as passive, despite it being their labour processes and social organisation that produces value in the first place. We are reminded of Gorz's question, with which we began, for in Marx's analysis, 'the tool of outside powers' is exactly what the individual in capitalism appears to be.

Marx proposes then, that we develop a new definition of wealth, one that would necessitate the explosion of the contradiction of value, and the hold that this contradiction exerts on the lives of individuals, through its consequences for the nature of work. We shall see that this redefinition would entail a radical reconfiguration of the meaning of work. The manner in which Marx conceives of this reconfiguration is revealing in terms of Marx's understanding of human freedom. As we shall see throughout the current book, this is not something that is unique to Marx. But does Marx propose a reconfiguration of work, or its abolition? In a letter to Arnold Ruge, Marx wrote; '...even though the question "where from?" presents no problems, the question "where to?" is a rich source of confusion' (Marx 1975a: 207). As is well known, Marx was more concerned with criticising the present than constructing utopian visions of a possible future. The idea of communism should not be written out of Marx, however, particularly in the context of a book such as the present one. The idea of the end of work is at the centre of Marx's vision of a future society; we inhabit a very different future, and Marx's alternative can provide useful critical insights for those who feel that our reality is still in need of criticism.

Often, scholarly commentators focus on Marx's proposals for an end to the division of labour. Marx's own comments, in *The German Ideology* have become well known;

> ...in the Communist society, where each one does not have a circumscribed sphere of activity but can train himself in any branch he chooses, society by regulating the common production makes it possible for me to do this today and that tomorrow, to hunt in the morning, to fish in the afternoon, to carry on cattle-breeding in the evening, also to criticize the food – just as I please – without becoming either hunter, fisherman, shepherd or critic (Marx 1959a: 1).

With the division of labour abolished, the individual would no longer have their identity defined by their economic function; their activity would be autonomously decided by the individual themselves. As Axelos writes; 'In the past, it was natural that men be led to the division of labour. But in the future, by transcending the stifling framework of the division of labour, they will be able to give themselves voluntarily to social activities' (Axelos 1976: 59). With the end of the division of labour would come the end of the class system, and individual identity would be just that – the autonomously created identity of the true individual, defined by the individual themselves. Clearly, although Marx proposes the abolition of the division of labour, the total scientific and productive knowledge of advanced society can not reside in every individual. The end of the division of labour, as Conly writes; '...does not preclude all specialization. It only means that the individual must produce what, when, and as he decides' (Conly 1978: 86). The famous phrase 'from each according to his ability, to each according to his needs' (Marx 1972b: 17) is part of a recognition that individuals do have different abilities, and may therefore choose to specialise in a particular area. This would be a matter of individual choice, and although this choice may be mediated by the needs of the community of which the individual is an integral part, it would not be dictated by the workings of capital. As for the division between mental and physical labour, Marx saw the key to eradicating this in education:

> As we can learn in detail from a study of the life work of Robert Owen, the germs of the education of the future are to be found in the factory system. This will be an education which, in the case of every child over a certain age, will combine productive labour with instruction and physical culture, not only as a means for increasing social production, but as the only way of producing fully developed human beings (Marx 1974, 522).

Having just used the word 'eradicating', it is necessary to admit that Marx did not very clearly explain how the division between mental and physical labour would be eradicated. We can presume that providing a high level of education to all individuals would allow people a greater degree of choice in terms of the nature of their labour.[6] It would also allow manual workers to engage in the intellectual activity of running the production process. We might suggest that Marx's comments on rearing cattle in the evening and criticising after dinner describe a situation where the individual will engage in manual or intellectual labour at different times, at the direction of their own will. Another conceptualisation is to see work being re-skilled, thus reintroducing an element of mental labour into previously mindless tasks. Perhaps the end of the division of labour would necessitate something like the combination of all these elements.

---

6 For an interesting discussion on the possibility of ending the division of labour through over-education, see Hegedus 1976: 106–124.

Marx, the end of work and the politics of time

It could be argued that the division of labour is so inextricably linked with the general concept of labour in capitalism that abolishing the former is essentially the same as abolishing the latter. This may be the case, but Marx does not restrict himself to discussing the abolition of the division of labour, and he appears at times to be explicitly advocating the abolition of labour, divided or not. We have already seen how Marx viewed advances in the technology of production as reducing the labour time necessary to fulfil human needs. We have examined also the reasons why this has not actually led to a reduction in working time. Despite its contradictions, capital 'is instrumental in creating the means of social disposable time, and so in reducing working time for the whole society to a minimum, and thus making everyone's time free for their own development' (Marx 1972a: 144). Marx proposes that were we to begin producing to meet the needs of society, if the 'labour time necessary will be measured by the requirements of the social individual' (Marx 1972a: 144), rather than the need to produce surplus value, the potential of modern technology could be realised. The realisation of this potential would be the reduction of necessary labour time to a minimum, leaving a greater space for the individual to develop themselves as a truly human being.

It is possible to see the reconfiguration of time as being at the centre of Marx's vision of a world beyond alienated labour. Booth relates Marx's analysis of the role of time in communist society to Aristotelian understandings of the good life. Certainly, it is possible to agree with Booth when he suggests that free time for Marx is understood as '...the realm of freedom and as the scope or space for human development' (Booth 1991: 9). Marx himself asserted that 'In the final analysis, all forms of economics can be reduced to an economics of time' (Marx 1972a: 75–76). Marx suggests that society '...must divide up its time purposefully in order to achieve a production suited to its general needs; just as the individual has to divide his time in order to acquire, in suitable proportions, the knowledge he needs or to fulfil the various requirements of his activity' (Marx 1972a: 76). Marx is proposing that society, and individuals, should no longer be dominated by time as an external force (the despotic bell being its most overt manifestation). Instead of working time being the abstract measure of value, free time should become the measure of real wealth, free time in which to develop one's identity as one sees fit. The abolition of work (or at least its reduction to a bare minimum) has both a negative and a positive element then; people would be free from degrading toil, and free to enjoy the possibility of personal development. Once again, one gets a strong sense of the importance, in Marx's analysis, of freedom, of liberation, as well as the development of true individuality. As already noted, these are themes that underpin the analyses of later writers on the end of work.

In the reconfiguration of time in communist society, as envisioned by Marx, is work to be eliminated entirely? If we define work as necessary productive activity, then the answer is no. Having established that the realm of freedom begins where necessity ends, Marx states that: 'Just as the savage must wrestle with Nature to satisfy his wants, to maintain and reproduce life, so must civilised man, and he must do so in all social formations and under all possible modes of production' (Marx 1977: 820). This passage can be interpreted as suggesting that some work will always be necessary, since basic human needs will always exist. Indeed, it is possible that these needs will increase in scope, with the continued development of society. Marx suggests that these new needs would indeed expand, but would be met by the ever increasing effectiveness of production. Continuing with our analysis of the concept of necessity, one could draw on another section of the previous extract;

> Freedom in this field [the realm of necessity] can only consist in socialised man, the associated producers, rationally regulating their interchange with Nature, bringing it under their common control, instead of being ruled by it as by the blind forces of Nature...achieving this with the least expenditure of energy and under conditions most favourable to, and worthy of, their human nature (Marx 1977: 820).

This is a description of a form of activity that bears little resemblance to work as it has existed historically, certainly not to capitalist work as described by Marx. In capitalism, as in previous stages of social development, it is not 'socialised man' that engages in work, but 'alienated man'; 'interchange with nature' (or possibly, work) is not something that is rationally controlled, it is in fact subject to the dictates of capital, which appears precisely as a 'blind force of nature'. Although necessary productive activity will still exist in communism, the individual, transformed by the developmental potentialities of free time, engages in this production not as work, but as 'experimental science, materially creative and self-objectifying knowledge' (Marx 1972a: 148–149). When the contradictions of capitalism have been overcome, with the social individual liberated from domination of time, from the domination of value as a measure of wealth, from the arbitrary division of labour, 'labour thus itself appears not to be labour any more but a full development of activity...' (Marx 1972: 86). It can be argued then, that although necessity will persist in communist society, the character of the productive activity that satisfies this necessity is so different from what has come to be called work, that it is not work at all.

The question of whether Marx advocated, and predicted, an end to work, or rather its transformation, could be seen as a matter of semantics, of course. At the start of this chapter, the idea of ideal work was discussed. Can this ideal conception of work now be considered not-work? How far need something be reconfigured before it ceases to correspond with the word used to define it before that reconfiguration? Many would argue that the prohibition of slavery changed little for the workers in the cotton fields of the American South, and yet almost overnight, 'slavery' was abolished.

Perhaps work, in Marx's communist society, takes on the character of play, and productive activity should be defined thus. Axelos considers this possibility:

…will not man's activity, in its polytechnical character, be of the order of Play? Does play constitute the sense of human action once it has surmounted the search for meaning, without for all that foundering in the absurd and the meaningless?... Will there be a global human activity in which productive and creative work, poetic activity and recreational activity will be fused in their singleness, and will this one activity be Play? (Axelos 1976: 313).

Unfortunately, Marx himself does not clearly answer this question. If anything, Marx can be seen as fighting shy of such a definition; he states that: 'Work cannot become a game, as Fourier would like it to be...' (Marx 1972a: 149). Elsewhere, Marx asserts that; 'labour can [not] be made merely a joke, or amusement, as Fourier naively expressed it in shop-girl terms' (Marx 1972a: 124). We should remember, however, that games, jokes, or amusements are not the same as play. Later theorists of work, such as Herbert Marcuse, have attempted to utilise the notion of transforming work into play, and interestingly, commentators in the field of policy and business consultancy have begun to investigate this very issue (see for example Kane 2004).

Conclusion

Ultimately, it serves no purpose to pursue with dogmatism at this point a single definition of what Marx saw as human activity beyond capitalist work; it is sufficient to show how Marx saw the radical reconfiguration of work as key to the realisation of human freedom, to the development of a truly human identity. For Marx, the abolition of work, at least work as we know it, is at the centre of a utopian vision. Utopias can be defined as 'blueprints of a future society that are incapable of realisation' (Levitas 1990: 35). Certainly, Marx would have balked at the suggestion that his analysis of the possibilities for social development beyond capitalism amounted to an utopia. We may wonder whether a classless, leisure oriented, workless society is a realistic proposition. We cannot know for sure, however, what is realistic and what is not.[7] Realistic or not, the contrasting of the ideal with the existing non-ideal can be a powerful method of social criticism,

---

7   One cannot help but be reminded of a slogan that appeared during the May Events of Paris in 1968, which read: 'Be realistic, demand the impossible!' (*The New Statesman* 1998, October 16). Marcuse, who will be the focus of the next chapter, was familiar with this slogan, as the following exchange shows:

'*Mr. Moyers*: There was another piece of graffiti from, I think, the Paris rebellion, that you once said was one of your favourites. Do you remember that?
Dr. Marcuse: Which one?
Mr. Moyers: "Be Realistic – Demand the Impossible".
Dr. Marcuse: Exactly. That is what I still think today. And I don't think you can call that mellowing' (Marcuse 2005a: 164).

what we might call, perhaps, critical utopianism. Marx uses an analysis of labour to highlight the ways in which individuals and society are confronted by forces seemingly outside of their control, stripped of their autonomy, their ability to act as free individuals. Since Marx's death, these issues have continued to preoccupy social theorists, who have sought to develop new analyses in the face of inevitable social change, often relating their insights to those of Marx himself. At the heart of some of the most powerful of these analyses lies the possibility of the end of work.

Chapter 5
Marcuse: Needs and Potentialities in the Age of Automation

Introduction

Herbert Marcuse never inspired a global political movement in the quite the same way that Marx did, and his profile has been subject to the same vicissitudes of sociological temperament that see Marxism's popularity vary from decade to decade. Yet in the context of this book, Marcuse is of great importance. With Marcuse, the theory of the end of work is refined, expanded and developed into the heart of a critical theory of society. By examining Marcuse's writings on this topic, we aim to achieve a number of objectives. Firstly, we hope to gain a distinctive perspective on the writings of Marcuse through a renewed evaluation of the cogency and criticality of his proposal of an end to work. Secondly, we shall situate Marcuse's theories within the discourse of the end of work that has been outlined in the foregoing chapters. As part of this second element of the discussion, we will gain a deeper and clearer understanding of the philosophical, anthropological, and political understandings that lie behind theories of the abolition of work. These understandings form a theoretical and discursive structure through which human society is understood and critiqued, and in which the end of work is something of an Archimedean point. The end of work, for theorists such as Fourier, Marx, Marcuse, and as we shall see later, Gorz and other more contemporary writers, represents the key to unlocking the human potential that capitalism denies; as a theory, it is both a clear and analytically coherent expression of the contradictions of capitalism, and a prescription for its resolution.

Marcuse's work contains many of the key elements of Classical, Fourierist and Marxist critiques of labour, but is responsive to the changes undergone by capitalist society during the twentieth century. The analysis in this chapter will attempt to demonstrate, by situating Marcuse in concrete historical, as well as intellectual context, how Marcuse's treatment of the end of work represents a transition and a progression from the theories of earlier writers, to those of individuals calling for the end of work in the twenty first century. In the chapters that follow, we shall discuss the role of theories of the end of work in the context of the development of social theory in the latter half of the twentieth century: Marcuse's writings will form an important element in this analysis, and the present chapter will provide some necessary background. The focus here will be on Marcuse's work itself, however.

Marcuse, needs, and the human essence

For Marcuse: 'The intention of the critique is to show that essential human needs and powers are being repressed and distorted in capitalist society' (Kellner 1984: 82). The ideal for Marcuse, like Marx, is a society in which human needs and potentialities are expressed and fulfilled free from repression and distortion. This can only occur when labour, in the sense of alienated work under capitalism, has been abolished. This analysis is based on a particular understanding of human nature, or human essence, if you will.

Marcuse's writings represent a continuation of Marx's critique, since like Marx, he sees both human needs and powers (or potentialities) as fulfilled and expressed, ideally at least, through work.[1] Marcuse's 1933 essay 'On the Philosophical Foundation of the Concept of Labor in Economics', while at times revealing a Heideggerian influence that was later to fade, contains some of the key conceptual positions on work and human essence that Marcuse was to hold throughout his career. Thus, Marcuse outlines the

> "place" of labour in the totality of human existence. In its broadest and most primordial sense labour is grounded in the mode of being human as historical being: in consciously developing one's own existence by means of the conscious mediating praxis of production and reproduction (Marcuse 1973: 29).

From early on then, we can see that what it is to be human is intimately bound up with work. Work and existence are further to be considered as historical; labour is the medium through which humanity creates itself – and this is expressed in the different social conditions extant at different historical stages. Thus society, and logically social critique, should proceed from an examination of the labour process, that is, work. Marcuse suggests in his later *Reason and Revolution*, that; 'Marx rests his theories on the assumption that labour process determines the totality of human existence and thus gives to society its basic pattern' (Marcuse 1969a: 295).

The relationship between the concepts of essence and work is not quite as straightforward as this kind of quote suggests however. Work, as we saw in the last chapter, is a kind of mediating and generative factor. Man is in essence a working, creative being, but this working and creating must be accurately understood; as well as being at the centre of man's essence, work is perhaps more crucially the means by which essence is expressed. This suggests that there might be, for Marx and Marcuse both, a human essence that is, if not independent of work and creative activity, at least prior to, or more 'essential' than it.

Already, in his 1932 review of the *Paris Manuscripts* (Marcuse 1972b), Marcuse had placed human essence at the centre of Marx's thought. Bourgeois

---

1   We will see that this statement is not as incompatible with the view of Marcuse as advocating the end of work as it might at first seem.

political economy is criticised as ignoring the central questions of existence, of what it means to be truly human. 'It disregards the essence of man and his history and is thus in the profoundest sense not a "science of the people" but of non-people and of an inhuman world of objects and commodities' (Marcuse 1972b: 11). Marcuse's methodology, in contrast, shares with that of Marx the tendency to counter pose the real, and the ideal, in order to highlight the tension between the two. Describing Marxism in 'On the Concept of Essence', Marcuse quite accurately describes his own form of critical theory: 'The tension between potentiality and actuality, between what men and things could be and what they are in fact is one of the dynamic focal points of this theory of society' (Marcuse 1972c: 69).

Perhaps paradoxically, and certainly rather confusingly, essence represents not something extant or real, rather it represents potentiality or 'what men could be'. Bourgeois political economy, and by extension much of mainstream social thought, confuses existence with essence, the is with the ought: Thus Marcuse is critical of the identity theories of positivist methodologies that accept only empirical reality, eschewing the second dimension of the ideal, of potentiality. Critical theory retains the idea of essence as a point of critique – it generates the tension, or creates the conceptual space, if you will, for critique to exist. Of course the ideal, for critical theorists such as Marcuse, and for Marx also, is somehow more real than reality; it is a representation of true existence in an undistorted state, an existence where essence is realised without distortion or perversion. In capitalist society, ideology prevents this state of affairs from being known, it obscures it from view. The task of critical theory then, is to go beyond ideology and seek out the reality, or more accurately the truth of the human condition, understand how this truth is denied in modern society, and suggest ways in which it could be realised.

We have already made some observations about the idea of essence; but we might continue to try and clarify exactly what is meant by the term. Essence can perhaps only be defined post festum (Marcuse 1972c: 73), since as Marcuse pointed out in his analysis of Hegel in *Reason and Revolution* (Marcuse 1969a), essence represents the stage of realization of something's potentialities. As Marcuse asserts in 'On the Concept of Essence' (Marcuse 1972c), 'The truth of this model of essence is preserved better in human misery and suffering and the struggle to overcome them than in the forms and concepts of pure thought' (Kellner 1984: 133). In a sense, Marcuse is here admitting the complexities associated with a definition of essence. Essence is better grasped by examining what makes us miserable and causes us to suffer, than through a reliance on philosophical concepts. However, philosophical concepts cannot be written out that easily. On the Marxian, and it could be argued, the Marcusean understanding, misery and suffering occur when an individual, or more generally the species as a whole, is prevented from satisfying their true human needs through fully exercising their true human potentialities. The following extended quotation contains Marcuse's definition of essence.

> Here the concept of what could be, of inherent possibilities, acquires a precise
> meaning. What man can be in a given historical situation is determinable with
> regard to the following factors: the measure of control of natural and social
> productive forces, the level of the organization of labour, the development of
> needs in relation to possibilities for this fulfilment (especially the relation of
> what is necessary for the reproduction of life to the "free" needs for gratification
> and happiness, for the "good and the beautiful"), the availability, as material
> to be appropriated, of a wealth of cultural values in all areas of life (Marcuse
> 1972c: 72).

So the individual is in essence a being with a set of needs that must be satisfied
through the realisation of their potentialities; the medium of this realisation is the
organisation of labour, and productive forces, in short, work. This conception,
of true needs which can be satisfied and developed through non alienated work
(the true expression of human potentiality), is hardly new; indeed it should be
familiar from our examination of utopian socialism, and of Marx. This conceptual
framework is developed to a fuller and more explicit extent in the work of Marcuse,
however.

Although understanding human essence through a theory of needs and
potentialities allows use more of an insight into the dynamics of the definition of
essence in Marx and Marcuse, it is hardly a final answer, since we are now left
with the question of defining true and false needs. For Agnes Heller, the concept
of people rich in needs is 'partly a pure philosophical construct' (Heller 1974:
45). Human essence, Heller argues, is, further to being a philosophical construct,
a value category. If the possibility of a future person rich in needs is merely
something existing in the mind of a philosopher called Karl Marx, however, who
will overthrow capitalism, and why? The answer for Marx was the proletariat, a
class that would eventually become aware of their true needs and the extent to
which they are alienated from them. For Marcuse, of course, this question was to
become rather more troubling.

Heller writes about Marx, although we might well extend many of her
observations to Marcuse,[2] for whom Marx is central to philosophical construction.
In the extended quote above from 'On the Concept of Essence', for example,
Marcuse refers to 'free' needs for gratification and happiness, for the 'good and
the beautiful' and a 'wealth of cultural values in all areas of life'. The fact that he
places 'free' and 'good and beautiful' in inverted commas suggests that Marcuse
himself was aware that in fact his definition of essence appears to rely on 'forms

---

2   In reading Heller on needs, it is all but impossible not to think that her analysis
is influenced, to some degree at least, by Marcuse. Witness the following passage: 'The
time has come to be more concerned with the alternative – how to organise the essentials
of social existence and human survival in such a way as to open better possibilities of
satisfying, more directly and more simply, the real needs of thinking, imagining, active,
loving human beings' (Heller 1974: 10).

and concepts of pure thought' – (the need for) 'freedom', 'good', 'the beautiful', not to mention gratification and happiness. (Here we might pause to note that through defining essence in terms of needs, Marcuse's critical theory remains true to its principles – the components of essence are not things we have, they are things we need.)

We seem to be left with a definition of essence that is somehow rather impressionistic and imprecise; a collection of concepts that themselves require definition. What is gratification, what is beautiful, what is freedom, happiness? Can these concepts ever be elevated above the realm of subjectivity? Possibly. Or at least, they can be shown to emerge not entirely subjectively, but rather to be linked to various discourses and perspectives that continue to inform social thought. Perhaps we must come clean and accept that there is no objectively verifiable human essence. There is merely a tradition of social thought extending from Ancient Greece to modern critical theory. Along the way, value judgements are made as to what is real, what is true, what is higher, what is lower. These judgements have been informed both by social context, and by developments in philosophical thought. Just as we saw in the last chapter that Marx's vision of an ideal, communist society (a society, we might now say, in which true needs are realised) was informed by Ancient Greek conceptions of the good life and the nature of work, as well as the aesthetic theory of Schiller, not to mention Fourier's utopia of the passions, so will we find that Marcuse develops his ideas in a definite intellectual context, of which Marx (and Marx's own influences, it turns out…) forms a central part. In accord with Andrew Feenberg (Feenberg 2005: 17), we suggest that Marcuse attempts to reconstruct essence historically, through encounters with Marx, Freud, German romanticism and aesthetic theory, and the artistic and intellectual avant-garde itself. This being the case, it is clear that our discussion of the concept of essence, and indeed that of true and false needs, is far from over. Although as we note, Marcuse himself never entirely escapes from the suspicion that needs and potentialities can indeed only be defined subjectively, and certainly with reference to philosophical tradition, it seems clear that Marcuse sees one element of human existence as a means through which freedom and happiness can be realised, and through which the extent of this realisation can be measured; this element is human historical species constitutive productive activity; work. As Marcuse wrote in 1945, 'We shall see how it is in labour that the distress and neediness, but also the universality and freedom of man, becomes real' (Marcuse 1972b: 22).

Work and Eros

For some, Marcuse's tendency to look at the fundamentals of human existence, or ontology, might belie the influence of his erstwhile mentor, Martin Heidegger (Feenberg 2005). For others, Marx provides both the conceptual framework (Agger 1992) and, in the case of Marx's early writings, the emphasis on the ontological dimension of social theory. Either way, as Douglas Kellner notes, Marcuse believed it essential to understand fundamental structures of human existence in order to provide an adequate foundation for social theory (Kellner 1984: 70). Throughout his career, Marcuse has indeed sought to uncover fundamental structures of human existence and use them as part of a critical framework. One of his best known attempts to do this was his 1955 book *Eros and Civilization*. This is also where the notion of the end of work receives its first extended exposition in Marcuse.

Eros and Civilization is usually seen as an attempt by Marcuse to integrate the work of Marx and Freud, with the latter's theory of instincts providing a more concrete basis to a theory of needs and human essence than had previously been the case. While we do not dissent from this view, it is worth noting that even the supposed arch rationalist Marx had already commented, albeit in a fragmentary fashion, on the psychological dimension of needs. As Heller has noted (Heller 1974: 42), Marx wrote of desires which are 'fixed and irremovable', and have in fact a biological basis. The notion that Marx saw men and women as equipped with biological drives is evident from the following quote, with which Charles Rachlis chose to open his account of *Eros and Civilization*: 'As a natural being... man is on the one hand equipped with natural powers...these powers exist in him as drives. On the other hand, as a natural, corporeal, sensuous, objective being, he is a suffering, conditioned and limited being' (Marx 1844, cited in Rachlis 1978: 64).

Marx's commitment to the idea of biological drives, however, should not be over emphasised. It may be the case that he was influenced by Fourier's writings on the passions, or perhaps we should understand these comments as made in the context of a Western intellectual tradition that has always presumed some biological dimension to human behaviour.

Interestingly, Marcuse in 1933 had argued against viewing labour in terms of biological need; 'The positing of man as a natural-organic being, however, is inadequate when dealing with his specific mode of being in the world...'(Marcuse 1973: 19). In the same piece, he had criticised Carl Bucher for explaining economic activity through drives (Marcuse 1973: 20). These points should not be taken as a serious contradiction to his later work, however, since their primary aim is to argue for the historically conditioned nature of needs, a line of argument that is in fact continued in the later Freud-influenced analysis.

In his 1938 essay 'On Hedonism' (Marcuse 1972d) Marcuse had introduced some of the arguments that were to be central in *Eros and Civilization*. These included the idea that repression is necessary to the maintenance of the status quo, and that the pursuit of pleasure and freedom should be central concerns of a liberatory theory. The idea that individuals labour under false needs and a false consciousness was introduced:

> It appears that individuals raised to be integrated into the antagonistic labour process cannot be judges of their own happiness. They have been prevented from knowing their true interest. Thus it is possible for them to designate their

condition as happy and, without external compulsion, embrace the system that oppresses them (Marcuse 1972d: 191).

In *Eros and Civilization*, Marcuse uses Freud's theory of the instincts to underpin his assertion that society represses the individual's essential urge towards pleasure, towards uninhibited self expression. Marcuse agrees with Freud's thesis, propounded mainly in his *Civilization and its Discontents* (Freud 1975), that social development depends on social labour, on work: 'Civilization is first of all progress in work...' (Marcuse 1987: 81). Again in agreement with Freud (and implicitly with Marx), Marcuse argues that work in industrial society is the very antithesis of pleasurable,[3] and is therefore anathema to the individual, whose opposition to work, and (essentially libidinous) drive towards pleasure, must be repressed in order for the institution of work and production to continue. This repression, Marcuse argues, is carried out under the aegis of a 'performance principle' that, in contrast to the pleasure principle, promotes the pursuit of production; it is, arguably, a concept closely connected with the idea of a work ethic. Performance principle is Marcuse's term, an adaptation of Freud's reality principle. The performance principle, Marcuse argues, is the form of the reality principle characteristic of modern industrial society. This repressive reality principle must be reinforced in a number of ways, since:

> left to itself, and supported by a free intelligence aware of the potentialities of liberation and the realities of repression, the libidinal energy generated by the id would thrust against its ever more extraneous limitations and strive to engulf an ever larger field of existential relations, thereby exploding the reality ego and its repressive performance (Marcuse 1987: 47).

Thus women and men must be occupied for the largest amount of time possible with the activity that reinforces most directly the performance principle, work itself. Marcuse suggests that we are left with little more than four hours per day of 'free' time; even this so called free time is colonised by the culture industry and leisure pursuits. This, Marcuse suggests, represents the extension of the realm of necessity into an already restricted realm of freedom, since in fact this realm of leisure is little more than an administered recuperation from the demands of work.

---

3   Although as Marcuse notes, some types of work are more acceptable than others. Displaying the by now familiar Enlightenment preference for artistic and intellectual work, Freud suggests that the work of the artist and the scientist allows them to gain a satisfaction that is 'finer and higher' (Freud 1975: 16).

Eros and automation

Moving to historicise Freud, Marcuse argues that while repression may have been necessary in historical periods dominated by scarcity, this is no longer the case, since modern production techniques, and above all automation through the use of advanced technology, mean that it is possible to free humanity (or at least that portion of it living in the advanced economies, of which the USA is exemplar) from the necessity of a life of toil. Under these circumstances, the current level of repression is disproportionate to that which is objectively necessary; it is surplus repression (Marcuse 1987: 35). Marcuse's aim is to show the necessity of exploding this system of repression, and abolishing the system of burdensome and unnecessary labour that it perpetuates. He is apparently calling for an end to work. In *Eros and Civilization*, Marcuse constructs a framework for critique that synthesises some of his earlier perspectives, and in fact provides the outline for much of his subsequent work. It may be in the interests of clarity to summarise this theoretical construction here, before analysing it in more depth in the rest of the chapter.

Marcuse argues that the objective potentialities of the affluent society mean we need not be enslaved by work, yet work continues to dominate the life of the individual in modernity. This state of affairs is explained through a theory of false needs and manipulated waste. Marcuse, or at least the Marcuse of *Eros and Civilization* and subsequent work, proposes that we could make work play, in a re-eroticised realm of freedom and creative activity. Marcuse's value judgements on why this should happen are informed not only by his conception of human essence, but by also by aesthetics, which in fact form part of his definition of what true human essence is. A new aesthetic state of re-eroticised work will require a new sensibility on the part of humanity – one that recognises both true needs and true potentialities.

Marcuse's observations on the potential in modern society of eradicating the need to toil are based around the idea that; 'Technology operates against the repressive utilization of energy in so far as it minimises the time necessary for the production of the necessities of life, thus saving time for the development of needs beyond the realm of necessity...' (Marcuse 1987: 105). And further: 'The more complete the alienation of labour, the greater the potential of freedom: total automation would be the optimum' (Marcuse 1987: 156). Marcuse is here restating Marx's idea that under capitalism, technology, although instrumental in the alienation and degradation of labour, in fact holds the key to its eradication. Marcuse's belief in automation is in accordance with both Marx[4] and some of the more openly utopian writers we have looked at. Throughout all end of work

---

4   We are in disagreement here with Edward Andrew who, in an article highly critical of Marcuse, suggests that Marx never entertained the possibility of complete automation (Andrew 1970: 242). See Schoolman for a contrary position to Andrew (Schoolman 1973: 295–302).

discourse, the idea of full automation is a common theme, recall, for instance, Marx's reference to the inventions of Daedalus, or engineer Etzler's dream of mechanical ease. Here we should also note the historical context in which Marcuse was writing; namely post war America.[5] As is illustrated by Amy Bix's *Inventing Ourselves out of Jobs*? (Bix 2000), automation was not only a hot topic in academic circles, it was frequently discussed in the press, and even inspired folk songs on the theme.[6]

The fact that Marcuse advocated total automation in theory is rather more clear than whether he actually thought this possible. Daniel Bell, whose work we know Marcuse had referred to, later characterised automation as a 'social-science fiction of the early 1960s' (Bell 1974: 463). Certainly, Agger considers that even for Marcuse, by 1969, complete automation represented a 'pipe dream at best' (Agger 1992: 173). Agger sees Marcuse, accurately, as advocating the fusion of work and play, productivity and creativity. It is worth noting that Marcuse tends to refer to the automation of labour, rather than work. 'Labour', Marcuse distinguishes from 'work'. Labour denotes the alienated productive activity, or 'toil' of the worker in capitalist society,[7] work serves more as a term referring to creative human activity, although this seems rather a problematic linguistic game to play, as we shall see later on.

Although a totally automated existence in the mould of Etzler is not what Marcuse has in mind, he does argue that toil/alienation are to be abolished, and that full or complete automation is the prerequisite. By full, Marcuse does not mean that every activity is to be automated, including the manufacture of machines themselves, rather that automation is to be utilised to the fullest possible degree; and further, while automation cannot lead to socially necessary work being performed, Fantasia like, as if by magic, automation can allow the worker to 'step to the side of production', in Marxian terms, and intellectual and creative work can be fused with socially necessary work. Automation in the first instance should be used to eliminate painful, repetitive work processes. Marcuse points out that critics of automation like Charles Denby often have in mind semi-automated factories where such work processes are still in place, but could be eliminated (Marcuse 1986: 25).

---

5 Although post-war France should probably be included as part of this context, since Marcuse maintained links with the *Arguments* group, which included writers such as Kostas Axelos and Serge Mallet.

6 The Chorus of this 1964 song ran:

'Oh, the wages were low and the hours were long

And the labor was all I could bear.

Now they've got new machines for to take my place

And you tell me it's not mine to share' (Ochs 1964).

7 The reader who might suggest we abandon any attempt to associate Marcuse with the end of *work* should remain patient. The use of the terms 'labour' and 'work' by writers like Marcuse rests on an epistemological/linguistic basis that we will have reason to discuss at the end of the chapter. We shall also see that Marcuse is not always assiduous in his differential use of the terms.

The status of work in the realm of necessity that is not repetitive in the sense of factory work, but that is equally unfulfilling at first sight (cleaning, for example) is not clear. Ideally, we assume that for Marcuse, even these tasks could become play. When writing about automation, Marcuse perhaps has in mind the highly automated industrial plants that were exercising the imaginations of various social scientists of the period. One wonders whether Blauner's *Alienation and Freedom* (Blauner 1964) was at all influential, although Marcuse does not cite it. Certainly it seems that Mallet's studies of the Caltex refinery (Mallet 1969) were a source for Marcuse's thinking on automation. Indeed, in *One Dimensional Man* Marcuse makes liberal references to empirical studies of automation, including those by Mallet. Daniel Bell is cited also, having made a study of the effects of automation in 1958 (Marcuse 1986: 29).

Given the central role that technology[8] plays in Marcuse's analysis of the end of work, we cannot avoid dealing with questions over his supposed technological determinism, however tedious and objectively unnecessary this may in fact be. Similar accusations of technological determinism have of course been levelled at Marx, sometimes based on his comments about steam power giving us the modern capitalist. As Joseph Chytry states; 'Although he does insist on the primacy of the productive element, Marx never abandons his early humanist position that the prime goal is control of production and technology by free and common deliberation' (Chytry 1989: 270). A virtually identical defence can be made of Marcuse, but this has not been enough for him to avoid accusations of technological determinism. Marcuse was fully aware, as was Lewis Mumford, one of the foremost twentieth century writers on technology and society that

> ...the machine is ambivalent. It is both an instrument of liberation and one of repression. It has economised human energy and it has mis-directed it. It has created a wide framework of order and it has produced muddle and chaos. It has nobly served human purposes and it has distorted and denied them (Mumford 1955: 283).

Marcuse does make some particularly ambivalent statements on technology, to be sure, and these could be used to support the notion that he is not only a technological determinist, but some kind of technophobe: 'Specific purposes and interests of domination are not foisted upon technology "subsequently" and from the outside: they enter into the very construction of the technical apparatus...' (Marcuse 1972e cited in Agger 1992: 205). On a superficial reading, this statement

---

8   Readers should note the following – discussions of technology in the realm of social theory, history and philosophy usually implicitly connect technology to work. Krell notes: 'Historians and social scientists define "modern technology" as the application of power machinery to production' (Krell 1993: 308). We must qualify this point, however, by noting that for Marcuse, particularly the Marcuse of *One Dimensional Man* and later, technologies orientated towards war or cultural manipulation are also targets for criticism.

could be seen as suggesting that domination somehow 'inheres' in technology. Certainly, there is no shortage of work by Marcuse that critiques the dominant technological rationality of modern capitalism. Note the word 'construction' however. Marcuse is arguing not that (advanced/industrial) technology is inherently dominatory, but that it is constructed as such by interested parties. The conclusion of the quote clarifies this point: 'Technology is always a historical-social project: in it is projected what a society and its ruling interests intend to do with men and things' (Marcuse 1972e cited in Agger 1992: 205). For Marcuse, technology is not inherently evil or inherently liberatory, neither is it something that autonomously shapes human existence; although for the worker, or the victim of mechanised warfare, technology appears oppressive, this oppression is actually a result of, and originates in, social organisation. Ben Agger expresses this particularly well in arguing that Marcuse views; '...science and technology as a transmission belt between human sensibility and the economy' (Agger 1992: 205). For Marcuse, the aim should be to transform all of these elements, including technology. Although at present technology is used to enslave people in pointless, but profitable drudgery, or to kill them in ever more efficient ways, the potential is there for a truly new, liberatory technology.

Work in one dimensional society

In his 1964 book *One Dimensional Man*, Marcuse does not cite Daniel Bell's 1956 essay *Work and its Discontents*, nor does he mention J. K. Galbraith's *The Affluent Society*, which was published in 1958. However, both books contain similar themes, even sometimes similar arguments to those of Marcuse. They also serve as evidence that the public imagination was very much occupied, and one would therefore think receptive, to these ideas. This was a period of unprecedented economic growth and stability, of rising incomes and fast developing technology. Already in 1956, Bell had begun to sketch the outlines of a theory of postindustrial society. Both Bell and Galbraith discuss the tendency for automation to lead to increased leisure time, and note the decreasing role of work in social identity. Bell writes that; 'The themes of play, of recreation, of amusement are the dominant ones in our culture today' (Bell 1956: 36). Of course, Bell uses the term play in a different, more conventional sense than Marcuse – more akin to leisure, than Marcuse's later idea of play. Galbraith's comment that one of the central economic goals of society should be to 'eliminate toil as a required economic institution' (Galbraith 1958: 264) shows that Marcuse was not alone in thinking along these lines during the (in some ways) optimistic, and certainly economically successful post war years. Galbraith comes even closer to Marcuse when he suggests that only 'an elaborate social camouflage' (Galbraith 1958: 264) has kept us from realising that a reduction of work is possible. Earlier analyses can be found which closely parallel the Marcusean line, as we shall see.

Lewis Mumford's Technics and Civilization was first published in 1934, and his analysis certainly contains elements prominent in Marcuse's writings on false needs and false consciousness.

> Unfortunately the capitalistic system...thrives by a denial of this condition [increased leisure]. It thrives by stimulating wants rather than by limiting them and satisfying them. To acknowledge a goal of consummation would be to place a brake upon production and to lessen the opportunities for profit (Mumford 1955: 396).

This logic is not unfamiliar to us. We have seen a similar analysis in the work of More, Fourier, Etzler and Morris. Indeed, most writers on the end of work argue that artificially stimulated consumption, whether by the production and promotion of unnecessary (luxury) goods, or through planned obsolescence, represents a primary obstacle to the reduction of working time. Marcuse develops this analysis most famously in *One Dimensional Man*, although the outline was sketched previously: '...whatever satisfaction is possible necessitates work, more or less painful arrangements and undertakings for the procurement of the means for satisfying needs...' (Marcuse 1987: 35). Capitalism creates an array of false needs in order to compel people to labour interminably for their 'satisfaction'. Thus the end of work is forever forestalled by the need to purchase, to consume, to enjoy. For Marcuse, unfreedom is already operative in the very needs and wants themselves, since they are but a wholly commodified simulacra of human satisfaction (Marcuse 1972d: 183). Note here the coincidence of false needs and unfreedom – that is, needs are false because they are unfree, and we are unfree because we are caught in the logic that compels us to satisfy false needs. False needs, for Marcuse, appear to be those that arise within a system of domination. Further, (and by extension) their satisfaction does not lead to true happiness; there is no happiness to be found in the commodity form, since this is but the objectification of alienation – in labour and from our fellow men and women. Any happiness that we derive from the consumption of the tawdry products of modern capitalism is both transitory and ultimately illusory. As Marcuse notes in *Eros and Civilization*, capitalist consumerism offers only illusory choices, and a distraction from the real issue, 'which is the awareness that they could both work less and determine their own needs and satisfactions' (Marcuse 1987: 100). Here we encounter another dimension in the definition of true needs; that they are self determined, autonomous.

In *One Dimensional Man*, Marcuse draws on contemporary commentators such as Vance Packard to illustrate the plethora of false needs created and satisfied in America's burgeoning consumer society.[9] Although we must look further to

---

9   In one passage in *One Dimensional Man*, Marcuse extends the idea of false needs to include actual occupations that merely reflect the need to sustain the performance principle/work ethic; thus public relations, advertising and many bureaucratic jobs are

determine positively what true needs are, Marcuse is explicit in his negative definition: 'Most of the prevailing needs to relax, to have fun, to behave and consume in accordance with the advertisements, to love and hate what others love and hate, belong to this category of false needs' (Marcuse 1986: 5). One criticism of Marcuse, levelled for instance by William Leiss, was that his criticisms of false needs in the consumer society represented ill-concealed snobbery (Leiss 1976 cited in Rachlis 1978: 79). Here we return to our earlier discussion on the definition of true and false needs. Marcuse's defence against such criticisms as Leiss's is disarmingly honest – he admits that judgements on needs are effectively value judgements, but that 'twas ever thus, from Plato to Hegel:

> To be sure, this is still the dictum of the philosopher…He subjects experience to his critical judgement, and this contains a value judgement – namely, that freedom from toil is preferable to toil, and an intelligent life is preferable to a stupid life. It so happened that philosophy was born with these values (Marcuse 1986: 126).

Rachlis's answer to Leiss's accusation is to define true needs in the way we suggested earlier, in negative terms. Conceiving of true needs also as 'autonomous needs', that is, needs developed autonomously, rather than as part of a system of domination, Rachlis equates them primarily with happiness – a happiness denied by the misery of an exhausting existence in capitalist society. The need for frenzied consumption and concomitant exploitation and environmental destruction are false because they degrade the individual (Rachlis 1978: 80), and because an existence of freedom (essentially from work) is possible, but is in fact denied by these very false needs. The first part of this statement is not entirely satisfactory, since it rests on a judgement of what is or is not degrading, and this is accepted by Rachlis. Rachlis acknowledges also that his further attempts to define true needs suffer from abstractness; 'needs for the free development of human faculties, for the happy deployment of the individual and collective desires, for the rebuilding of the natural and built environment…' (Rachlis 1978: 81). This is in line with Marcuse's explicit definitions of what he means by true needs, which are expressed in a fragmentary way, and of which the following is typical. '…the need for peace, calm, the need to be alone, with oneself or with others whom one has chosen oneself, the need for the beautiful…' (Marcuse 1970: 67).

---

seen as parasitical – a 'planned diversion of labour' (Marcuse 1986: 48); serving both to decrease those employed at entirely necessary labour (and thus increase their workload), and to maintain a significant sector of the population in work that is superficially satisfying, but has the ultimate aim of creating and servicing false needs. We should note that this idea, like many others, is not new; the idea that parasitical employments merely increase the workload of those usefully employed was propounded in More, Bellamy, Fourier and Morris.

We must not forget that work is the key factor in any discussion of false and true needs. As Agger notes, '…needs are false because they do not unite creativity and productivity' (Agger 1992: 90). This after all, is the aim for Marcuse; we cannot separate freedom and happiness from the question of work – as noted earlier, Marcuse shares with Marx the view of work as praxis; 'Thus, praxis in the "realm of freedom" is the authentic praxis and "goal" to which all other labor is directed: the free unfolding of existence in its true possibilities' (Marcuse 1973: 31). Since human essence is both expressed through, and defined by, praxis, or what Marcuse is prepared to call work, the truth or falsity of needs, freedom or domination are expressed through work – sometimes referred to as labour precisely to indicate that it is not free from domination.

Work and aesthetics in Marcuse

So the individual's essential and authentic need is self developmental, self directed and free creative activity. At present of course, a life expressed through this kind of activity is the province of certain classes; the intellectual, the bohemian, the sensualist, the artist. For these groups, the boundary between work and non work, even work and play is sometimes ill defined. Marcuse's aim is to abolish the boundary between work and play for all. Although we shall see that some of Marcuse's thinking on 'play' was informed by psychoanalytic research, the sphere of aesthetics was also to supply Marcuse with the framework for his liberated existence governed by a 'new sensibility'. It is hard to define quite what we mean by aesthetics, since one's thoughts immediately turn to art, and this was not Marcuse's only concern. Aesthetics in Marcuse, as will hopefully become clear, represents a way of judging existence, as well as a way of existing, that is somehow informed by what is good, and beautiful, creative and free, rather than miserable, ugly, deadening and imposed.

Work, play and aesthetics are linked in Marcuse's writing, just as they are in Schiller's, from whence Marcuse takes many of his cues on the topic. As Kellner notes: 'The notion of aesthetic education and the transformation of work into play as the basis of a new civilisation was the cultural ideal of Schiller' (Kellner 1984: 178). As early as the 1930s and before the influence of Schiller on Marcuse's (published) work had become more obvious, Marcuse was writing of play as the defining feature of a free existence. In play, he argued, '…one comes precisely to oneself, in a dimension of freedom denied in labour' (Marcuse 1973: 14). Play at this stage however, is relegated to the realm of freedom; he stops short of suggesting a fusion of play and work. Indeed, play is still here seen in terms of sports and games; '…in a single toss of a ball, the player achieves an infinitely greater triumph of human freedom over objectification than in the most powerful accomplishments of technical labour' (Marcuse 1973: 15).

We should note that Marcuse was not alone in writing about play in relation to work. Indeed, Marcuse was not the only writer of the twentieth century to suggest that work could become play. Again, Mumford's writing strikingly presages Marcuse's: 'When automatism becomes general and the benefits of mechanization are socialized, men will be back once more in the Edenlike state...work itself will become a kind of game' (Mumford 1955: 279). It was not until the 1950s that Marcuse was to suggest that work could in fact become play – something that can be seen as an abolition of the boundaries between the realm of freedom and the realm of necessity.

In *Eros and Civilization* and later writings, Marcuse attempts to incorporate Freudian concepts into his analysis. Thus, he suggests that sexuality, repressed under capitalist productivism, and desublimated only in the repressive forms of the culture industry, can be introduced into the activity of work. He hopes to activate the individual's 'polymorphous perversity', to free sexuality from its current genital locus. Drawing on a 1943 article by Barbara Lantos entitled 'Work and the Instincts', Marcuse suggests that it is the purpose and not the content that makes an activity work or play. If work could be made into an expression of polymorphous eroticism, it would be gratifying and play-like regardless of its work content. Lantos describes the activities of a playing child, his pleasure in free activity. This, she suggests, is 'auto erotic pleasure', a theory she takes from Freud (Lantos 1943: 114). 'Every organ is an erotogenic zone, every function is coupled with auto-erotic pleasure' (Lantos 1943: 114). Lantos does not argue, however, as Marcuse does, that the pleasure principle can be the governing factor in work, as it is in child's play. This element of Marcuse's argument sees him at his most radical, his most utopian perhaps. Certainly Marcuse's proposal that work can be eroticised is one of the most difficult to follow. All is fine if we define erotic loosely as pertaining to Eros, with connotations of pleasure and refinement, narcissism and display. The more straightforwardly sexual elements in Marcuse's work do seem over reliant on Freud's somewhat questionable theories, and relate to debates on sexuality that have become veritable relics of 1950s intellectual fashion.

Marcuse stops short of criticising Marx in the terms that Kostas Axelos did. For Axelos:

> Marx had reduced human reality to work, to making tools, to conquering nature, to producing efficient machines that led to automation; what he did not call enough attention to was that human reality also had to create itself, in Rimbaud's words, 'to change life', not only to satisfy material needs, but to maintain the full satisfaction of desire...subjectivity was reduced to tool making, and had no right of satisfaction of its own (Poster 1975: 226).

Axelos was a member of the French Arguments group, closely associated with humanist Marxism and the existentialism of Sartre. This was a group with which Marcuse was acquainted. Axelos, like Marcuse, saw play as a key factor in a liberated existence, for him, the most appropriate realm of thought and action in the post scarcity world is play (Poster 1975: 226). Unlike Marcuse, Axelos (in the postmodernist fashion that emerged partly as a result of writing such as his) sets off into an exercise in poetics (Poster 1975: 226). Marcuse took another path, although one in which poetry retained a role, in content if not in form.

It is not surprising that Marcuse draws on Fourier, since in some ways our utopian from Besancon can be seen as representing something of a connection between Marx and Freud himself, given his preoccupation with work, coupled with an interest in the 'passions' that form the instinctual substructure of humanity. It is possible that Marcuse's references to Fourier in his 1922 dissertation *Der deutsche Künstlerroman* were his first (Lowy 1980: 26). Here, Marcuse compares Fourier's position to the Romantic writers that were the doctoral student's main subject, with both seen as seeking a radical change in the nature of human existence, informed in large part by a search for a more pleasurable, and aesthetically informed life (Lowy 1980: 26). We saw in Chapter 3 that in Fourier's theories the aesthetic element is of great importance. In *Eros and Civilization*, Fourier represents perhaps the finest example of a thinker whose goals matched those of Marcuse. 'The transformation of labour into pleasure is the central idea in Fourier's giant socialist utopia' (Marcuse 1987: 217). The reassertion of Fourier's position in the context of late 20th century conditions, that labour could indeed be transformed into pleasurable play, is perhaps Marcuse's most important contribution to the end of work debate. Incredibly, even Charles Fourier was found lacking in terms of radicalism by Marcuse, who balked at the prospect of administered communities in the Fourierist mould (Marcuse 1987: 218).

Thus Marcuse's writing incorporates the analyses of Freud, Marx and Fourier.[10] A discussion of how Marcuse sees work being transformed into play is incomplete however, without a discussion of aesthetics per se, particularly in the context of German romanticism. We should not forget that these influences are also key to understanding not just how work and play might be combined, but why, in terms of what authentic human existence might look like, this combination should be carried out. Schiller's influence is clear, on both Marx and Marcuse. In a passage that can be read as an indictment of human alienation under the division of labour, Schiller observes that;

> Eternally chained to one single little fragment of the whole, Man himself
> grew to be only a fragment; with the monotonous noise of the wheel he drives
> everlastingly in his ears, he never develops the harmony of his being, and instead

---

10   We leave out the possible influence of Heidegger. Andrew Feenberg (Feenberg 2005) argues that Heidegger was perhaps the primary influence on Marcuse. This seems a difficult position to maintain. A preoccupation with the idea of authenticity is one possible link, but Marcuse clearly draws on other writers whose central concern is with the authentic human essence. We shall see later that Feenberg argues for the relevance of Greek notions of *techne* in Marcuse and Heidegger. Ancient Greek visions of creative work, like those of the good life, are not the preserve of Heidegger's critique of technology, they represent the very DNA of social critique since the enlightenment, particularly that which focuses on work (such as Marx).

of imprinting humanity upon his nature he becomes merely the imprint of his occupation, of his science (Schiller 2004: 40).

Play, for Schiller, is 'everything that is neither subjectively nor objectively contingent, and yet imposes neither outward nor inward necessity' (Snell 2004: 8). He is in no doubt that the authentic existence is the existence of play: 'Man plays only when he is in the full sense of the word a man, and he is only wholly a man when he is playing' (Schiller 80: 2004). Schiller's vision of the authentic individual is one who leads a creative, self directed life. The form of activity, both in terms of creating, and enjoyment, that embodies this kind of existence is, for Schiller, the fine arts. Schiller's is a view of human essence where freedom and beauty are closely linked (Chytry 1989: 78). As Marcuse himself pointed out, for Schiller, aesthetics is the new, or rather – potential – liberatory reality principle that will transform human existence (Marcuse 1987: 180).

In Marcuse's later work avant-garde art, poetry, creative writing, all represent a kind of ideal-type realm of freedom, a realm where aesthetic principles (as described by Schiller and Kant before him), rather than those of the commodity form, serve as the reality principle. As Chytry suggests, surrealism for example, represents for Marcuse something that: '…benefited revolution by demonstrating that the Marxist 'necessity' of material productive life ought to be transcended by the 'freedom' of surrealism, which strengthened the content in the "utopian concept"' (Chytry 1989: 412). Crucially though, art is not to be confined to the cultural realm. In Marcuse's liberated post work society, art will be incorporated into the process of production; this was the position, at least, that Marcuse had come to hold by the time he wrote *An Essay on Liberation* (Marcuse 1972: 39). Interestingly, Marcuse here suggests that art recover some of its more 'primitive elements' (Marcuse 1972: 39). Thus cooking and gardening are to be defined as 'artistic' activities in a future liberated society. It seems that although Marcuse continued to view the dimension of art, conventionally viewed, as holding a critical impetus in capitalist society; in a liberated society, the boundaries of art are to be generalised to include all self directed creative activity. Ultimately, society itself would become a work of art.[11]

For work to be transformed into a pleasurable compound of art and play, and for society itself to become a work of art governed by authentic needs such as love, peace, creativity and cooperation, Marcuse accepted that two phenomena must emerge; a new technology a new sensibility.

---

11   Those familiar with Marcuse's *oeuvre* will be aware of his 1978 essay *The Aesthetic Dimension*. With this short piece, Marcuse engages in debates around Marxist theories of literature and art, and the possibility of autonomous art. I have included no extended analysis of it here because a discussion of Marxist aesthetics is perhaps a digression too far in the current context. There is enough in the material covered in this chapter to establish the relationships Marcuse saw between work, aesthetics, and liberation.

Marcuse and the new sensibility

The new sensibility in Marcuse's liberated future society, which we are surely entitled by now to admit is a utopia, is to be based on new needs. Here we are back to the familiar problem of defining new (or true) needs. However, we have made some headway in this direction, and have noted that in a fragmentary manner Marcuse does make specific references to peace, beauty etc. These new needs can be summarised as aesthetic-erotic needs – needs for self realization and non repressive gratification (Kellner 1984: 342). At times, supposedly feminine qualities are seen as representing those in accordance with the new sensibility, and by definition representing negation of those dominant in the status quo... 'receptivity, sensitivity, non-violence, tenderness and so on' (Marcuse 2005c: 168).

Marcuse's reference to feminine values as containing liberatory potential is related to his more general observations on the women's movement that was becoming increasingly active during the 1970s. Marcuse was preoccupied with identifying groups with values in accordance with a new sensibility, since in actual fact, a 'transvaluation of values' was seen as a precondition for a transformation of society, and the emergence of a new sensibility. Feminism, of course, can be seen to emerge out of a particular set of socioeconomic and historical circumstances. In more general terms, Marcuse saw late capitalism as producing prevailing sets of individual and group values that would ultimately come to undermine the system itself. Changes in the nature of work and technology are of course crucial. Marx had seen increasingly scientific production processes as creating individuals with ever more developed faculties. In 'The End of Utopia', Marcuse self consciously follows a similar logic, suggesting that automation would lead to '...a creative experimentation with the productive forces' if it were freed from the fetters of capitalism (Marcuse 1970: 66). Although this has not happened, Marcuse does suggest that increasing use of technological production systems that demand intellectual development and creativity has led to an increase in revolutionary potential among certain social groups. Marcuse had, by the 1960s apparently given up looking to the working class as sole bearer of revolutionary potentiality; thus he looked to other social groups as potential candidates. Mallet's studies of the engineers in the Caltex refinery (Mallet 1969) provided a possible example of capitalist logic producing new values orientated towards creative and self directing work. As Poster has observed[12] (Poster 1975: 368), however, Marcuse was one of many commentators who looked on this particular social group rather too optimistically. By the time he wrote *An Essay on Liberation*, Marcuse had acknowledged that this group was just as integrated into the capitalist system as the rest of the working class (Marcuse 1972a: 60).

---

12 Poster does not refer to Marcuse by name, we should note.

Given the following description of the events of May–June 1968 in France, it is not surprising that Marcuse detected the stirrings of new needs, of a possible new sensibility amongst the students and the wider counterculture:

> ...schools throughout France were relinquished to the students...Ten million workers went on strike...Everywhere the smooth hum of the technocratic machine was silenced...the French paused and then began relating to each other in new ways, ways that evidenced creative powers that had hitherto lain dormant. In the eyes of many, the monstrous spectacle of meaningless toil and passive consumption gave way to an exhilarating, joyous festival (Poster 1975: 373).

The students, the counterculture, for Marcuse, did not represent a revolutionary force in themselves (Marcuse 1969b: 21). They did, however, represent a group that rejected productivist forms of socialism, and whose emphasis on freedom from expression and liberated sexuality Marcuse equated with an emerging consciousness that liberation, and the construction of a qualitatively new, and free, society, may be possible. Marcuse also associated these tendencies with an emerging view that the realms of necessity and freedom might become indistinguishable, that work itself could be initially rejected, and ultimately transformed. Radical youth were at least, Marcuse suggested, prepared to take the crucial step in developing a critical perspective, to 'think the unthinkable'. This, for Marcuse, represented perhaps the most critical aspect of a potential 'great refusal'. As for the hippies and psychedelia, the trip represented a liberation of the senses only in a distorted form (Marcuse 1972a: 44).

Ultimately, Marcuse's theory of liberation rests on a seemingly interminable contradiction, much the same as did Schiller's before him:

> But are we perhaps not arguing in a circle? Is theoretical culture to bring about practical culture, and yet the practical is to be the condition of the theoretical? All improvement in the political sphere is to proceed from the ennobling of the character – but how, under the influence of a barbarous constitution, can the character become ennobled? (Schiller 2004: 40).

Marcuse too admits the circle in which he is trapped;

> ...in order for revolutionary needs to develop, the mechanisms which reproduce the old needs must be abolished. In order for the mechanisms to be abolished, there must first be a need to abolish them. That is the circle in which we are placed, and I do not know how to get out of it (Marcuse 1970: 80).[13]

---

13   Note that in *Eros and Civilization*, Marcuse had suggested that some kind of educational dictatorship may be the only answer (Marcuse 1987: 225).

Marcuse's vision of a liberatory technology is a radical and exciting one, but it is largely conceived of in characteristically negative terms; certainly, the new technology is to be new indeed, since the real liberating tendencies of technology will only become apparent after 'capitalist industrialization and capitalist technology have been done away with' (Marcuse 1970: 68). We have already shown that Marcuse is not a technological determinist, but he was a critic of both the form of technology under capitalism, and the uses to which it is put. From *One Dimensional Man* onwards, Marcuse shows how technology is a crucial part of the machinery of repression. We have encountered this implicitly in the discussion of false needs that are transmitted largely through the electronic channels of the culture industry. In the realm of production, technology is constructed not with the aim of enhancing it as a creative and fulfilling experience for the worker, but is purely oriented towards profit. Not only is the worker demeaned and degraded by technology, the environment too is subject to capitalism's brutal logic; technology in Marcuse's future society is to be used not to dominate and destroy the environment, but to facilitate an equitable and non-destructive exchange between humans and nature. Even the scientific thinking underpinning capitalist technology is to be transformed – metaphysics is to become a guiding principle, replacing formal scientism; since the former can be used to project possibilities for liberation that a reconstructed technology can then be used to fulfil.

In the liberated society, as we have already noted, labour and art are to become one, and clearly, the technology of the work process is to be important. Feenberg understands Marcuse's utopian demand for a liberatory technology as 'an implicit recovery of the idea of techne in a modern context, freed from the limitations of Greek thought and available as a basis for a reconstructed modernity' (Feenberg 2005: 4). This is an interesting observation; we have already discussed the concept of work in ancient Greece, as well as their influence on Marx. It seems that the Greek conception of autonomous, self directed creative activity as the only true and authentic mode of existence is particularly influential.

Conclusion

For Aristotle, as for Marx, so for Marcuse, existence is seen as divided up into a realm of necessity, and a realm of freedom. The Greeks asserted theory as the highest order of praxis, the form of activity that most directly expressed the 'truthfulness of human existence' (Marcuse 1973: 31). Likewise for the early Marcuse, this hierarchical ordering is maintained, and art and science are placed in the realm of freedom, with labour or unfulfilling, exploitative work relegated to the realm of necessity. This is the dichotomy, enforced by the modern division of labour and the division of society into classes corresponding to this, that Marcuse was to explore for the rest of his career. In his essay 'On the Philosophical Foundation of the Concept of Labor in Economics', written in 1933, Marcuse criticises this division as leading to the bifurcation of praxis; the separation of the realms of necessity produces a one dimensional existence, whereas praxis should constitute the self creating activity of men and women in a unified totality.

Throughout our exploration of Marcuse's thought, we have portrayed him as someone advocating the end of work. Although we have hinted at complications in this portrayal, we have left it until now to fully justify it. Fortunately for us, Marcuse was himself asked to clarify his position; his answer is worth quoting at length:

> *Express*: Are you saying that labour should be totally abolished?

> *Marcuse*: I have wavered in terminology between the abolition of labour and the abolition of alienated labour because in usage labour and alienated labour have become identical. That is the justification for this ambiguity. I believe that labour as such cannot be abolished. To affirm the contrary would be in fact to repudiate what Marx called the metabolic exchange between humans and nature. Some control, mastery, and transformation of nature, some modification of existence through labour is inevitable, but in this utopian hypothesis labour would be so different from labour as we know it or normally conceive of it that the idea of the convergence of labour and play does not diverge too far from the possibilities' (Marcuse 2005b: 111).

This answer contains elements of the both 'early' and 'late' Marcuse. In 'The Concept of Essence', Marcuse asserts that 'Nature remains a realm of necessity: the overcoming of need, and the satisfaction of human wants will remain a struggle – a struggle, to be sure, which it will only then be possible to conduct in the manner worthy of man...' (Marcuse 1972c: 86–87). This indeed suggests that work in the realm of necessity, which we might possibly term labour, if not alienated labour, then routine and non creative work, would remain. Note, however, that it is to be conducted in a manner worthy of man. Marcuse is here suggesting that alienated labour is to be eliminated, even if socially necessary labour is not. In 'On the Philosophical Foundation of the Concept of Labor in Economics' also, Marcuse proposes an end to alienated labour. Certainly, taking Marcuse's work as a whole, including later material that proposes eliminating toil through automation, we can confidently assert that he argues, as Marx did, in fact, for the abolition of alienated labour.

For some commentators however, including Marcuse,[14] Marx retained an analysis of work where true freedom is restricted to a realm outside of necessity, beyond socially necessary work. Although we have argued that Marx can in fact be seen as advocating a complete transformation of work itself, Marcuse ultimately advocates going beyond Marx, and moving closer to the Fourierist idea that work, all work, can be essentially transformed into pleasure, into play. This, as we have seen, was not always the case in Marcuse. In 'Some Social implications of Modern

---

14 But not in my analysis – see Chapter 4 of this book.

technology', for instance, Marcuse continued to argue that it was only beyond the realm of work that truly free individual existence was possible. 'Beyond the realm of necessity, the essential differences between men could unfold themselves' (Marcuse 1998: 64). By the time he wrote *Eros and Civilization* however, Marcuse had indeed gone beyond Marx – we have seen how he proposed the transformation of work into play, and not merely the eradication of (alienated) labour. This is not a freedom from work, but rather a freedom in work. It can be persuasively argued that this represents in fact the eradication of the distinction between the realms of freedom and necessity, and is so radical a transformation of what we understand by the term 'work', that we can call this 'the end of work'. On the first point, Marcuse is certainly in accordance; this we know from his essay 'The Realm of Freedom and the Realm of Necessity: A Reconsideration' (Marcuse 1969b) where he makes it clear that the realm of freedom is to be extended into the realm of necessity – that is, work is to become subject to the free play of human creativities. In the same essay, Marcuse explains that he is not writing merely of the shortening of the working day, but of the 'transformation of work itself' (Marcuse 1969b: 24). For clarification, we can draw on an answer given by Marcuse in a 1968 interview published as 'Marcuse Defines his New Left Line'. When asked about the status of work in a future society, Marcuse replies that: 'We must have machines instead of slaves, but without returning to the feudal system. It would be an end of work' (Marcuse 2005b: 111). It seems that here we have some kind of an answer. Of course we cannot be sure that Marcuse was not mis-translated; he might have been persisting with the distinction between labour and work, and in fact meant the former. Alternatively, he may have accepted that such linguistic distinctions had become rather unnecessary by the late twentieth century, since in contemporary English at least, there is little distinction between the two concepts. In conventional usage, 'work' refers to alienated activity in capitalist society, just as 'labour' did for Hannah Arendt and the early Marcuse. Certainly, Marcuse would never suggest that human productive and creative activity would ever end, since this is the very essence of humanity. We might suggest then, that Marcuse was in accordance with our analysis on this point also, that the transformations he proposes to what we now call work would render this term wholly inappropriate. That the end of work may require us to choose alternative words to denote our most basic activities is something that we need not be concerned with here.

Marcuse represents a high-point in the utilisation of a theory of the end of work as a tool for critical social theory. Marcuse's imagination is unmatched – appropriately, since he himself emphasises the importance of imagination in creating the conceptual space for social change. Lowy is correct in claiming that Marcuse was both a romantic and a rationalist (Lowy 1980: 26). He is correct also in asserting that these poles are not contradictory. Marcuse's work is illustrative of the manner in which theories of the end of work combine the romantic and the rational to powerful effect. Although Marcuse's descriptions of a world without work sometimes read like an 'utopian novel' (Lowy 1980: 26). This apparently romantic conception is underpinned by rationalist observations based on changes in society, and in the sphere of production – specifically, the tendency for advancing technology to make alienated labour unnecessary. Both these theoretical understandings perform the same critical role – they counter pose the existing with the possible, the idea with the reality – this is the essence of critical theory. These two conceptions revolve around a demand that work be abolished, and the reasons that this demand is made are grounded in a particular set of beliefs about what it is to be truly human.

I hope to have shown that these beliefs arise within a set of specific discourses, which typically tend to revolve around a critique of work since it is in work, that humanity is both expressed and constituted. Beginning with Ancient Greek thought, attempts to realise the potential of the true human being have developed their theoretical groundings to incorporate the aesthetics of German Romanticism, the utopianism of Fourier, the anthropology and critical method of Marx, and Freud's theory of an instinctual dimension to subjectivity. Each writer we have encountered, and many we are yet to encounter, has added their own perspective on what a truly-human individual fulfilling true needs looks like, and indeed what these true needs are. These perspectives have been constantly informed by changing social conditions, from the industrialisation of Marx's England, to the automation and cybernation of Marcuse's affluent American society.

Charles Rachlis suggests a particularly useful simplification when he proposes defining the authenticity of existence in relation to the amount of happiness it allows. This is only a superficial simplification however, since we are no nearer defining happiness now than we ever were. We know, however, that under current conditions unhappiness prevails for the vast majority, and that conceiving of conditions where this would not be the case remains largely the province of philosophers and social theorists. Perhaps then, we should conclude, again with Rachlis, that the search for freedom, truth and happiness is the essential element in a critical process that seeks to formulate alternatives to our current distorted reality. Defining 'true' needs, as both justification for the abolition of work, and as key to understanding what a post-work world would look like, is a stimulus to constructing a vision of another form of society. As we intimated at the start of this chapter, theories of the end of work represent utopian thinking with a strongly rational basis that uses observations on a changing social reality to unlock the potentialities that are inherent in this reality; that these theories are utopian does not negate their status as a particularly powerful form of critical social theory.

Chapter 6
The Future of Work and Leisure

Introduction

All accounts of the end of work that have been examined so far have been couched in terms of the future. For the socialist utopians, Marx, Marcuse and Gorz alike, work had not *ended*; such an outcome depended on some form of social change – a revolutionary transformation of consciousness and society, typically. In this sense then, we have been dealing with the future of work from the outset of the book. The purpose of the present chapter is to examine discourses that for the most part are, unlike those connected with Marcuse or Gorz, apparently outside of the sphere of twentieth century Marxism. That Marx's influence is often relevant, if less apparent, will however – somewhat predictably perhaps – be found to be the case.

From Adam Smith and J. S. Mill to the Luddites and the followers of Captain Swing, commentators on work in industrial society have noted the tendency for machinery to replace and displace human labour. As we have seen, this dynamic was at the centre of Marx's vision of the transition to a communist society. B.K. Hunnicutt has provided an engaging account of how American workers achieved reductions in working hours during the latter part of the nineteenth century, and the first two decades of the twentieth. This trend of falling hours coincided, and was probably not entirely unconnected with, a growing interest in the concept of the end of scarcity (Hunnicutt 1988: 33–34). By the 1920s, particularly in North America – the most technically advanced of the industrialised nations – these changes began to be discussed in both the management press, and in the public sphere more generally. The debate over the future of work, and the apparently ascendant concept of leisure, was given extra impetus by developments in worker efficiency (and control) such as those introduced by Gilbreth, Taylor, and Ford, by advances in mechanisation, and by increasing concerns over technological unemployment.

Some writers appeared to take the depression of the 1930s as indication that technology was at the stage where people were being permanently eliminated from the production process. In both the USA and Britain, predictions of a leisured future were made; worrying for some, but for others replete with a certain promise.

In the USA, the briefly popular technocracy movement looked to a more rational organisation of production, and society in general, than the capitalistic 'price system', which the Depression appeared to suggest had had its day (Segal 1985: 121–123). One of the leaders of the technocracy movement, Harold Loeb predicted a leisured future in *Life in a Technocracy: What it Might be Like* (1933) (cited in Segal 1985: 141–145). Not only did the technocrats predict declining working hours, they also placed this in the context of a society beyond the wasteful vicissitudes of the profit motive, which continued to respond to inevitable technical increases in productivity with built in obsolescence and the burgeoning consumer culture. Technocracy proposed a kind of developmentalist utopia (Segal 1985: 141–145). Not for them idleness and dissolution, rather the flowering of art and creativity. Although technocracy's prediction of a 14 hour (or less) work week before the end of the century was never fulfilled, technocrats more recently continue to argue not only for an end to unnecessary work, but to the manufactured scarcity and widespread poverty with which they associate it (Nicholson 1996).

Shortly before the Wall Street crash, Walter T. Pitkin predicted a future of ease, but also of dissipation and decay, and declared; 'Better a world less good and [more] busy. Better a sea of trouble than a desert of ease! Better the burning dust of tired men than the twilight of the best minds' (cited in Hunnicutt 1988: 48). Others of the period were similarly wary; the end of work and the rise of leisure may be upon us, but this situation is not without its risks being the prevailing sentiment. Walter Lippman (cited in Hunnicutt 1988: 261) worried, for example, that the working classes were spending too much time going to parties, the cinema, and listening to the wireless. In fairness, this apparently conservative take on the emerging leisure society relates, in the case of this critic and many others of the time, less to a patrician desire to limit the free time of the workers, than to a concern that the rise in *so called* free time was being matched, and apparently absorbed, by the expansion of the culture industries, and what would later be called 'mass leisure' (Larrabee and Mayerson 1958). Across the Atlantic, John Maynard Keynes, writing in 1932, similarly viewed the prospect of the end of work with mild trepidation (although he does not relate it to the rise of mass leisure in quite the same way as many of the American commentators):

> ...the *economic problem* may be solved, or at least be within sight of solution, within a hundred years...thus for the first time since his creation man will be faced with his real, his permanent problem–how to use his freedom from pressing economic cares, how to occupy the leisure, which science and compound interest will have won for him...Three-hour shifts or a fifteen hour week may put off the problem for a great while. For three hours a day is quite enough to satisfy the old Adam in most of us! (Keynes 1932: 366–369).

We will not know for another few years whether Keynes's prediction of the future of work was accurate, but he at least restrained himself from suggesting that the end of labour, and the rise of the leisure society was actually imminent.

Hunnicutt's detailed historical account of what are in effect early twentieth century debates over the end of work is difficult to improve on, and interested readers are directed to this material. Of particular relevance in the present context is the quote with which Hunnicutt chose to end his book; it relates, appropriately, to his thesis on why the fight for shorter hours was abandoned, and to a central element of our own examination of the end of work. Hunnicutt quotes Marcuse, whose analysis we have already examined in some detail. An extract from *Eros and Civilization* mirrors Hunnicutt's own findings, that while some social commentators worried that the growing free time of the masses might be diverted into marketised consumerism, industrial and commercial elites worried that they might *not* be:

> …automation threatens to render possible the reversal of the relation between free time and working time: the possibility of working time becoming marginal and free time becoming full time. The result would be a radical transvaluation of values, and a mode of existence incompatible with the traditional culture. Advanced industrial society is in permanent mobilization against this possibility (Marcuse 1987: vii).

According to Hunnicutt, this mobilization was conceived of fairly explicitly by capital, and found its ideological manifestation in the expansion of consumerism, through the intensification and extension of advertising, part of which included an unprecedented denigration of domestically produced goods, with the aim being their commercialisation. 'The new "gospel of consumption" was designed specifically to ensure industrial advance and save work' (Hunnicutt 1988: 50). As the choice of quote from Marcuse illustrates, Hunnicutt did not pluck this account from a theoretical void.

The use of detailed historical evidence to support the assertion that work has been deliberately maintained through the engineering of the expansion of consumerism follows in the tradition of writers such as Ewen, whose contribution is seminal (Ewen 1976). Interestingly, despite the interdependency of work and consumption, Ewen notes that advertisers considered the mere mention of work to be 'bad copy' (Ewen 1976: 79). This view supports the argument made in Chapter 8 of this book, that the obfuscation of the importance of work is more befitting of advertising copywriters than social scientists. Of course, earlier writers had noted the elevation of consumption over production, at least in ideological terms, and the concomitant tendency for the general population to emulate the leisure class's image of a life free from the necessity of working (Veblen 1915: 103–104).

One might wonder whether those in charge of kick-starting modern consumer society as a response to the decline in the objective necessity of work during the pre WWII period were influenced primarily by their own observations of social, industrial and technological change, or whether they were reacting to commentaries on the future of work. It would be rather ironic, would it not, if the latter were the case? On Hunnicutt's account, however, it appears that business leaders were acting on more concrete observations; those concerning the bottom line, with the wider issue of economic growth adding to their anxiety.

> If basic needs were being met by industry, and if workers chose to devote less and less time to their work, then extended periods of general unemployment

would not be necessary to halt progress. Free time in the form of leisure could create the same conditions as free time in the form of unemployment: reduced production and consumption, idle productive capacity, limited investment opportunities, and even a mature and stable economy (Hunnicutt 1988: 39).

The relationship between the consumerist nature of contemporary society and the maintenance of toil was observed by various other writers during the twentieth century, including Lewis Mumford, J. K. Galbraith, Marcuse, and more recently, André Gorz. As we will see in the present chapter, debates over the future of work often centre on an essential dialectic, between some kind of 'higher' existence, of free expression, enlightenment, and self development – which tends to be associated with the end of work – and an existence based on consumption and commodification, in which real autonomy is limited, both by the perpetuation of toil, and what appears to be the chief means of this perpetuation, the ideological dominance of consumerism, fuelling a growth based economy. In forecasts and predictions of the future of work, the *end* of work, and the rise of leisure, is often a central element. The concept of the end of work seems to provide a wide range of commentators with a means of highlighting the supposed irrationalities in the way contemporary Western society is organised, in terms both of consciousness and empirical social conditions. It offers the promise of a more fulfilling and authentic existence, whilst simultaneously compelling us to wonder why the routes to this existence remain blocked.

Automation, the affluent society and the future of work

The onset of The Second World War, not surprisingly, meant that '[t]he entire context for talking about workplace technological change had shifted' (Bix 2000: 233). Discussions about the future of work, technology and leisure, while no doubt extant in the interim, only came to the fore once again in the late 1950s, particularly in the USA. This time it was not worker activism, unemployment and recession that stimulated debate, but economic success and unprecedented material abundance. At the same time, advances in workplace technology continued, having themselves been stimulated by war.[1] Words like cybernation, robot and computer began to appear in reports and commentaries on work.

In 1956, Daniel Bell (who was later to distinguish himself by introducing the theory of post-industrial society to a wide sociological audience), suggested that 'The themes of play, of recreation, of amusement are the dominant ones in our culture today' (Bell 1956: 36). This super-structural development was a reflection of the fact that 'The vast development of automatic controls and the continuous

---

1   'The first all-electronic computer was built at the University of Pennsylvania, to solve problems in ballistics and aeronautics for the U.S. Army' (Fry 1975: 8). ENIAC, as the computer was known, entered service in 1946.

flow creates the possibility of eliminating the workers from production completely' (Bell 1956: 45). Looking back to the utopias of the past, Bell suggested that industrial civilisation had reached a stage where bygone hopes could actually be realised.

By 1958, when a group of well known American sociologists published the volume *Mass Leisure* (Larrabee and Mayerson 1958), churches and academics alike were worrying about people having too much leisure time. According to some, a three day week was 'imminent' (Lynes 1958: 346). Once again, the role of technology was emphasised, and if a thinker as sophisticated as Daniel Bell could submit to what appeared to be technological determinism, it is no surprise that others followed suit, with Russell Lynes declaring that reduced labour time was less the result of labour's activism, than of the telos of technology; 'Machines not men have created the three day weekend' (Lynes 1958: 346).

For these critics, as for those of thirty years previous, the issues of consumption and needs were central; and once again, some accounts struck an ostensibly conservative tone. Riesman, for example, seemed worried by the prospect of the uneducated masses falling victim to the temptations of abundant leisure time.

> For many people today, the sudden onrush of leisure is a version of technological unemployment: their education has not prepared them for it and the creation of new wants at their expense moves faster than their ability to order and assimilate these wants (Riesman 1958: 363).

However, it is not the classical, enlightened model of leisure that such writers were critical of. Rather, their concern continued to be with both the nature of consumer society, and the values underpinning it. Whatever the misgivings of liberal commentators during this period, the future was widely perceived as one characterised by decreased working time, and the increasing dominance of leisure, for the masses at least. It was even suggested that work might become the privilege of a ruling elite (Riesman 1958: 374).

By 1962, it seemed to some that, for Americans at least, the land of Cockaigne was theirs for the taking. Sebastian De Grazia, however, offered a classic account of the paradoxical relationship between leisure and abundance in industrial society (De Grazia 1964). Although De Grazia is not seen as writing from a radical standpoint, his analysis has some parallels with Marcuse, whose writings on the radical transformation of work we discussed in Chapter 5. Marcuse, we may recall, suggested that false needs were being created by capitalist society in order to keep workers in a state of permanent dissatisfaction, and therefore willing to continue lives of toil. He agreed with many more mainstream figures that technology, particularly automation, held the key to a workless world, and even at the level of the 1960s, was capable of vastly reducing labour time. The capitalist system prevented this from happening however, presumably afraid that the masses, faced with expanded free time, might choose to expand their consciousness as well, something that could threaten the status quo. In this analysis, humanity appears trapped in an ontological circle – for work to be abolished, people's attitudes, to consumption, economics, and politics must change, but for attitudes to change, people must be free from the cycle of work and spend that characterises life in late industrial society. So the abolition of work remained part of a future utopia. In the analysis of Marcuse, the fact that the social system prevents the future of work becoming the present was used as part of a global critique of capitalist society (Marcuse 1964).

De Grazia, like Marcuse sought to comprehensively explode the myth both of a leisured present and a leisured future. In a sense, of course, one person's present was somebody else's future, and De Grazia drew attention to the fact that predictions of the decline of work were nothing new:

> Every half century from the time of the industrial revolution on, we have men of wisdom and vision predicting more time to come. One of the things that bids us be cautious about accepting glowing prophecies of the future of free time that up to now they have all been wrong about it (De Grazia 1964: 285).

Despite a growing plethora of labour saving devices, and advances in technology and communications, the worker of 1960s America was little better off than his or her counterpart a century before. Not only did the increased dominance of clock time and the use of machinery mean that working days were more regulated and intense than in the past, according to De Grazia, domestic appliances, radios, wristwatches and automobiles merely added to the diurnal clutter of life in high modernity: 'Wherever timesaving appliances, communications, and transport abound, time – harried faces appear at every turn' (De Grazia 1964: 315). Work remains dominant, and consumerism is once again the main culprit, with the good life characterised by 'whatever industry produces, advertisers sell, and government orders' (De Grazia 1964: 279). For the individual, the central dilemma of consumer society is the fact that the more one spends on prestigious goods, both to save time and to ensure one's status, the more one must work, and the less time one has to enjoy them, and indeed life itself. Just as in Marcuse's analysis, the false needs of the consumer are never satisfied, and the road of abundance leads only to more toil.

Like many other writers on the cultural position of work, De Grazia has a critical understanding of its antithesis, leisure. His is the utopian, the developmentalist view of time that should be truly free, and yet remains merely a commodified restorative for further work. '[C]reativeness, truth, and freedom…discovery and creation' (De Grazia 1964: 395), are the qualities associated with authentic leisure. This is the ideal with which the reality of passive consumerism is contrasted. Under such a system, the future holds out the promise not of less work and more truly free time, but of 'patriotism and work, war and fighting…'[2] (De Grazia 1964: 279).

---

2   As of 2009, such a prediction seems to have been reasonably accurate.

Both writers were sure that the issues of work and free time were political ones, since they ultimately beg the question 'what to do with one's life here and now' (De Grazia 1964: 392). The future of work is posed as a question of essence, something at the core of what it means, should, and could mean, to be truly human. In the same way that Marcuse saw humanity trapped in a kind of double hermeneutic, with radical change and a transformation of values almost fatally interdependent, De Grazia saw the dialectic of exhausting toil and tranquilising leisure as preventing any meaningful discussion of their own legitimacy: 'With work dominant, free time raises no such question: work takes care of the answers' (De Grazia 1964: 392). De Grazia, like Marcuse, does detect changing values amongst certain sections of the population, but does not specify who, and his prediction of how this situation may develop is far from revolutionary. It seems the best we can hope for is that the future of work and time will come under ever increasing scrutiny. We will see in the present chapter that in the Anglo-American context at least, this has not happened.

One key difference between De Grazia and Marcuse's often similar accounts is, of course, the fact that the latter is much more closely associated with Marxism. Marcuse was fairly explicit in his analysis that for time to be truly free, and truly free from work, capitalism must come to an end. De Grazia makes no such assertion, and although he is certainly aware of the relevance of Marx (De Grazia 1964: 333), is never quite able to propose that it is the domination of capital that prevents consciousness of the possibility of a world free from capitalist work, from ever emerging in depth.

Futurology and revolution: Towards the year 2000

America's fascination with the brave new world of automation, and the social changes supposedly associated with it, continued through the 1960s. Accounts began to appear suggesting that work was reducing itself, or rather, that the new technologies of cybernation[3] were doing so. Kahn and Wiener's *The Year 2000* (1967) is typical of non Marxist commentary on the future of work during this period. Their account is seen by some as archetypal of the futurology that proliferated during the 1960s; funded by Rand or the Hudson institute, spurred on by an increased state commitment to social planning, and the growing prominence of science and technocracy during the era of space travel (Kumar 1978: 186). Although it is possible to see accounts by writers such as Kahn as merely apolitical relics of the era of 'hyperexpansionism' (Robertson 1985: 5), these non Marxist analyses are not without their insights, and are less outlandish in their claims than is sometimes supposed.

---

3   'The combination of the computer and the automated self-regulating machine' (Bell 1974: 463).

Kahn and Wiener are, like De Grazia (whom they reference) initially sober in their assessment of the so called age of leisure, both in terms of the present and the future. Noting that work time had not dramatically decreased in the post-war period, their future scenario is far from extravagant, with annual hours seen declining from 2000 to 1700–1900 by the year 2000. Hardly the end of work. However, elsewhere, Kahn and Wiener predict a declining dominance of the cultural significance of work.

> Let us assume, then, with the expanded Gross National Product, greatly increased per capita income, the work week drastically reduced, retirement earlier (but active life span longer), and vacations longer, that leisure time and recreation and the values surrounding these acquire a new emphasis. Some substantial percentage of the population is not working at all (Kahn and Wiener 1967: 194).

This non working class are to be supported by an increased commitment to welfare, although Kahn and Wiener do not explicitly propose a guaranteed minimum income. Unlike some other writers of the period, they say little about the possibility of social polarisation in the future.

Like the other commentators examined in the present chapter, Kahn and Wiener have much to say on changing values, and like most other analyses of this phenomenon, particularly of this period, their statements are pure speculation. While Marx, Marcuse et al looked to a change of values in the direction of an increased emphasis on self realisation, Kahn and Wiener depict this as a rise in the number of 'sophists, epicureans, cynics, primitive or humanist sensualists, other materialists, and various kinds of dropouts…' (Kahn and Wiener 1967: 125). They remains ambivalent however, and fight shy of any prediction of an end to the work ethic, pointing out that there will always be people for whom the idea of extra work for extra pay, and the luxuries it can buy, is attractive.

Kahn and Wiener are at their most insightful when discussing the difficulties of making predictions regarding the future social and cultural position of work. While it is possible, as they note, that a decline in working hours may lead to a decline in the cultural importance of work, it is equally possible that the opposite could prove to be the case. Work could in fact grow in importance. That is, if work were to become scarcer, it could come to be seen as something of a privilege, and therefore valued more highly.

> One of the greatest problems…of sociological speculation has to do with the dialectical quality of the processes involved…For example, if work will occupy fewer hours of the average person's life, it is plausible to speculate that for this reason work will become less important. On the other hand, it is at least equally plausible that the change in the role of work may cause work as an issue to come to new prominence (Kahn and Wiener 1967: 194).

The ideology of work has the potential to either wax or wane, or do both simultaneously, but amongst different sectors of the population. It is possible to conceive of a split in the ideology of work serving the functional priorities of a society, with the underlying population being encouraged to prioritise leisure, since little work is available to them, with an administrative elite encouraged to continue to emphasise the ideology of work, since it remains necessary for society to be administered. This conception is, admittedly rather similar to various scenarios imagined in works of science fiction, a point we will return to later in this chapter.

If further evidence were needed to confirm that the future of work was a major concern in the public sphere during the 1960s, particularly in the USA, we might briefly examine the letter sent by the 'Ad Hoc Committee on the Triple Revolution' (Agger et al 1964) to President Lyndon B. Johnson in March 1964. As Bix notes, this report had 'overtly socialist implications' (Bix 2000: 269), the most radical being, that a guaranteed minimum income was necessary to prevent social polarization and breakdown. The report is a classic statement of the problem of technological unemployment:

> The cybernation revolution has been brought about by the combination of the computer and the automated self-regulating machine. This results in a system of almost unlimited productive capacity which requires progressively less human labor. Cybernation is already reorganizing the economic and social system to meet its own needs (Agger et al 1964).

The labour that tends to be eliminated first, according to the letter's signatories, is low skilled. Unlike *The Year 2000*, the *Triple Revolution* letter paints a picture of growing social polarization: '"The confluence of surging population and driving technology is splitting the American labor force into tens of millions of 'have's' and millions of 'have-nots'"' (Agger et al 1964). Arguing that 'wealth produced by machines rather than by men is still wealth', the committee 'urge, therefore, that society, through its appropriate legal and governmental institutions, undertake an unqualified commitment to provide every individual and every family with an adequate income as a matter of right' (Agger et al 1964). The idea of a guaranteed minimum income, conceptually, seems straightforward enough, despite the possible practical complexities of its implementation, but the apparently equally straightforward idea that wealth produced by machines is still wealth, is a contentious one, and goes to the heart of the idea of the end of work. Most theories of the end of work share this idea, but rarely is it made clear quite how opposed this notion is to the economics of capitalism. That the proposals of the *Triple Revolution* report were rejected by the government of the day is no surprise, since the capitalist system depends on a definition of wealth that involves the extraction of surplus value from human labour, not mechanical.

The authors were, in effect, calling for a transition to the prioritization of use value over exchange value. The *Triple Revolution* report at least acknowledges that production for people, rather than profit, is not the current *raison d'être* of the American state; 'national policy has hitherto been aimed far more at the welfare of the productive process than at the welfare of people. The era of cybernation can reverse this emphasis' (Agger et al 1964). The latter part of this statement appears highly technologically determinist, as do other statements within the report. However, the fact that the authors make recommendations of policies to ameliorate the unemployment and poverty that cybernation has caused, shows that they understand the key factor in social change to be human decision making, rather than technology; that is, human agency and social forms are *prior to* technology. It is possible to *choose* to use technology differently, or for different social aims. Whether capitalism is characterised by the absence of control over technology, a decision not to exercise control, or indeed depends precisely on such control, is thus far a moot point.

What is missing from the *Triple Revolution* report, as from the other accounts examined here, is an understanding of the radicality of their own proposals. Unlike Marx and Marcuse, few of the future of work writers of the 1960s considered it necessary to argue for a complete transformation of society, although the *Triple Revolution* group came close. While for Kahn and Wiener, work was likely to decline naturally, and without causing massive social problems, under capitalism, the *Triple Revolution* committee members seem unaware that their prescription for a future of declining work would entail American capitalism, arguably the most powerful and stable social system the modern world has known, abolishing itself.

The future of work in postindustrial society

The period 1968–1973 can be seen both as the peak of an era of economic growth, and also the climax of protest movements apparently oriented around demands for greater autonomy in the university and the workplace (Rose 1985). In the realm of sociological theory, the 1970s also saw the rise to prominence of the idea of postindustrial society, due in no small part to the publication of Daniel Bell's *The Coming of Post-industrial Society* in 1974.

Bell's *Post-industrial Society*, it should be noted at the outset, is not a book that diagnoses or predicts the end of work. Nor are many of its ideas radically different from those that we have already come across whilst discussing books from around the period it was being written. The two most significant trends discussed in *The Coming of Post-industrial Society* were, arguably, the shift in emphasis from the production of goods to the delivering of services, and the growing importance of knowledge as a key factor in ordering late twentieth century economy and society in the West.

As is typical of future of work literature, the role of technology is central. However, Bell has revised downwards, by 1974, the claims he had made for automation in 1956, and suggests that predictions such as those made in the *Triple Revolution* letter were merely 'one more instance of the penchant for overdramatizing a momentary innovation' (Bell 1974: 463), in this case cybernation. Bell, whilst agreeing with the analysis of American society as having gone beyond the realm of necessity, does not see productivity as having risen enough to liberate humanity from work. Time, rather than being liberated entirely from the fetters of labour, has itself become 'an economic calculus' (Bell 1974: 466).

Also of interest is Bell's view that consumerism had led to a hedonistic way of life and a destruction of the protestant work ethic. Capitalism, in this reading, has undermined one of the founding principles of its existence. The post scarcity society has allowed a class to develop for whom the bourgeois attitudes of high capitalism are increasingly irrelevant, and who instead increasingly inhabit a realm of 'prodigality and display', of '*carpe diem*' (Bell 1974: 78). This, strangely, appears to be sustainable without an equally prodigious amount of work, although Bell at least acknowledges that the world of work is still dominated by the values of industriousness and self control, bringing it into ontological conflict with an increasingly post-bourgeois cultural sphere. The fact that consumerism has emerged as, essentially, the replacement for the protestant work ethic in that it obliges people to work more, rather than less, is not picked up by Bell at this point. A close reading, however, reveals that this analysis anyway refers only to the rising knowledge class, while the working class continue to covet 'ever expanding goods and production' (Bell 1974: 479). Bell sees the new modernists, the ascendant knowledge manipulators, as being the key meaning bearing group of the future, and suggests that they dominate the media and culture. He seems to have underestimated the extent to which apparently anti-bourgeois attitudes can coexist with a willingness to promote consumerism to a surprisingly numerous working class, which is essentially the role of the media and 'culture'. Moreover, Bell has underestimated the allure that consumerism or 'expanding goods', hold for the new knowledge elite, as well as the working class, whilst overemphasising the so called anti-bourgeois attitudes of the former. Like many others writing during the early 1970s, in the wake of 1968 in France, the campus disturbances in the USA, the anti Vietnam struggle, and the civil rights movement, it is likely that Bell was guilty of what he had criticised in others, over-dramatizing a momentary innovation, in this case, the anti bourgeois affectations of the youthful demimonde. Bell is not the only commentator to be guilty of over-dramatization, as we shall see.

The revolt against the work ethic and the revenge of work

Diagnoses of a declining work ethic were common currency in the 'peak' period of 1968–1973: Indeed by the early 70s they were reaching something of a feverish pitch, particularly in the pages of American newspapers and magazines. It seemed to many that in terms of work's future – it simply did not have one. In 1973 A special government task force was established to try and gauge the levels of 'blue collar (and indeed white collar) blues' amongst the American population, and this resulted in a book entitled *Work in America* (U.S. Department of Health, Education and Welfare 1973). The following articles represent merely a sample of those appearing in wide circulation print media during 1972 and early 1973 (it is taken directly from an article by John Zerzan, who we will come to shortly): 'Barbara Garson: 'To Hell With Work', *Harper's*, June 1972; *Life* magazine's 'Bored On the Job: Industry Contends with Apathy and Anger on the Assembly Line', September 1 1972; and 'Who Wants to Work?' in the March 26 1973 *Newsweek*' (Zerzan 1974). The *Work in America* report concluded, contrary to sensationalist media accounts, that there was no great weight of evidence supporting claims of a 'new "anti work ethic"' (U.S. Department of Health, Education and Welfare 1973: 43). Research by Yankelovitch was cited which suggested that 79% of young people still believed a career is a meaningful part of one's life (U.S. Department of Health, Education and Welfare 1973: 43). Leaving to one side the reliability and ultimate usefulness of such attitudinal research in itself, we can at least see that not all commentators were taken in by the media's portrayal of revolting workers.

The 'theory', or more accurately perhaps, *the claim* of the revolt against work in the late 1960s and early 70s was not totally without foundation. Absenteeism,[4] turnover,[5] sabotage[6] and strikes[7] did all appear to be on the rise during this period, not just in the USA, but throughout the industrialised world. Particularly badly hit in the US was the auto industry, and this branch of production seems to attract the attention of sociologists and commentators quite like no other. 1973 witnessed what appeared to be an unprecedented upsurge of labour activism amongst car workers, labelled by some the '73' Wildcats' (Ramirez and Linebaugh 1992: 153). John Zerzan, writing from what might be seen as an anarchist perspective, can be seen as one of the main proponents of the idea that the sabotage, absenteeism and a series of strikes at factories such as Dodge Truck (June 1974) and GM Lordstown (1970–1974) represents a significant development in worker consciousness, and an oppositional statement against capitalist hegemony. Zerzan, like others of this ilk, provides supporting material that is heavy on examples, but rather less weighty in terms of analysis. Still, sabotage, wildcat strikes, and absenteeism are seen as

---

4   Absenteeism in the US auto industry doubled between 1965 and 1970 (Kumar 1978: 284).

5   In 1969 turnover at Volvo in Sweden reached 52% (Linebaugh and Ramirez 1992: 150).

6   Rates of sabotage are hard to measure, and evidence of them is often semi anecdotal. Literature on sabotage from the 1970s gives examples such as the following: 'In 1970 the electrical fittings of several cranes were disconnected in the France Dunkerque yards...In 1971 iron bars were inserted into the lines in the Brandt works at Lyon, causing them to stop instantly' (Dubois 1979: 25) Commenting on the overall trend, Dubois suggests that 'forms of sabotage have never been so numerous as they are today' (Dubois 1979: 58).

7   The strike at LIP in France, which lasted 8 months, and the miners' strikes in 1972 and 1974 in the UK are better known examples from Europe. The latter will forever be linked in the British historical consciousness with the three day week. Some American cases are discussed in the text, above.

'the vital movement of the negative that will finish off bourgeois values such as sacrifice, discipline, and hierarchy' (Zerzan and Zerzan,[8] March 1977). Similarly, Peter Rachleff's analysis of the revolt against work has much in common with theories of the end of work generally:

> Our future society, and our role in it, cannot be defined simply by the "socially necessary labour" that we do. Rather, for the first time, we will meet as human beings and define our own needs and the paths to their realisation. While labour will be part of this, there is no way that this activity can exhaust either our desires or the solutions to our problems (Rachleff 1977).

His final suggestion, however, is highly questionable. 'It is this future which is pre-figured by the "revolt against work"' (Rachleff 1977).

It is questionable for precisely the same reasons as Zerzan's supposition of sabotage etc. as a 'vital moment' in the struggle against work and the bourgeois values supporting it. As Charles Reeve suggests,

> ...attempts to show how the revolt against work constitutes the new, radical tendency of the class struggle – appears...to be far from achieved. Uncritical confidence in the opinions of the ruling class on this subject don't seem to me to be a sufficient argument for accepting such a thesis (Reeve 1976).

Reeve is referring to the fact that much of the supposedly radical revolt against work literature takes the reports of *Harper's* and *Fortune* journalists at face value. Other factors undermine the thesis that sabotage and phoning in sick are the very acme of radical opposition. Firstly, sabotage and absenteeism are hardly new, nor have they proved insurmountable odds to capitalism's continued survival. As Pierre Dubois points out; 'even though, overall, forms of sabotage have never been as numerous as they are today, increases in productivity have never been so great' (Dubois 1979: 58). He suggests that sabotage might serve as a kind of amelioration of fatigue, and workers tend to be more productive when not exhausted. Worker revolts may even spur on capital to develop and invest in new technology and new, more efficient methods of organising work that minimise the possibilities for worker interference, thus raising productivity again.

To some extent, there may be an element of subjectivity in how one views sabotage. It may appear as a rather futile and even petty reaction to the colloquial privations of wage labour, done more out of frustration and perhaps exhaustion than revolutionary zeal. To some though, it is an uncompromising radical act, a sign of radical consciousness on the part of the workers. It seems clear, however, that such individualistic, spontaneous activities have had little mitigating effect on

---

8   Writing in *Fifth Estate*: an American anarchist periodical. I am grateful to Andy Smith of Middle Tennessee State University (as of October 28, 2005) for bringing this periodical to my attention.

the forward march of capital, and of course work itself, which has only intensified as a result of them.

Part of this debate hinges on the motivations of the revolting workers, in the following case, typically, American auto assemblers. Stanley Aronowitz, in his influential *False Promises* suggests that the Lordstown workers were driven by resentment against 'working conditions that robbed them of their autonomy and control more than by issues of speedup [of the assembly line] or pay' (Aronowitz 1974: 287). This stands in direct contradiction to the assessment of Rose (Rose 1985: 71) who suggests that the events at Lordstown were indeed a reaction against speedup, rather than an attempt to oppose the alienation and exploitation inherent in such industrial work. Aronowitz points out that relatively high pay levels for auto workers have not been enough to reduce high absenteeism and dissatisfaction among the younger employees, so presumably, pay is not an issue, which leaves more intrinsic matters in the frame. This brings us to another key point – the social and economic conditions under which the so called revolt against work took place.

It could be argued, contra Aronowitz, that far from high pay being something of an irrelevance, it is the very reason that workers were able to revolt in the first place. Revolutionary history shows that revolt tends to occur as conditions are improving, rather than when they are at their most dire. We saw in Chapter 2 how writers such as E. P. Thompson suggested that the natural, and certainly the preindustrial attitude to work is to labour only until one's needs are satisfied, and this would certainly fit the context of the revolt against work. Some of the best paid members of the working class, a country at the peak of unprecedented affluence, and relatively low levels of unemployment. As Charles Reeve points out, if support from the welfare state is considered as part of the equation, a downward move in this respect, and an upswing in unemployment will likely lead to

> the collapse of the myth of absenteeism as a radical form of struggle, in the same way as today already the slogan of the 'revolt against work' is collapsing in the face of rising unemployment. As always there will then remain for the workers only an open struggle against the wage system or else submission to it and to the barbarism it engenders (Reeve 1976).

As the Oil Crisis of 1973 took effect, this is precisely what happened. Some have suggested, in fact, that the supposed economic woes of the mid to late 1970s were in fact a reaction by capital to a worryingly restless working class. Claiming that the Yom Kippur war was 'financed on both sides by the same capital' (Montano 1992: 121), Montano, writing in 1975, suggests that the crisis was not a temporary recession to cure inflation but 'the imposition of a *long term austerity for the purpose of enforcing work* with the maximum feasible violence' (Montano 1992: 115).

Whether the recession was orchestrated, or a genuine result of imbalances and conflict in the international economic system, the result was the same. A future without the work ethic, with falling working hours, rising wages, increased leisure, and a guaranteed minimum income, began to look like a work of science fiction. The 1980s saw American society combine austerity with economic expansion and a renewed commitment to accumulation and acquisition. There was little room for discussions of the end of work in the America of yuppies and Reaganomics.

The end of work, or work resurgent?

In Britain, the picture was rather different, and there was a veritable flood of books on the future of work during the 1980s. From the late 1970s books began to appear that predicted a workless future. Aside from the American socioeconomic (and ideological) context, two further factors may help explain why the focus of debates about the future of work shifted from America to Europe. Firstly, Britain in particular had begun to experience what some considered catastrophic levels of unemployment. It appeared to many that this was to be a permanent situation, and in fact unemployment would continue to rise almost ad infinitum. Charles Handy, for example, suggested that 'there are not going to be enough conventional jobs to go around...That much seems certain' (Handy 1984: 1–2). Secondly, computers had entered the national consciousness, and were seen by many commentators as not only responsible for existing unemployment to some extent, but having the potential to eliminate ever greater proportions of the population from productive work.

Books such as Charles Handy's *The Future of Work* (1984), James Robertson's *Future Work* (1985), Barry Jones's *Sleeper's Wake* (1982), and Jenkins and Sherman's *The Collapse of Work* (1979), all appear to share many of the same certainties. It was clear to all that, in the words of Handy, 'Britain is no longer primarily an industrial nation' (Handy 1984: 24). Bell's prediction of a postindustrial society, it seemed, had been accurate. Commentaries such as these tended to follow a similar pattern. After asserting that automation and computerisation will continue to eliminate jobs in the 'traditional' manufacturing sector, they suggest that although the expanding service industries will absorb some of the surplus, these too will become increasingly computerised, and may themselves decline as a source of employment. Many of these writers offer a range of future scenarios, all of which emphasise the decline of work, certainly in quantitative terms, and often with a concomitant qualitative or ontological reduction in importance. For those still in employment, Handy suggests lifetime working hours will halve, from 100,000 to 50,000. Many, however, are likely to be unemployed. Surveying the range of scenarios posited, the nomenclature for which includes terms such as 'hyperexpansionist' or 'Sane, Humane, Ecological' (Robertson 1985: 5), we can summarise by suggesting that society is seen to face two basic alternative futures. In the first, a small elite retain employment in highly productive, high technology and knowledge based sectors, while the remainder languish, stigmatised, impoverished and restless, with only insecure menial work, or crime, as options. Robertson describes it thus:

> Full employment will not be restored. All necessary work will be done by a skilled elite of professionals and experts, backed by automation, other capital intensive technology, and specialist know how. Others will not work. They will merely consume the goods and services provided by the working minority – including leisure, information, and education services. Society will be split into workers and drones (Robertson 1985: 5).

This vision of a society polarised around the fulcrum of work is a common one. Therborn, for instance, terms it the 'Brazilianisation of advanced capitalism' (Therborn 1986: 32). This is what Jose Nun calls the 'marginal mass' thesis (Nun 2000). Bellini painted a similar picture with his book (and TV series) *Rule Britannia* (1986), but with more emphasis on the criminal element taking hold amongst a superfluous rabble.

One point of interest is that many (Bellini, Handy, Gershuny, Jones) of the future of work accounts during the 1980s refer to Kurt Vonnegut's *Player Piano* (1953) in their discussions of a polarised, dystopian future.[9] Also referenced (by Gershuny, for example) is Huxley's *Brave New World*. References to science fiction are surprisingly common in future of work literature.

Kumar has noted that the image of industrial society that became established during the 19th century owed more to the literature of Dickens, Charles Kingsley, and Mrs. Gaskell, and the cultural criticism of Carlyle and Ruskin, than to rigorous empirical investigation (Kumar 1988: 48). It seems that images of the future of work and society might be similarly inspired by works of science fiction. However, it could be more likely that this is a case of science fiction moving in the direction of social comment, rather than the other way round. Literature, like sociology, reflects social reality, and extrapolates from social conditions at a given time. Literature can also be expected to pick up on social trends in the same manner that social commentary does.

In contrast to this vision of a polarised society, future of work writers in the 1980s often attempted to supply something of a blueprint for a better future. This tended to involve the acceptance of computerisation and automation, since there is no objection to the reduction of work in itself, indeed, it is to be welcomed. Alongside this, however, there must be a shift in consciousness. In the polarised society discussed above, the ideology of work is maintained as a central feature, the most salient aspect of this ideology being the fact that work is used to distinguish the elite from the marginalised. In that it perpetuates many of the negative aspects of conventional capitalism – social inequality, alienation, ecological degradation, this ideology of work is seen as a dysfunctional remnant of industrial, employment

---

9 *Player Piano* is noted by Suedfeld and Ward as a text that foresees 'overwork for a minority with a lack of meaningful work for the majority' (Suedfeld and Ward 1976: 22).

based society. In the more favourable future scenario of writers such as Robertson, Jones, Jenkins and Sherman, society must undergo what Marcuse, back in the early 1970s, had called a transvaluation of values. Handy predicts that, 'The job will no longer be the whole measure of one's identity, one status, one's finances, or one's purpose in life' (Handy 1984: 11).

A common theme is that the progressive elimination of work as traditionally conceived is accompanied by some kind of escape from economic imperatives. As Jones writes; 'we ought to reject the idea that only things which generate economic profit are worthwhile' (Jones 1982: 97). The idea of going beyond the economic is a familiar one by now. We saw how Marx and Marcuse saw true human existence beginning where economic imperatives end. Work, in the futures literature, as in Marx, is seen as the ontological and ideological, indeed the essential link between the individual and the economy. In the society of work – contemporary capitalist society, it is the irrationality of economic rationality that prevents work from being transformed.

In practical and infrastructural terms, since society will be unable to supply everyone with work as conventionally understood, work in the formal economic sector should no longer be the precondition for an income. A Guaranteed Minimum Income scheme is to support the population as they discover new and self enhancing forms of activity beyond the realms of traditional work. Indeed, such activity is hardly to be considered work at all. This new form of quasi work typically involves horticulture, crafts, research, sport, and DIY activities. More often than not, there is to be a community element to this new sector, which is seemingly beyond capitalist economic rationality. In many accounts (see for example, Robertson 1985: 42), each community is to have communal workshops, equipped with the latest technology, with which the citizens can manufacture goods to satisfy many of their needs.[10]

Conclusion

From the perspective of 2009, predictions of a future of leisure, or the abolition of work and its ethic, appear almost quaint. During the 1990s, some high profile treatments of the future of work did appear, primarily in the USA. Stanley Aronowitz and William DiFazio, published *The Jobless Future* and Jeremy Rifkin produced *The End of Work* at around the same time – the middle of the decade. Both books were widely read and in the context of the restructuring[11] of many large American

---

10 Some went as far as sketching these out. See, for example, the illustrations in Richards 1990: 149–154.

11 A euphemism for laying off as many employees as possible. Other terms developed by management gurus of the time include downsizing and streamlining. For an excellent analysis of the way management discourse seeks to present baseless and ideological pseudo analysis as an insightful science see Gantman 2005.

companies, it was not surprising that they caught the public imagination. Aronowitz and DiFazio are prominent members of America's left intelligentsia, with histories of labour and political activism which continue to influence their allegiances (Aronowitz and DiFazio 1994: 342), so one expects references to Marx in their text. More surprising, perhaps, is that Rifkin uses Marx's *Capital* to help explain how automation progressively eliminates the worker from the production process (Rifkin 1994: 16–17). That workers are being permanently eliminated, rather than merely displaced, is something the authors of both books agree on (Aronowitz and DiFazio 1994: 299, Rifkin 1995: 3). Like many of the British based writers of the 1980s, Aronowitz, DiFazio and Rifkin share a concern over social polarisation, and again in accordance with commentators such as Robertson, see a third sector (Rifkin 1995: 249–274, Aronowitz and DiFazio 1994: 352, 358) of socialised work in sustainable communities as the preferred outcome. All profess an interest in guaranteed minimum income schemes (Rifkin 1994: 258–260, Aronowitz and DiFazio 1994: 353–354).

Lerner, another American writer, provides an analysis which draws on the work of Gorz to propose that national governments should give more consideration to supposedly 'far out' ideas such as the guaranteed annual income (Lerner 1994: 191). Interestingly, Lerner's article represents something of a reversal of the situation discussed earlier, and Lerner even refers to the UK as *setting a trend* towards underemployment and contingent employment (Lerner 1994: 85). That is, this seems to be a case of Britain being even more advanced than the United States along the road of labour deregulation, or perhaps of Britain having overcome the mass unemployment of the 1980s, leaving the spectre of unemployment now hovering over the USA. This is the impression, of course, of one particular American commentator. Also relevant is the fact that by 1994, when the article was written, the issue of 'jobless growth' was gaining in prominence in North American debates, as evidenced by *The Jobless Future* and *The End of Work*. While politically supported rapid deindustrialisation was highlighted in 1980s Britain by the miners' strike and urban unrest, awareness of industrial decline in the USA was heightened during the 1990s because it was accompanied by a plethora of relatively well publicised restructuring programmes in the service and professional sectors (International Business Machines, for example). Rifkin's book, in particular, draws together a plethora of reports on the effects of this restructuring from the business press as evidence for its thesis.

In the twenty first century so far, in both Britain and America, unemployment, while still higher than official figures suggest, has not reached catastrophic levels, although being unemployed remains a catastrophe for the individual. Having said that, the economic crisis that began in 2008 with the so-called 'credit crunch' has seen levels of unemployment rise.

An increasing proportion of the population as a whole are part of the workforce, people are working longer hours, are working harder (Green 2001) and will need to retire later. The tendency for working hours to increase, even in the face of increased productivity, was seen by Rosenberg as a trend characterising the 1980s

(Rosenberg 1993). Rosenberg predicted, on the basis of a continued 'employer driven' scenario (labour surplus, weak unions), that paid time off would not increase, and that the labour market would continue to be increasingly polarised into a core of overworked employees, and a group in more precarious employment.

For many workers today, remaining employed requires that one show ever more extreme levels of commitment, to one's 'team', to competitiveness, to satisfying the client, to 'adding value'. Or, one may be out of work, marginalised and stigmatised, or working in an expanding sector of menial, precarious, and almost equally marginal low paid jobs, both in the so called service sector, and in a manufacturing sector that refuses to disappear in a puff of silicon tinged smoke. There has been, in the words of Juliet Schor, an 'unexpected decline of leisure' (Schor 1993). Since technology has continued to advance, and productivity increase, our present situation is indeed unexpected; why has there been no significant reduction in work, let alone its elimination?

One explanation, proposed by some Marxists, relates to the labour theory of value, and can be seen as part of an explanation of why the optimistic predictions of our 1980s futurists have not come to pass. Since the only source of profit for capitalists is unpaid labour, that is, the proportion of labour performed by workers after they have done enough to pay their wages, capitalist society would indeed be abolishing itself if it were to abolish work. Having invested in labour saving technologies, the capitalist, paradoxically, needs workers to operate that technology as intensively and extensively as possible, requiring harder work and longer hours. At the same time, unemployment is kept high, and wages low, whilst consumerism, in ideological terms particularly is cranked up to ever more dizzying levels. There has been a revamped commitment to promoting the work ethic through social policy and welfare reforms. Under such circumstances, the work ethic is unlikely to decline. The apparent paradox, and apparent irrationality of rising productivity alongside the extension of work might lead some to the conclusion that work is today less an economic phenomenon, and more a strategy of political control (Bowring 2002: 171).

And what of developing 'third sectors' beyond the rationality of profit, sectors that have the potential to slowly eclipse the world of conventional work in the money economy? Far from economic rationality declining, it searches out more spheres to colonise, thus we are faced with the phenomenon of cash (or work) rich, time poor couples employing what amount to new servants (time rich, but cash poor) to care for their children, home, shopping, pets, garden, etc. etc. (Gorz 1989: 39). The sphere of work then, expands. Time is to be filled with work virtually to the last second, as evidenced by the 'Slivers of Time'[12] scheme, initiated by the British government in 2005:

---

12   The Slivers of Time scheme was brought to my attention at the Cardiff Futures Conference 2006 by Jamie Saunders of Bradford City Council.

Slivers-of-Time Working is for anyone who can only be available for work around other commitments in their life (e.g. childcare, studying, existing part-time work, caring for a dependant adult, medical commitments, hunting for an ideal job or starting their own enterprise). These people typically have a few hours when they could work each day but only know which hours, if any, on a day-to-day basis (Office of the Deputy Prime Minister 2005).

On the question of discourse that explicitly engages with the future of work, one might suggest that much of it has used the fact that work is a central element of both base and superstructure in modern society to allow a wider social critique, often with a utopian bent. In Britain at least, the future of work has rarely been discussed during the boom years of the early twenty first century, and there is a faint sense of embarrassment surrounding previous wild predictions of thinking machines, robot workers, and dreams of ease.[13] A 2005 report for The Work Foundation, a British think tank, noted the absence of debates on work and its futures at the level of national politics in particular;

> …despite its recognised importance, the quality of work as experienced by the majority has not featured on the political agenda for some considerable time. This is a genuine surprise, not least because a political party that can speak directly to the experience of most workers might expect to be rewarded with a substantial electoral dividend (Coats 2005).

Debate at the level of policy, with the exception of occasional, brief discussions of the 'work life balance', has indeed been surprisingly lacking, in the British context at least, during the twenty first century so far. Certainly, policy makers appear not to be positively attracted to predictions of a decline in work, although they are likely to be aware, at some level, of some of the more mainstream commentaries such as those of Handy or Rifkin. They are still less interested in changes that would fundamentally threaten existing political and social structures. Rather, policy continues to focus on attaining and maintaining full employment. Citizens are to be endowed with skills and attitudes that will ensure national competitiveness in the global capitalist economy, and key to this, clearly, is the ideological and ontological dominance of work. Whether or not it is desirable that work and life remain separate entities to be balanced, rather than combined, remains a question that few stakeholders seem willing to discuss.

---

13   Discussion of work in the media appears to be increasing in volume as the recession takes hold, one notices. See for example *The Observer* Review section special edition on work (15 March 2009).

Chapter 7
André Gorz:
Postindustrial Marxism and the End of Work

Introduction: Gorz in intellectual context

Marcuse's friend André Gorz,[1] has placed the end of work at the centre of his major published output since the appearance of *Farewell to the Working Class* in 1980, and indeed, conceived of slightly differently, in earlier work such as *Strategy for Labour*, published in 1964. Although Gorz is an important figure in his own right, we will see many parallels with Marcuse. Gorz has been called 'the French Marcuse', and has been said to be 'taking up where Marcuse left off' (Lodziak and Tatman 1997: 1). Although Bowring (Bowring 2000: 60) suggests that Gorz avoids the 'globalising critique of mass culture' associated with the Frankfurt School, it is far from clear that this is the case. It is appropriate then, that in the process of examining Gorz's not inconsiderable contribution to the end of work debate within social theory, we leave intellectual space for the recognition of the importance of Marcuse to this contribution.

Strategy for Labour is routinely ignored by writers making reference to Gorz, despite the fact that it had a huge impact on the New Left internationally, according to Mark Poster (Poster 1975: 363). Dyer-Witheford, for example, in an article on Autonomist Marxism (specifically its leading light, Italian theorist Antonio Negri) and the information society, claims that Gorz 'is in fact directly influenced by the autonomists and draws on the same passages of *Grundrisse* which they find so fertile' (Dyer-Witheford 1994: 21). Dyer Witheford, however, makes no reference to Gorz's work prior to *Adieux au proletariat* (1980). Although Gorz does refer to Italian trade unionists such as Bruno Trentin (Gorz 1964: 21) and Vittorio Foa (Gorz 1964: 15) in *Strategy*, these are not figures normally associated with autonomist Marxism (Wright 2002: 15, 77). Certainly at the time of writing *Strategy*, Gorz would have found limited use for Negri's works, largely consisting as they did up that point of writings on State and Right in the young Hegel, essays on Dilthey and Meinecke, juridical formalism in Kant, and another piece on Hegel and the philosophy of Right (Negri 1989: 273). However, there are in fact some interesting parallels between Autonomist Marxism and Gorz's work, most notably Negri's conception of the social factory and Gorz's notion of economic rationality. We shall examine this parallel in the course of this chapter, just as we will explore these authors' respective understanding of the role of technology in the abolition

---

[1] Gorz sadly died in September 2007, during the completion of this book.

of work, and the ways in which Negri and Gorz have understood the relationship between the end of capitalist work and the social subjects created by, or within, advanced capitalism.

Gorz's changing theoretical perspective?

Like many social theorists, including Marx himself, Gorz is sometimes seen as a writer whose work can be divided into different periods (Lodziak and Tatman 1997: 9). In Gorz's case, we might say three periods, since as Finn Bowring has shown, (Bowring 2000) books such as *La morale de L'histoire* (1959), bear the imprint of Sartrean existentialism in a way that later work does not, or at least not as obviously. These existentialist explorations, as Bowring is happy to note, are not the essential keys for understanding Gorz, since 'all Gorz's books are an attempt to start out from nothing and to say something personal and original' (Bowring 2000: 85). Although it is difficult to entirely agree with this assertion that all Gorz's writings start out from nothing, for our purposes, some of Gorz's books are better left to Sartre scholars such as Bowring. It is with Gorz's 1964 book *Stratégie ouvrière et néocapitalism* (*Strategy for Labour*) that we begin, since it is here that the themes with which we have already become familiar through our exploration of other writers on the end of work start to emerge in depth; themes such as the role of technology in the liberation of work, the relationship between the realms of freedom and necessity, and so on.

Strategy for Labour appears at first to be significantly different from Gorz's later work, however, and represents a possible second stage, in a periodisation or categorisation of his output. Although such a periodisation remains plausible at the level of emphasis, the deeper level of Gorz's analysis remained remarkably consistent over the 43 years since Strategy was published. Much of the change of emphasis, such as it is, is largely a result of changing political and social conditions.

During the 1960s, the status of Marxism became a central concern for the French Left. Some commentators highlight the role of Sartre in promoting the centrality of existential concerns vis-à-vis Marxism, during this period (Hirsch 1982: 5). Certainly, Sartre had a role to play in the growing division between those who would prioritise traditional Marxist concerns such as exploitation, ownership, and the state, and those moving towards a more 'humanistic' interpretation of Marxism, which emphasised the denial of individual autonomy and creativity that was seen as symptomatic of late modern capitalism. The growing significance of what are sometimes known as Marx's more humanistic writings, the 1844 Manuscripts in particular, was of course a wider trend in Western Marxism. Marcuse is, if not a typical, at least a paradigmatic example of this trend, and the same might be said of the Frankfurt School as a whole. There was considerable transatlantic interchange of ideas amongst the left intelligentsia of the 1950s and 60s; in addition and in terms of social context, both Europe and North America were experiencing high rates of economic growth and rising levels of affluence, which contributed to shared notions of Western societies having moved beyond scarcity.[2] Coupled with relative physical improvements in working conditions and the establishment of a system of welfare, the target for sections of the left shifted from pauperisation and the possibility of an imminent revolution of the toiling masses, to more qualitative concerns: 'The theme of alienation thus became the rallying point for the critics of traditional Marxism. What is wrong with capitalism, they argued, is that it alienated the individual from one's authentic being' (Hirsch 1982: 17).

The end of work, a strategy for labour

Strategy for Labour is a product of this intellectual milieu, the contours of which we have sketched but briefly and in broad strokes. For an equally brief summary, this time of Gorz's first book to be published in English, we turn to Mark Poster: 'To [Gorz], the chief evil of capitalism was not exploitation but the alienation of the workers' creativity. Gorz's conclusion anticipated the events of May: to combat alienation, worker self management, *autogestion*, must be the focus of the socialist movement' (Poster 1973: 363). Gorz's writings are primarily concerned with highlighting the possible, rather than the actual. For Gorz, liberatory social theory, as well as the labour movement, must concentrate on a range of key possibilities. The possibility that has come to be seen as the central concern for the Gorz of *Strategy* is the possibility of humanising production, of eliminating alienation at work.

Like Marx, Gorz saw the industrial worker as existentially mutilated, their true human identity as a freely creative being denied. Gorz suggested that the repetition, boredom, and regimented hierarchical control associated with labour since the mechanisation of production, were far from inevitable; '...repetitive work, regimentation at the places of work, and authoritarian division of labour are no longer technical necessities' (Gorz 1967: x).

In relation to the possibility of eradicating alienation at work, Gorz made some observations that he later contradicted. Even when production takes place in the context of a global combine, where distant plants fulfil different elements of the manufacturing process, Gorz argued that the worker tended to develop knowledge of the production process as a whole. He goes as far as to suggest that '[i]t is impossible in a modern production unit, even of medium size, to be on top of one's job without becoming familiar with world history in the process' (Gorz 1967: 117). And further: 'It is impossible to produce turbines in Grenoble without knowing what

---

2   As was the case with Marcuse, Gorz was well aware that poverty and misery still exist amongst large sections of the population, even in the developed world. The contention of both of these writers was that we have entered a period where scarcity is objectively surmountable, and is in fact artificially perpetuated.

is being done in Milan, Ljubliana, in the Ruhr, and in Scotland' (Gorz 1967: 117). One might question how accurate a description of large scale industrial production this is, in terms of the consciousness of the workers involved, and as we shall see later, Gorz's view on the matter was indeed to change. To confuse matters, Gorz was apparently referring here to cooperatives (Gorz 1967: 117), so we might assume that this tendency for workers' comprehension to increase, is something of a potentiality (since most industrial combines are not cooperatives, although a high level of technical cooperation may exist amongst their workers), a tendency that is blocked from fruition by current repressive management practices.[3]

Whether or not Gorz actually thinks workers have developed a truly global perspective, he certainly sees increasingly scientific and knowledge based work leading to the development of some kind of (albeit generally latent or repressed) higher cultural consciousness amongst the workers. This is the case especially amongst skilled technical staffs, for whom the denial of creativity and autonomy at work comes to be experienced almost as physical pain. Gorz cites Mallet's classic 1963 study *La Nouvelle classe ouvrière* (*The New Working Class*), (Gorz 1964: 105) and clearly shares the conviction that skilled technical workers represent the vanguard of the workers' movement by dint of their real, but more importantly, their *potential* level of autonomy in the workplace. It is not clear whether or how much Mallet influenced Gorz as such, or whether the similarities in their analyses stem from a coincidentally shared involvement in, and perspective on, the workers' movement in post-war France. It is interesting to note that Mallet, like Gorz, is clearly influenced by the Marcuse of *One Dimensional Man* – he makes numerous references to *l'Homme unidimensionnel* in his introduction to the 4th edition of *The New Working Class* (Mallet 1975: 1, 9, 12, 20, 26). Whatever Mallet and Gorz's relative positions in the intellectual map of the New Left in 1960s France, the following quote from Mallet gives an indication of the affinities between his and Gorz's analysis.

> It is these...workers, technicians and *cadres*, profoundly "integrated" into industrial society, in the most "sensitive" and decisive sectors who are in a position to formulate possibilities for a human liberation which does not reject technological progress, and which rises against its distortion (Mallet 1975: 12).

Workers tend to develop qualitative needs for satisfying and creative work under conditions of advanced capitalism, but are bought off not with greater autonomy in the workplace, but with quantitatively higher rewards in the form of wages and possibilities for consumption. The new technical elite represent the group for whom this contradiction is most apparent.

---

3   The matter is far from clear, it must be acknowledged, and it is entirely possible that Gorz was referring to modern, medium-large scale industrial enterprises both formally cooperative and commercial in nature, and rhetorically emphasising the fact that large scale industry increasingly demands cooperative work.

> For the highly skilled workers…the dominant contradiction is between the active essence, the technical initiative required in their work, and the condition of passive performers to which the hierarchy of the enterprise nevertheless still condemns them (Gorz 1967: 36).

Gorz is here restating, in contemporary terms, Marx's analysis of the way modern, technicised production tends increasingly to create workers for whom work is no longer merely labour, but rather a form of *praxis*.[4] While we have suggested that the *Paris Manuscripts* were influential on the left intelligentsia of the 1960s and 1970s more generally, the influence of Marx's *Grundrisse* is evident here, and Gorz acknowledges the importance of this part of Marx's writings. It will be seen that the *Grundrisse* remains important for Gorz throughout his later and indeed final works.

It is difficult to know whether or not Marx considered such a situation as Gorz describes extant at the time the former was writing, and most likely he did not. For Gorz however, production techniques, particularly in the most advanced sectors, had reached the stage where the workers concerned do indeed 'step to the side' of production. Further, the advanced societies produce surpluses of goods to a magnitude indicating that scarcity is no longer objectively predestined, and produce this surplus ever more efficiently, suggesting that people could move from quantitative concerns to qualitative, or what might be seen as more authentic, or truly human needs; 'once a certain level of culture has been reached, the need for autonomy, the need to develop one's abilities freely and to give purpose to one's life is experienced with the same intensity as an unsatisfied physiological necessity'(Gorz 1967: 105).

---

4   The influential passage from the *Grundrisse* reads: 'No longer does the worker insert a modified natural thing [*Naturgegenstand*] as middle link between the object [*Objekt*] and himself; rather, he inserts the process of nature, transformed into an industrial process, as a means between himself and inorganic nature, mastering it. He steps to the side of the production process instead of being its chief actor. In this transformation, it is neither the direct human labour he himself performs, nor the time during which he works, but rather the appropriation of his own general productive power, his understanding of nature and his mastery over it by virtue of his presence as a social body – it is, in a word, the development of the social individual which appears as the great foundation-stone of production and of wealth. The *theft of alien labour time, on which the present wealth is based*, appears a miserable foundation in face of this new one, created by large-scale industry itself. As soon as labour in the direct form has ceased to be the great well-spring of wealth, labour time ceases and must cease to be its measure, and hence exchange value [must cease to be the measure] of use value. The *surplus labour of the mass* has ceased to be the condition for the development of general wealth, just as the *non-labour of the few*, for the development of the general powers of the human head' (Marx 1993: 705). We might also note the fact that Gorz draws a distinction between essence and existence in the above passage, something that runs through his career; since this tactic is a key element in what is called Critical Theory, it can, and will be argued that Gorz's work should be seen as just this.

Gorz is following Marx by analysing contemporary society in terms of the possibilities of transcending the economic, of moving instead to the genuinely social – that is, a state where people relate to each other *as people*. Just as Marx wrote of a so called history, to be transcended by a society where individuals exist in and for themselves, rather than as alienated desiderata of the market, so Gorz suggests that production could be devoted to creating women and men who are truly human (1967: 70).

Gorz was of course following Marcuse also, and includes the latter's assertion from *One Dimensional Man* that 'economic freedom would mean freedom *from* the economy' (Gorz 1967: 128). It is interesting to note that Gorz, like Marcuse, drew on Galbraith – in this case for his analysis of the 'post scarcity' society as one in which, 'the priority accorded to economic goals comes to focus in a conflict with truth and aesthetics'(Galbraith 1964, cited in Gorz 1967: 115).

In *Strategy for Labour*, Gorz proposed that in the sphere of production, the technical, organisational and intellectual infrastructure exited at a level where workers can and should organise production themselves. It appears at this point then, that Gorz is advocating freedom *in* work, rather than freedom *from* work. In later books such as *Farewell to the Working Class* (1983) and *Paths to Paradise* (1985), Gorz seems, on the contrary, to emphasise freedom from work, by means of a radical reduction in working hours. However, it is possible to see Gorz's emphasis on the workplace as something of a strategic move, hence the title of his earlier book; that is, during the period when he wrote *Strategy*, Gorz as an activist with links to the labour movement, saw *autogestion* as the first step towards the transformation of society. Not only are workers to self-organise in the context of the industrial enterprise, but also in the key institutions of advanced societies, with which the industrial or productive sphere is interconnected. In a kind of 'overflowing' process, the autonomous power of the workers will,

> inevitably tend to extend beyond the framework of the large enterprise, because the policy of a monopoly or of an oligopoly is in such close reciprocal relation with the economic policies of the State, the life of the city, the community, and the region (Gorz 1967: 10).

The ultimate objective in political terms is in one sense quite unambiguous – 'replacing capitalism' (Gorz 1967: 10).

Post scarcity society and the new sensibility

In the case of *Strategy*, Gorz made the end of work, or at least the end of the alienated labour of modern capitalism, the keystone of his wider vision of a radical transformation of society. For Gorz, the transformation of work can lead to the transformation of consciousness – to people becoming conscious of their 'true' needs in the Marcusean sense. 'When an individual discovers himself as a praxis subject in his work it is no longer possible to make him consume and destroy superfluous wealth at the price of the essential element, his free disposal of himself' (Gorz 1967: 128). Capitalism satisfies the alienated worker with similarly alienated cultural products, that is, with the products of the consumer society; more than this, according to Gorz, it subordinates consumption to production (1967: 73), adjusting the former to meet the demands of the latter. Gorz's criticism of this state of affairs in *Strategy* clearly shows that he does not wish to denigrate consumption as such – indeed, he is scathing of notions of 'virtuous austerity' (1967: 73). He wishes to see consumption freed from the dictates of monopoly accumulation, or industrial capitalism, in other words.

Previously, dehumanised work had left individuals fit only for 'sub human and passive leisure and consumption' (Gorz 1967: 128). In a society where workers organise production to maximise their creativity and self expression, and coordinate the key institutions of society to operate along similar lines, fundamental questions will emerge, as the miasma of mystification (for the purposes of ensuring alienated production/consumption) dissolves, questions such as the 'orientation which production ought to have in view of felt needs and of the existing scientific and technical potentialities' (Gorz 1967: 73). Clearly, in political terms, Gorz was describing a socialist society – one in which people subordinate production and the economy to human needs, and not vice versa.

Gorz seems to be proposing a strategy of escape from the ontological circle which we have discussed in the context of Marcuse's writings. This ontological circle, we may recall, represents the contradiction inherent in the emergence of a transformed consciousness – which values self expression, cooperative work, the environment, etc. rather than one which is prepared to accept meaningless toil in return for alienated leisure – where this emergence appears to depend on the transcendence of the system which is in turn its prerequisite. Marcuse ultimately admitted that he did not know how this contradiction could be overcome. For Gorz, it is the nature of production in an advanced, post scarcity society that may provide the necessary transformative power. Clearly technology has a role to play here, but the emphasis is on the organisation of production in the context of high technology capitalism, rather than technology itself. Gorz's formulation is in accordance with almost all modern theories of the end of work in proposing that it is capitalism itself which created the conditions for the radical transformation of work, and by extension, society as a whole. This can be seen as something of a restatement of the Marxian theory of capitalist productive development escaping the institutional and ideological bounds of capitalism, and Gorz quotes Marx at length, including the following from the *Grundrisse*:

> Productive power and social relationships – which are different sides of the development of the social individual – appear to capital only as means, and are only means to allow it to produce on its restricted base. But in fact these are the material preconditions to blow this base to pieces (Marx, in Gorz 1967: 130).

It is clear that Gorz, like Marx, and indeed Marcuse, does not read off social relationships, and social transformations, from the sphere of work in a mechanistic manner. People do not just produce themselves as (albeit potentially) truly human individuals in the context of work – narrowly defined, but in the social and cultural spheres of societies where objective scarcity has been overcome.

> ...this production takes place not only in the work situation but just as much in the schools, cafes, athletic fields; on voyages; in theatres, concerts, newspapers, books, expositions; in   towns, neighbourhoods, discussion and action groups – in short, wherever individuals enter into relationships with one another and produce the universe of human relationships (Gorz 1967: 117).

From a more critical perspective, it is possible to question the theoretical rigour of statements such as the one above. Gorz appears to be saying that people produce themselves throughout the entirety of everyday life. Sociologically speaking, this type of analysis might not be particularly useful, since it appears to be explaining a social process with a rather vague reference to multiform human interaction. The essence of the point Gorz is making here appears to relate to the post-scarcity status of modern societies, where everyday life, like work and economic production, is increasingly illustrative of the victory over material want, and over nature itself. In such a situation, human activity comes to approach the status of *praxis* in the Marxian sense. As this becomes increasingly evident, Gorz argues, the contradictions of advanced capitalism at the level of human development, in the sense of freedom from necessity, come more clearly into view.

Although we have implied that Gorz does not reduce social and individual development to an epiphenomenon of work, it is notable that moving beyond scarcity, and therefore into the realm of the multi sided development of the human individual, is dependent at least in the first instance on work. It is through work, and indeed capitalist work that scarcity is overcome, after all. Gorz appears to accept this, and quotes Marcuse in support of the notion that 'Labour must precede the reduction of labour, and industrialization must precede the development of human needs and satisfactions' (Marcuse 1964, cited in Gorz 1964: 122). It is to the reduction of labour that we now turn.

Reduction of work in *Strategy* and beyond

We have already discussed the idea of freedom from the economy in terms of freedom from the ontological and existential domination of capitalist productivism. Freedom from the economy can also be understood in terms more akin to the notion of freedom from necessity, which in turn is usually understood in end of work literature as freedom from the necessity of working. Gorz proposes that as part of the unfolding of potentialities that will lead to people understanding themselves as ends of society and production, rather than means (Gorz 1967: 128), free time should become the measure of wealth. Again, this is clearly a Marxian idea, and Gorz follows this statement with a very long quote from the *Grundrisse* (Gorz 1967: 128–130). Based on the assumption (largely correct in many of the sectors that 1960s sociology held as central; motor car production, for example) that '[a]utomation will be a reality in the industrialized societies before the end of the century' (Gorz 1967: 130), Gorz asserts that the left should concentrate their energies on the reduction of work time; traditionally conceived in the form of the work week. It is necessary to be as clear as possible here in terms of what Gorz means by free time. Gorz makes it explicit that he understands free time not as idle time, but as time for the individual who is free to develop themselves culturally and socially. 'The increase in free time is not an increase in idle time, but an increase in the socially productive time which is objectively and subjectively necessary for the production of human individuals and a human world' (1967: 118). Gorz criticises the Unions for wanting an increase in leisure, but without a radical change in the nature of work (Gorz 1975: 85).

The unfulfilled potential of capitalist technology

Work time, as Gorz was aware, has not been dramatically reduced in the industrial societies in the second half of the twentieth century. Certainly there has been no significant opening up of a realm of freedom beyond necessity – at least not one free from the grip of mass/consumer culture, which might be characterised as a slightly more garish version of work itself. The necessity to work remains pressing for the majority. In his early books such as *Strategy for Labour* and *Socialism and Revolution*, and indeed in later work, Gorz highlighted the gap between the possible and the actual. In this context, the possible uses of the advanced technological production resources developed under capitalism include 'the abolition of poverty, squalor, ugliness, ignorance, and degrading forms of work'. In contrast, this technology has been used for 'armaments, space exploration, color television, specialized repressive and counter guerrilla military formations' (Gorz 1975: 54). In attempting to answer the question of why this is the case, Gorz suggests that the values associated with free time – creativity, the meaning of life (Gorz 1975: 79), the richness of human relationships – are *extra economic* values, and therefore incompatible with profit and capitalist domination; the former being the motive for and the essence of the latter, perhaps, although Gorz fails to make this clear. Capitalist society operates on the basis of economic rationality, according to Gorz. The transcendent values Gorz, after Marcuse, has discussed, appear so unattainable largely because they go not only against some form of ideology or even public opinion, but because they run counter to a system of thinking, to reality itself. Reality, of course, in the analysis of critical theorists such as Gorz and Marcuse, need not inhibit theory and imagination, being as it is contingent and open to analysis and challenge.

From alienation to heteronomy, the end of work in the electronic era

By the time he published *Adieux au prolétariat* in 1980, Gorz's emphasis had shifted from what could be called the humanisation of work, to the possibilities offered by high technology, particularly the then emergent trend to universal computerisation, for the radical reduction of work. More precisely, Gorz appears to move away from the possibility of freedom *in* work, and towards an analysis that emphasises the possibilities for freedom *from* work. *Farewell to the Working Class*, as it is known in English, is without doubt Gorz's best known essay. Unfortunately, most commentators read little beyond the deliberately provocative title. It would be useful, perhaps to provide a blow by blow account of how Gorz's admittedly provocative polemic has been misinterpreted, but this has already been done creditably well (Lodziak and Tatman 1997, and Bowring's 1996 article *Misreading Gorz*), and furthermore, we must continue to concentrate on our central issue – the end of work.

In *Strategy for Labour*, Gorz had suggested that workers could gain an almost global perspective on the production process, leading to the possibility of self organised, unalienated work. In *Farewell*, however, Gorz points out that we live in a 'complex, machine like society' (1982: 9), where a high proportion of production involves complex scientific and administrative structures that are beyond the grasp of individuals. Thus, '[t]he effects of alienation can be attenuated, but never entirely eliminated' (Gorz 1982: 9). Necessary labour, Gorz asserts, will never be defined as art or craft activity, and it is a 'dangerous illusion to believe that "workers' control" can make everyone's work gratifying, intellectually stimulating and personally fulfilling' (1980: 9). Gorz even criticises his own previous characterisation of a new knowledge class of technical workers as a vanguard of self organisation. In the modern factory, apart from management, nobody knows why things are being produced, and nobody 'gives a toss' ['*on s'en fout*'] (Gorz 1982: 48, 1980: 73).

The *Grundrisse* is an important point of reference in *Farewell*, and in its successor, *Paths to Paradise*, just as it was in *Strategy*. In particular, the reduction of work time is emphasised, and we should be in no doubt that the central theme remains 'the liberation of time and the abolition of work – a theme as old as work itself' (Gorz 1982: 1). Given that work in the realm of necessity can never be entirely free from alienation, Gorz proposes that we accept some heteronomous work, that is; work that is not entirely self directed, free and always creative, and concentrate on expanding the realm of autonomy outside work. This realm of autonomy consists of freely chosen activities, and equates broadly to Marx's realm of freedom beyond necessity, where one might hunt in the morning and criticise in the afternoon, and so on. The self directed activities Gorz has in mind may be familiar in character, since we have discussed them briefly in our chapter on the future of work; they centre on workshops and community centres where facilities are provided for repair activities, exercise, arts and crafts, and even small scale farming (Gorz 1986: 199–206).

The reduction of heteronomy and the concomitant expansion of the autonomous realm are to be facilitated by the vast advances in productive efficiency which computerisation increasingly offers. Rises in productivity have already been great enough, Gorz asserts, for the autonomous sphere to be supported by a guaranteed minimum income, which Gorz calls a social income (1985: 45) for all citizens. Gorz advocated, up until recently, that a guaranteed income scheme should include an obligation to work, so that people would not be excluded from the wider framework of rights and obligations that make up the ontological infrastructure of society. This standpoint is abandoned in *Reclaiming Work* (1999), where Gorz proposes a wholesale uncoupling of income from the necessity of work, since extending income into the sphere of voluntary and caring work may leave those doing such work voluntarily feeling resentful, and would in effect aid the extension of economic rationality into the private sphere.

In terms of Gorz's utopian vision of the good life in an autonomous sphere of self realisation, we might note that some of his proposed activities cross over somewhat into the realm of production, with mention of constructing solar panels (Gorz 1986: 199–206) or house building (Gorz 1985: 104). A possible criticism might be that Gorz uses such as flexible definition of autonomous activity that it loses the distinction with work. In fact, Gorz would accept that his autonomous activities do involve work under a particular definition; however, Gorz proposes, and it is easy to agree, that work in contemporary society is generally understood as work for a wage. Further, work is not usually self directed – overwhelmingly, for all but the most privileged in society (academics, artists, company directors), it is performed under instruction, if not under financial duress, and the needs which work is oriented towards satisfying have been chosen by capital, rather than socially conscious human individuals.

The other half of what Gorz terms the dual society (he will later use the term differently), the realm of heteronomy, is equally subtle in its conceptualisation, and equally open to question. Gorz uses examples of large scale organisations such as the postal service or power generation to illustrate the fact that workers' self management is not possible in every branch of production (Gorz 1989: 32). This has led some commentators to characterise Gorz as someone who is happy to abandon the cause of abolishing alienation in work (Sayers 2000). However, heteronomy need not be a hell or a purgatory, asserts Gorz. For example '[m]aking joints, bearings or microcircuits in a medium sized factory...can be...a skilled, interesting and pleasant activity' (1985: 51). It is clear that autonomy within work is to be maximised too. In addition, work in the larger scale organisations required to support the infrastructure of a metropolitan state can even be a relief from the more emotionally involving environment of the family or local community. Gorz also has in mind, perhaps, the pleasure to be derived from a diversity of activities, not always in the sense of a temporal palette of creativity, but with the option of more mundane work. Such work, collecting rubbish or factory labouring, for example, may become alienating and oppressive if done all day and every day for the entirety of a working life, but if shared out more equitably amongst a universally well educated population, it could comprise a small part of the working life of a range of individuals, and a potentially satisfying part at that.

It is worth noting here that Gorz's conceptualisation of the realms of heteronomy and autonomy bear a striking resemblance to the spheres of freedom and necessity which Marx used in his discussion of the possibilities for a liberation from work (see Chapter 4 of this book). We have already noted that Gorz's realm of autonomy is similar to that described in Marx's *German Ideology*, and much of Gorz's writing on the dual society (as so-far conceived) is reminiscent of the Marxian assertion that the realm of freedom begins only where the realm of necessity ends. Gorz suggests that necessary/heteronomous work can be humanised as far as possible, but not entirely, and again, it is easy to interpret this as an echo of Marx, who pointed out that 'labour can [not] be made merely a joke, or amusement, as Fourier naively expressed it in shop-girl terms' (Marx, 1972a: 85–86). It is not the purpose of this book to prove the originality, or lack of originality in Gorz, or indeed anyone else, but a juxtaposition such as this reminds us that there is very little new under the sun, and to a great extent, social theories of the end of work are no exception. The power of the legacy of Marx, in simple terms, is very clearly illustrated in Gorz's work, however original much of it appears, and however contemporary the examples used.

New social subjects: The non working non class

Where Gorz is often seen as deviating significantly from Marx, or perhaps developing his theories in the light of contemporary conditions, depending on one's perspective, is in his analysis of the position of the working class in advanced capitalism. Once again, we find ourselves faced with the debate on the end of class, particularly on the disappearance of the working class. Once again, we will decline to enter into this debate fully, since it represents a topic warranting (and receiving) entire treatments of its own. The end of work represents a goal to be worked towards, for Gorz – it is a future point towards which society is progressing, or should progress. In this analytical context, it is worth discussing the social groups who Gorz sees as having the potential to move society decisively in the direction of the abolition of work – the non working non class of post-industrial neoproletarians.

Whereas the Gorz of *Strategy for Labour* proposed that the technical intelligentsia, and perhaps the intelligentsia in general, represented the vanguard class in the battle to abolish alienated work – that is, work as we know it, and transform society into the bargain, by the 1980s he had modified this view. This was partly a response to social conditions; the growth of mass unemployment in Europe, for example, and the increasing tendency for work to take on a contingent form. There is also a sense that Gorz detects a tendency for technical elite to be co-opted by capital.

In something of a theoretical reversal of his earlier position, Gorz suggests in *Farewell* that since work now comprised little more than pre-programmed activity in the service of the capitalist megamachine (Gorz 1982: 67), the idea that any individual or class could identify itself with work was illusory, hence the title of his most well known book. Further, a 'majority' of the population is now either unemployed, or in 'probationary, contracted, casual, temporary jobs and part time employment' (Gorz 1982: 69) – the social conditions mentioned earlier.

Since 1982, Gorz has characterised the advanced societies as increasingly polarised between a privileged, fully employed elite, or core, installed in the key sectors of production and administration, and a growing periphery of *précaires* (Gorz 2003: 98) – people in precarious, contingent, flexible and non standard employment. These are workers in what Beck, after Douglas Coupland, and rather glibly, calls 'McJobs' (Beck 2000: 83). This type of bifurcated social structure Gorz (from 1989 onwards) terms the 'dual society'.[5] In *Farewell*, Gorz contends (Gorz 1982: 69) that the *précaires* comprise a majority of the population, but in *Critique of Economic Rationality*, he cites figures of one third of the population of Britain in 1985 as typical (Gorz 1989: 67). This is roughly in line with current analyses which suggest that 'about one third of the labour force is employed currently on a non-standard basis' (Edgell 2007: 13). Gorz asserts that a large proportion of this group are over qualified for the work that they find themselves intermittently doing, and it is therefore not surprising that '[t]hey prefer to "hang loose", drifting from one temporary "McJob" to another, always retaining as much time as possible to follow the favoured activities of their tribe' (Gorz 1999: 61). Because of their ontological, and to a large extent temporal disconnection from the world of work, and their tendency instead to focus on extra-economic goals, these neoproletarians are the group most likely to develop the consciousness that will move society beyond the grip of the rationality of capitalism/work, and towards the abolition of work, and the realisation of freedom. This group represents, if not a revolutionary subject in the classic Marxist sense, then something pretty close, *'le principal acteur future d'une mutation culturelle antiproductiviste et anti-étatiste'* (Gorz 2003: 92).

To some extent, Gorz is following Marcuse in suggesting that it will be society's outsiders and aesthetes who will develop a new consciousness. On another, he is following the logic of writers such as Offe in suggesting that the lack of stable or rewarding jobs, or high unemployment, will lead to a diminution in the ethical or ideological status of work itself. Gorz does cite some empirical evidence in *Reclaiming Work* (Gorz 1999: 63, 64), including findings of the 1993 British Social Attitudes Survey, which supposedly suggest that 57% of Britons 'refuse to let work interfere with their lives' (Gorz 1999: 64). Gorz's background is in journalism, rather than academic sociology, and typically, the statistics he uses are

---

5　We saw earlier how Gorz used the term 'dual society' to describe the division of life into heteronomous and autonomous spheres. It seems he chooses to use the same term to describe a different phenomenon later on.

drawn from the work of others – Ray Pahl, in this case (Gorz 1999: 157). Indeed, in his commentary on 'Generation X and the unheard revolution' (Gorz 1999: 59–64), Gorz relies heavily on *Demos 4* (1994) and *Demos 5* (1995). There is nothing necessarily wrong in the way Gorz uses statistics to support his view that the work ethic is being abolished alongside work, but other writers have been able to use similar statistical sources to argue quite the opposite. Shaun Wilson, for example, drew on the British Social Attitudes Survey from 2000. When questioned on whether or not they would work, even if they didn't have to, 72% of respondents suggested that they would prefer to continue to work, with only 24% saying the opposite. The figure for preferring to work is even higher for the 24–28 year old group, Wilson notes, casting doubt on the characterisation of young people as turning away from the work ethic (Wilson 2004: 112).

In Gorz's defence, he does seem to express an appreciation, in *Reclaiming Work* and elsewhere, that the work ethic continues to be perpetuated by business and the state, through socialization at school, for example (Gorz 1999: 64–67). This is a case, Gorz suggests, of politics lagging behind culture – yet another ideological structure that has been overtaken by objective social conditions. It is possible that one's social context can influence one's analysis of social conditions, and one may wonder whether conditions in 1990s France and Germany – massive youth unemployment, and a vibrant radical/alternative scene amongst the same constituency – influenced Gorz to any extent. It may be unwise to write off the cultural persistence of the work ethic across the developed world, just as it is unwise to underestimate the potential for economic restructuring, government policy and propaganda, combined with consumer culture, to perpetuate this ethic. Gorz mentions an increasing tendency for Americans to 'downshift' (Gorz 1999: 64), but Lefkowitz was noting similar trends in the USA in the late 1970s, and North America is yet to undergo any *mutation culturelle antiproductiviste.*

Gorz and Negri on immaterial labour

We have earlier briefly discussed possible commonalities in the analyses of Gorz, and another prominent (in the rarefied theoretical circles of post 1968 European Marxism) Marxist writer for whom the abolition of work is a theme, Antonio 'Toni' Negri. One striking parallel between Negri and Gorz is in the conception of new social groups with liberatory potential emerging as a result of, and being instrumental in, the development of capitalist production. This, of course, is Marxist social theory, *avante la lettre*. Negri's work is more explicit than Gorz's, perhaps, in emphasising the dynamic or dialectical way in which such groups and tendencies, emerge.

Negri suggests, throughout his writings (but see for example Hardt and Negri 1994: 272–273 and Negri 1989: 214), that rather than automated work processes and computerisation emerging as part of a more neutral drive for efficiency on the part of capital, facilitated by advancing technology, these changes were in fact a response to increasingly refractory labour during the 1960s and early 1970s. Negri in fact refers to a 'refusal of work' (Hardt and Negri 1994: 273). We have raised this possibility briefly in our discussion of the so called revolt against work in Chapter 6. Put simply, the thesis is that capital sought to rid itself of labour wherever possible, and to make those still at the centre of the productive process as secondary as possible to increasingly panoptic machines. Further disciplinary momentum was provided by combining rising unemployment with restructuring in the welfare state. These measures were backed up by increased spending on police anti-insurgency operations.

The changes Negri describes had another consequence however. Having eliminated one antagonist from the field of battle – the 'mass worker' of factory, mine and shipyard, capital furthered the development of a 'social worker', for whom work and life are increasingly intertwined, and who produce as part of a cooperative of active, thinking agents. In the era of the techno – scientific social worker, 'productivity is now found entirely within the time of cooperation' (Negri 2005: 71). The social worker has the potential to transcend capitalism conceptually because their labour, being largely immaterial and intrinsic, is hard or impossible to measure in terms of value in the capitalistic, economic sense. Ontologically and at the level of lived experience, there is also a tendency towards 'self valorization'; that is, producing and organising actively and cooperatively in work and life, beyond the boundaries of capitalist rationality. Capital seems to have inadvertently created a group whose development as subjects useful to capital in the era of emotional labour and the weightless economy means it is actually poised ready to demolish the master's house with his own tools; to become conscious of its nascent new consciousness, conscious of the desirability of transcending capitalism, and capable of doing so. It is, in effect, a new proletariat.

We have, of course, heard something like this before, and Gorz himself cannot resist pointing out that *Strategy for Labour* provided a very similar analysis indeed (Gorz 1999: 39). Gorz is in fact here responding not only to Negri, but also to writers such as Lazzarato who write from a similar standpoint. Negri's more recent work follows Lazzarato in emphasising the idea that it is those involved in 'immaterial' labour who have the potential to explode the restrictions which capitalism imposes upon them (they are encouraged to be affective, autonomous and creative, yet capitalism wishes to "write the script"). Somewhat unfairly, Gorz, among others, criticises authors such as Negri for writing as if such potentials, or tendencies, are instead a reality (Gorz 1999: 41). There is an element of hypocrisy in this line of criticism; Negri's style is similar to Gorz's in that it tends towards the polemic and the utopian. Both figures, after all, are committed to promoting radical social change. This means that they must make statements in the realm of the not yet. Their strategy is to point out that the objective conditions for a new society are in place, but that somehow capitalism persists in its domination.[6]

---

6   The closing lines of the *Communist Manifesto* spring to mind: 'The proletarians have nothing to lose but their chains. They have a world to win. Working men of all countries

Both Gorz and Negri know that capitalist work continues, and both know that this is because abolishing capitalist work in reality would involve abolishing really existing capitalism, which from the point of view of capital, cannot be allowed to happen. It is surprising to find Gorz criticising Negri for saying that '"Capital becomes merely an apparatus of capture, a phantasm, an idol"' (Hardt and Negri 1994, cited in Gorz 1999: 40), when Gorz uses a similar rhetorical flourish – living dead capitalism[7] – to emphasise, as Negri does, that capital's lifeblood, work, has been rendered obsolete in the form which capital has always conceptualised it; that is, it has been abolished in abstract terms.

We will examine the notion of living dead capitalism in the next section, and return now to Gorz and Negri's notes on the social subjects capable of escaping the domination of capitalism through realising the abolition of work. It is clear that various criticisms can be made of the idea of a knowledge class, a new working class, or a class of immaterial workers. There is scope for considerable, and considerably tedious debate over whether or not immaterial workers make up a majority of the population, how immaterial their work in fact is, whether the concept is an ethnocentric one applicable only to the global north, and so on and so forth (for a discussion along these lines see Wright 2005: 34–45). Negri and Hardt, as Wright notes, have recently responded to such criticisms by stating explicitly that they understand immaterial work as having hegemonic tendencies, rather than being something that already involves a majority of the population (Wright 2005: 37). In an earlier period, they found it necessary to show that they understood the persistence of exploitation, and that they continued to be Marxists.

Of course, saying something represents a tendency, rather than an actuality, implies an element of futurology. Caffentzis (Caffentzis 1998) in particular has been critical of theories which seek to predict the future by extrapolation from present conditions, and points out, in essence, that social change is a result of class conflict rather than inexorable laws. Something of a contradiction becomes evident when we consider the fact that class conflict as a historical motor is a familiar concept to Marxists, and Caffentzis seems happy to project worker's struggles into the future (almost like an inexorable law), if nothing else.

Negri is notoriously light on empirical evidence, and we have seen that Gorz does at least attempt to apply some statistical rigour to his claims. We have seen also, that this rigour is sometimes open to question. It is also worth considering the issue of definitions here. Gorz occasionally attempted to present empirical evidence for the existence of a neoproletariat or non working non class, but this is an exercise that is beset with greater difficulty than Gorz acknowledged. It is left to the reader to consider the option of searching out the studies to which Gorz refers and fully apprising themselves of the categorical definitions on which they are based. How, exactly, is 'unstable' work defined (Gorz 1989: 67)? In this very chapter, Edgell is cited in support of Gorz's claims, but it is not clear that his

---

unite!' (Marx and Engels 1996: 55).
  7   'A spectre is haunting Europe' (Marx and Engels 1996: 2).

understanding of non standard work matches that of Gorz's concept of peripheral work, given that the former includes self employment in the 'non-standard' category. Even less helpfully for Gorz, Edgell points out that 'it is virtually impossible to generalise about the incidence' of non standard work (Edgell 2006: 148). Rhetorically speaking, Gorz attempts something of a compromise, offering statistical evidence on the one hand, but retaining a sense of tendency, rather than actuality, on the other.

On one level, the analyses of both Gorz and Negri are impressionistic, and the persuasiveness of their accounts may ultimately depend not only on their presentation of reality, but on the readers' own perception of it. Many will have got a sense in the 1980s that stable employment was undergoing something of a crisis, thanks to news coverage (or experience) of mass unemployment. Many young people will have experience of precarious, low paid McJobs, and those who don't may have read accounts of those who do in the press, or in popular literature (see for example Fran Abrams, *Below the Breadline* 2002). Many readers will work in the creative industries, in publishing, academia, web design. It is likely that to some extent they are a self selecting readership where accounts of 'culture and politics after the net'[8] are concerned, and it may be easy to accept an overestimation of the importance of pseudo bohemian intellectuals when you yourself, and your peer group, fall into exactly this category.

During the 1980s in particular, Gorz looked to the non working non class as a social subject. He always maintained however, that they were often highly educated – too well educated for the work they were expected to do. In a sense then, he never moved completely away from the link between the intelligentsia and revolution. In his latest book (on social theory) he retained the concept of the neoproletariat in the context of a polarised society, and emphasised more than ever the tendency towards higher learning (which they won't get the chance to fully use) amongst this cohort (Gorz 2003: 90). However, in an era where the instant global communication which he discussed in Strategy (Gorz 1967: 117) has become a reality, he appears to look to a sort of coalition of 'university students, economists, writers, scientists, with, and radicalised by oppositionalist groups, postindustrial neoproletarians, ethnic minorities, landless peasants, the unemployed and the precariously unemployed' (Gorz 2003: 98, my translation). There is also a role for those espousing the 'hacker ethic' of a 'creative commons' – an online realm of freely available information and interchange. Although there is indeed a political dimension occupied by radical direct action groups and website designers alike (they even have their own publications, *Mute* magazine, for example, which features numerous discussions of immaterial labour),[9] their radical spirit and anti

---

8   This is the sub-title of the journal *Mute*, which deals with technology and intellectual property issues from an immaterial worker perspective.

9   Another example is the radical arts and culture publication *Variant*. Those with an eye for detail may have noticed that both organs are funded by the same organisation,

economic cultural impulse is yet to explode decisively in the direction of political change.

In the absence of a guaranteed income, all but a tiny minority with independent incomes must work. And even for those in the most advanced immaterial sectors, this is likely to be work in the service of capital, or perhaps once removed – in the service of the state. As those who campaign against the so called new enclosures (which are decreasing the liberatory potential of the internet by turning it into a privatised commercial resource) are aware, those in control of the cutting edge of communication in the immaterial world are, and increasingly will be, the same social forces that have traditionally turned common property into economic resources to be quantified and traded. The *ne plus ultra* of internet age virtuality/ immateriality, Second Life, the name of which is absolutely self explanatory, even has its own virtual currency, which is exchangeable with the dollar, and a GDP of $500,000,000. The owner of the company which controls Second Life enthuses: 'We have learned a lot about monetary policy! I love it' (*The Guardian* 2007a, May 17). Workers at Google may be pampered, but they still work for shareholders, and must bend to the wishes of the Chinese government, who are busy installing their own version of ultracapitalism. Scientists at Qinetic may scale the heights of metallurgical and chemical science, but like almost all other workers, material or immaterial, they have little say in the needs satisfied by what they will produce, or the means to which it will be put. 'In a world based on exchange they have to produce for strangers who do not share a project or common interests with them' (Anonymous 2006: 35). As far as creativity and the free expression of ideas is concerned,

> what is thinkable is what is objectively realisable within a landscape of undeniable, objective constraints: the finances available, the reality of market demand, the availability (in terms of cost!) of means, materials, labourers; the reasonability (in terms of cost!) of the design itself; the state of competition, etc. (Anonymous 2006: 35).

At least the neoproletarians of the 1980s, like the proletarians of the 1880s could be seen as having little to lose. Although immaterial workers are by no means universally highly rewarded, one has to assume that many of them occupy relatively privileged positions, and therefore question the strength of their antipathy to the status quo. In an atmosphere where the latest lifestyle illness is known as 'affluenza' (James 2007), where consumerism accelerates along with individual debt, and home ownership approaches the status of entry to King Arthur's Camelot, in terms of both desirability and feasibility, it seems sensible to assume that the revolutionary consciousness of the neoproletarian immateriat will remain at the level of underground publications and websites for some time yet.

---

the Arts Council, a cultural arm of the state. Presumably then, these forums for discourse amongst the creative elite are funded through tax on the labour of the masses.

Autonomy at work, as Gorz himself notes, is nothing without cultural, moral and political autonomy (Gorz 1999: 40). Cultural, moral, and political autonomy, as Gorz clearly states, arises not from the work situation itself, but from activism and cultures of resistance, hence the importance of encouraging alliances amongst the groups most likely to be culturally receptive to liberatory messages, and have the expertise to disseminate them. Whether through numerical scarcity, or because of the humdrum restrictions of everyday life, the new social vanguards of Gorz and Negri have yet to develop the ability to transcend the structures of capital within which they are contained. Indeed, rather than capitalist logic being purged from a widening sphere of existence, both Negri and Gorz detect the opposing tendency, something which we will discuss in the following section.

Living dead capitalism and the ghost of work

Both Gorz and Negri argue that since capital, through automation, has made capitalist work obsolete, and therefore fatally undermined itself, it represents a fetter, in Marxist terms, on the further development of humanity. 'The disappearance of market laws (as Marx showed in the *Grundrisse*), just like the disappearance of the law of value, is an inevitable consequence of automation' (Gorz 1985: 45) writes Gorz, and Negri's analysis is not dissimilar: 'The law of value, in the process of its extinction, is replaced by the regulation of exploitation according to the will of capital' (Negri 1988: 148). Capital becomes, in the words of Gorz, 'living dead capitalism', and for Negri, 'a phantasm, an idol'[10] (Hardt and Negri 1994: 282). And yet both writers are fully aware that exploitation and capitalist work continue. We are faced with two questions then. Firstly, if work is now objectively outdated, how is it perpetuated, and secondly, why is it perpetuated? The two questions are, of course, closely interrelated.

For both Gorz and Negri, perhaps the primary way in which work is perpetuated is by extending it as far as possible into realms that previously constituted life outside of work. This is what Negri terms the social factory or the diffuse factory:

> *...the emergence and growth of diffused forms of production...while it enlarged the labour market enormously, also redefined as directly productive and*

---

10   A rather esoteric field of literature is devoted to debating the status of the law of value, and the labour theory of value. See for example Caffentzis's chapter in Davis et al 1997. Both Gorz and Negri, although rather unclear, seem to accept that society continues to function according to capitalist logic, of which the law of value is a part. Their point is that this logic is no longer applicable, since the value of immaterial labour is almost impossible to measure, and automation has reduced necessary work to the degree that society should shift to a theory of free time, rather than surplus labour, as the key element in a theory of value.

"working class" a whole series of functions within social labour that would otherwise be seen as marginal or latent (Negri 1988: 208–209 [his italics]).

Gorz has a very similar conception of what he calls economic rationality being extended into private life. This, in simple terms, is the transformation into work for a wage, activities that would previously have been intrinsic to social reproduction. Gorz (and perhaps Negri, although he is less clear) has in mind domestic activities such as shopping and housework, for example (Gorz 1989: 154). A new servile class emerges to clean houses, look after children, and deliver shopping.[11] Rather than this saving time over society as a whole, it in fact increases to total quantum of labour time. These are activities that would take less time and manpower if they were done, as in the past, as private activities outside the commercial sphere. As more and more activities in the sphere of reproduction are turned into jobs, those whom the new servants wait upon must in fact devote more time and effort to earning the money with which to purchase their services. From the point of view of the perpetuation of work, this is rather an effective strategy. '"Making work", "creating jobs": these are the goals of the new tertiary anti-economy' (Gorz 1989: 155).

There are of course other ways in which capitalist work and the extraction of surplus labour power are extended and perpetuated. Not everyone can be employed; the paradox of the work oriented society is that although it places great emphasis on work, it is unable to create genuine full employment, and it must mask unemployment through subsidising 'eternal students', 'endless apprenticeships', 'increased arms production', and 'limited wars' (Gorz 1985: 36). Both Gorz and Negri are also aware of the tendency for the capitalist logic of work to expand not just intensively, within a society, but also extensively; something which has become known as globalisation. The tendency for capital to seek out new spaces for expansion was, of course, observed by Marx in the Communist Manifesto (Marx 1996: 5). This latter tendency has been usefully analysed from an autonomist Marxist perspective in the work of George Caffentzis.

Gorz and Negri are less clear on why the strategy of continuing to impose work exists, and who is behind it. Both authors understand work as the lynchpin of capitalism, and so see perpetuating the former as key to the survival of the latter. Capitalism and capitalists, presumably, are responsible for maintaining the necessity of alienated work artificially. A closer investigation of how capitalists perpetuate the work ethic and promote economic 'rationality' is left to writers such as Sharon Beder (Beder 2000) or Ernesto Gantman (Gantman 2005). As a basic level we might presume that since profit can only be extracted from surplus labour, the capitalist's werewolf thirst for profit can only be satisfied by the continuation, and expansion of waged work in sectors where automation has not yet eliminated

---

11   It is acknowledged, of course, that a servant class is not a recent innovation. Large sections of the population were engaged as servants in Britain up until the Second World War, for example.

it. In both Gorz and Negri however, one is never presented with such a clear explanation.

There is more of a sense in Gorz and Negri that work continues as a form of imposed discipline, as command, which is more than ever 'voluntaristic, subjective and precise in its will to dominate over the extinction of the law of value' (Negri 1988: 148). Gorz suggests that the chief objective of work is simply '"to keep people occupied", and thereby to preserve the relations of subordination, competition and discipline upon which the workings of the dominant system are based' (Gorz 1982: 72). Elsewhere Gorz emphasises the role of work as an ideology. If the work ethic collapses, he asks 'what would become of the social and industrial hierarchy? On what values and imperatives could those in command base their authority?' (Gorz 1982: 131). One could contend that essentially, Gorz proposes that work is continued so that people simply do not have time to think about any alternative.

In his more recent work, Gorz continued to see work as reinforcing domination (Gorz 1999: 44). However, there can be more orthodox economic reasons for creating a dual society, split between a peripheral class of servants, and a highly productive, highly integrated core. It is more functional for capital, according to Gorz, to have a smaller number of highly loyal, well rewarded workers working as intensively and extensively as possible. This not only allows the cutting of costs at the practical level of subsidiary employment fees, it promotes the creation of an elite with the 'correct attitude' (Gorz 1999: 45) to work – without which, they are made increasingly aware, their future lies amongst the servants, on the periphery of an increasingly unequal society.

Conclusion

In Negri's analysis, when the whole of life becomes work, the whole of humanity becomes working class. The class struggle comes to operate at the level of the entirety of life. For both Negri and Gorz, the objective is to integrate work and life not in the negative sense of subsuming life under wage labour, but by transforming work into an activity that serves the development of the autonomous individual, in the context of a society where needs are defined by society as a whole. As we have already pointed out, this is very much in the tradition of Marx. Although Gorz and Negri attempt to identify the ways in which Marx's theory must be adapted to present conditions, they face a by now familiar theoretical and practical problem. Critical theory operates at the level of rationality. That is, it attempts to show how an existing state of affairs is irrational, and how it should be replaced by, in effect, another rationality.

End of work theories such as those of Gorz and Negri are supposedly an advance on Marx in that the obsolescence of wage labour, and therefore capitalism, is more evident now, in the age of immaterial labour, than it has ever been. Like all critical theorists however, they are unable to account for the fact that it is only they who are able to perceive reality clearly, and to think according to a transcendent rationality. They also, perhaps, underestimate the power of the ideology of work, and overestimate the forces ranged against it. Both writers follow Marx in viewing historical social change as the result of class conflict, or more specifically, the struggle over work, and both are aware of the importance of combining revolutionary consciousness with practical political activity. Gorz even suggests alternative ways of living in a future utopia where work has been eliminated as far as possible. Although Gorz and Negri succeed in demonstrating the irrationality of work as we know it, they offer only a partial solution to the problem of how liberatory consciousness should be developed, and the power of their social subjects to abolish work remains at the level of potentiality rather than actuality.

Chapter 8
Sociology and the End of Work:
Classical, Cultural and Critical Theories

Introduction

Already this book has explored how writers such as Fourier, Marx, Marcuse and Gorz wish to see work as we conventionally know it transformed; in essence, abolished. Their writings seek to give critical support to the actual end of work for individuals in society. The current chapter, however, is primarily concerned not with the theory of the end of work in an empirical sense; that is, work being eliminated *in society as such*, although this aspect is of course pertinent. Rather, the focus here is on the move away from work as the key sociological category; the supposed end of work as a category of paramount importance for sociology and social theory, rather than in the social world itself. Readers should bear in mind that some discussion of the latter will be involved in any examination of the former. The following discussion of work's status as sociological category will begin in earnest with the most explicit treatment of this issue within recent sociology, Claus Offe's 1983 article 'Work: The Key Sociological Category?', republished shortly after as a chapter in his *Disorganized Capitalism* (1985). We will follow this with an examination of the work of Jürgen Habermas. While our discussion of Offe is focused on a particular essay, we will see that Habermas's analysis of the relevance of work to the social sciences must be drawn from across his oeuvre. We will move on to discuss one of the most notable changes within academic sociology, the supposed move from a paradigm of production, to one of consumption. First however, it is necessary to make some preliminary statements on how the categorisation of social thought will be understood.

The categorisation of social thought

Quite what is meant by a key sociological category is something that needs to be clarified. It is easy to pass over the term without considering the meaning of the word 'key', in this context, but it should briefly be commented on. The word key is used here to denote something that once grasped, can be used to understand, or unlock the meaning of, other phenomena, experiences or structures.

In general terms, one might suggest that the idea of a key sociological category has three levels, although it is clear that, typically, these levels are closely interconnected, and most analyses of work and society touch on all of them, whilst choosing to emphasise a particular one. Firstly, there is the discursive, disciplinary, or paradigmatic level. Self reflectively, the focus here is on the way sociologists, throughout the course of the development of the discipline, have described industrial societies, and the way sociology seeks to understand these societies. In this case, a sociological category is exactly that, a way of thinking about society, rather than an actual empirical state, phenomenon, or materially observable structure. It may seem strange to separate this level off from the second and third levels; structural/objective and individual/subjective. However, it is important to show that social thought at the paradigmatic level has a life of its own, so to speak. If social thought were able to simply apprehend with exactitude the social reality, there would be nothing for social theorists to discuss – there is clearly a separation between social reality and social thought or perception, but this does not exclude perception itself from analysis. That is, the way people think about something is just as real as the thing itself. Before moving on to accounts that posit the decline of work as a category at all three analytical levels, let us look next at the way in which work became the key sociological category, at the paradigmatic and conceptual level, in the first place.

The establishment of work as sociological category

According to Offe, 'to questions relating to the organizing principles of the dynamics of social structures, we can safely conclude that labour has been ascribed a key position in sociological theorizing'. This has been the case, he suggests, from the late eighteenth century to the end of the First World War (Offe 1985:129). The centrality of work, labour, production, whichever term one chooses to use, is clear from the work of the three key figures in classical sociology; Marx, Weber, and Durkheim.

The early development and establishment of sociology as an autonomous discipline roughly coincided, as various writers have noted with the French Revolution and the Industrial Revolution (see for example Nisbet 1970). The question of whether the French Revolution had its roots in economic dynamics in the context of French commercial and industrial development is beyond the scope of the present investigation, but is worth considering *en passant*. The importance of economic dynamics for the Industrial Revolution is in far less doubt. This was, after all, a revolution in *production* first and foremost. Sociologists were unsurprisingly concerned with investigating the radical changes in production, in both technological and relational terms, that, crucially, lay behind many of the changes in society more generally. To clarify further, and without wishing to appear unduly determinist, it is the case that many of the so called social problems (problems of order, of morality etc.) that exercised the imaginations of early sociologists and social commentators were linked with radical changes in the relations of production. The separation of home and work, the concentration of mechanised production in towns and cities which developments in technology (and ideology) had made possible, and the erection of an urban-industrial infrastructure all gave rise to new ways of living. This was evidently a period not only of change but of construction; the public sphere of the time was replete with accounts of homo faber scaling new heights in metal, glass, and velocity.[1] The prime mover behind this construction was work, newly defined as abstract labour power. These achievements could be seen to be happening not through magic, but through work applied in a rational and systematic way.

We come now to the second and third levels of meaning used in our examination of the concept of work as a sociological category. From the above discussion it should be becoming clear that the discursive/paradigmatic level is premised on the categorical importance of work at the objective/structural and subjective/individual levels. That is, work is important at the discursive level because what sociology wishes to discuss, social conflicts and structures, as well as everyday life, have work at their centre.

If the link between rationality and work was clear, it was also clear that this was rationality operating as a logic of capital, and wage labour was the organising principle in the new capitalist societies. This was in turn connected, as Offe notes, to the 'processes of pauperization, alienation, rationalization' and the new forms of resistance 'inherent within these processes' (Offe 1985: 132). Social forces; political conflict, changes in political consciousness, tended to be organised around the issue of work. Political parties were even *formed* ostensibly to represent the interests of labour.

Crucially, for Marxist sociology in particular (although by no means exclusively), class became the structural, as well as the existential and cultural form through which capital's logic was expressed. As industrialisation progressed, sociologists began to observe new industrial communities, in a spatial as well as cultural sense, coalescing around this or that form of work, communities for whom steel, clay, or coal, represented the centre of life. Relations of production have been the defining principle of class, in one way or another, for the vast majority of sociologists up until the present day. For many social thinkers, the *working* class represented the class whose creation, and ultimate destiny, was most intimately connected with those of the capitalist system.

For the working and middle classes, work took up a lot of time, that is, it had both a physical and existential hold on the population by dint of its extent. In terms of intensity also, work was as often seen as problematic, if not harmful, even if an ideal of work was usually portrayed as virtuous. Further, it was obvious that work, and lack of it, was at the heart of the extreme levels of poverty and social inequality evident in the industrial countries.

In the realm of beliefs, as Offe points out (Offe 1985: 139), and as discussed in Chapter 2 of this book, work was elevated to a new ethical status – a process with which early sociology had a particularly ambiguous relationship, being both an observer and at times a protagonist.

---

1   For an excellent survey of this see Harvie et al 1970.

An ongoing exploration of the different levels of sociological categorisation need not be abandoned, it will be continued in a less explicit fashion, through an examination of the central question, the status of work as key sociological category. This will, in fact, entail an assertion that work continues to be key, at all ontological, existential, and material levels.

Offe and the decline of work: Heterogenisation and rationality

Offe's first set of reasons for the dissolution of work as the key sociological category centre around the increased heterogeneity of work at the end of the twentieth century. '[W]ork situations are marked by a wide variation in income, qualifications, job security, social visibility and recognition, stress, career opportunities, communication possibilities and autonomy' (Offe 1985: 135). This change at the subjective level of work activities, Offe argues, leads to work losing its significance as a factor around which workers collectively identify and organise, and therefore in this latter sense its significance at the structural level declines also. As Cleaver has noted, however (Cleaver 1989: 117), the heterogeneity of work is nothing new, and this is perhaps the weakest point in Offe's argument.

After a brief appearance from the once ascendant notion that informal work was increasing in significance relative to formal, Offe moves on to the familiar observation that service work predominates in contemporary society. His assertion that jobs in the professional, caring and intellectual sectors are somehow outside the sphere of profit, of the law of value, and the command of capital, was doubtful in 1983 however, and has become increasingly so in the last quarter of a century. Offe is aware that service workers are essential to the reproduction of the status quo, and he intimates as much when he suggests that many service workers are tasked with containing the social problems of capitalism. More interesting is his description of the eclipse of the economic rationality of traditional productive work by the apparently empathetic rationality of the service sector.

Offe suggests (Offe 1985: 138) that 'inputs and outputs can often not be fixed and utilised as a control criterion of adequate work performance' in the service sector, particularly in the realm of normalising professions such as education, care, etc. We may *hope* that the 'economic-strategic criteria of rationality' is 'faltering', (Offe 1985: 138) to be replaced with empathy and normatively based substantive rationality, but in recent years the dominant tendency has been towards the opposite. Increasingly, performance is closely monitored, and educational and healthcare institutions alike are run as capitalist enterprises, replete with budgets, strategies, and a crypto Stalinist system of targets and league tables. In fact, increasingly is something of a misnomer, since the application of capital accounting and the rationality of profit are by now established in the service sectors of the advanced industrial nations at a high level; this should be as obvious to those working in the university sector, as it is to those working in the government agencies where staff are required to clock in and out of the office.[2] Even at the less obvious level of non temporal control of performance, far from pay being separated from (work) performance, remuneration, indeed maintenance of position, often depends on proof that one has delivered results (of one's work) in a measurable form, be it changes in the local rate of teenage parenthood, GCSE results, or amount of funding from successful bids. The latter represents a convoluted form of intellectual piece-work, it could be argued, and in general terms, the economic rationalities that have always governed industrial capitalism, far from drawing back from a growing autonomous sphere of service work (which in Offe's analysis ceases almost to be work), creep inexorably into ever wider spheres of activity (Gorz 1989).

The debate over the work ethic: Taylorisation, morality and necessity

Work's position as key sociological category is further eroded, according to Offe, at the level of ideology, by the decline of the work ethic. Offe contends that work is no longer seen as a moral duty, since the Taylorised nature of modern production does not 'allow workers to participate in their work as recognized, morally acting persons' (Offe 1983: 141). Leaving aside the fact that this line of argument apparently contradicts Offe's previous claim regarding service work, this understanding of the moral status of the work ethic is still problematic. There is, as Cleaver notes in his own response to Offe (Cleaver 1989: 122), limited evidence for the existence of a work ethic amongst the labouring classes at any point under capitalism, with the possible exception of skilled craftspeople. However, this counter argument shares some of the faults of that which it seeks to contradict, as we shall see.

Certainly there is evidence that workers resisted the imposition of capitalist work norms during the early stages of industrialisation, but Offe is almost certainly referring to the work ethic that was developed as part of this process, the work ethic of established industrialism. As Cleaver concedes (Cleaver 1989: 122), various sections of the working class have tended to organise politically and socially around the fulcrum of labour. It should be acknowledged however, that while organised labour conflict has often been the territory of skilled workers, twentieth century struggles in Britain and elsewhere have shown that this is not always the case. And though Cleaver suggests that workers' struggles for a shorter work-week indicate an anathematic relationship with work, is it not the case that in periods where work is in short supply, the same social subjects are at the forefront for the fight for the right to work (which may of course be better conceptualised as the right to a wage)? Indeed, a shorter work week may even be seen as a solution to the problem of mass unemployment.

---

2   Information from Tim Vernon, formerly a union activist in North West England (personal interview 2006).

Both sides of the argument here face the same problem; it is extremely difficult, if not impossible, to confirm, deny, or gauge the level of the work ethic in a society where work is a necessity. Put simply, it is impossible to know whether or not people would work if they did not have to, since work they must. It is true that it is possible to survive on handouts from the welfare state, and it is still just possible for some individuals to do this on a semi-permanent basis. However, there is little evidence that a state of mere survival in abject poverty is becoming a lifestyle that people are comfortable with. Whether or not we ascribe to the belief that modern society is one in which consumption is seen as increasingly important, poverty has never been popular.

It is possible to argue that Offe underestimates the cultural embeddedness of the work ethic. While it may be the case that a purely instrumental attitude to work is widespread amongst the unskilled working class (Edgell 2006: 16) – and this assertion is questionable – individuals from all social classes, in Britain at least, feel the moral obligation to work very strongly, perceive work as a moral duty, and consider worklessness nothing short of morally dubious; thus, work is perceived as a moral necessity. Offe suggests that Apostle Paul/Stalin's principle of 'he who does not work, does not eat', is 'not strongly institutionalised in liberal welfare states' (Offe 1985: 145), but it is far from clear if, in cultural terms, this principle can be dismissed so lightly.

Increasing unemployment, decreasing work time

Offe contends that increasing levels of unemployment, coupled with falling working hours, will further marginalise work as an element of social life. Under such conditions as described in the previous section, however, it is highly unlikely that, as Offe claims, increasingly high levels of unemployment (which, although high in real terms have failed to become catastrophic) could lead to the de-stigmatization of unemployment. It is possible that such a thing could occur, and may already have occurred, within a marginalised underclass, but this is nothing new; there has always been a group perceived as the undeserving poor – undeserving since they apparently refuse to work. It is even entirely possible that should unemployment rise to unprecedented levels, worklessness could continue to hold a negative connotation. One might guess that Liberians or Palestinians, or even citizens of the former East Germany do not have a terribly sanguine view of unemployment, and the recent mass migration west from the countries of Eastern Europe, points to a similar conclusion. Poverty in countries such as the USA and Britain is seen as highly undesirable, yet large proportions of the population remain poor. Like poverty, and as a key component of it, unemployment can perform something of a disciplining function; those who manage to stay in employment may wish to moderate their calls for higher wages and better conditions, since any job seems preferable to falling into the maw of poverty and unemployment.

Offe suggests that 'The proportion of work-time in people's lives has been declining considerably; free time has expanded and seems likely to increase further' (Offe 1985: 142). As we discussed in Chapters 6 and 7, this is not quite the case. Although working hours in Britain did indeed fall in the post-war decades, they reached a plateau around 1980 (Green 2001: 54). Bunting, in her long hours themed polemic *Willing Slaves*, notes that in Britain, the number of people working more than forty eight hours a week increased from 10% of the labour force to 26% between 1998 and 2004 (Bunting 2004: 9). Both Bunting and Francis Green, whose findings she draws on, note that such statistics hide a growing polarisation in the distribution of work, with two fifths working harder than ever (Bunting 2004: 19), but 16.4% of households having no one in work (Bunting 2004: 9). It is difficult to know what to make of the significance of this polarisation in terms of the continuing importance of work. It has already been noted, however, that it is possible for a work oriented society to maintain a large non-working population. In conditions where it is scarce, work could increase in value, as rare goods have a tendency to do (see Basso 2003: 197). As the calumny of apartheid era South Africa demonstrated, it is quite possible for a minority to be privileged, and a majority marginalised, based on the possession of certain fairly arbitrary characteristics, and it is entirely possible for a marginal mass (Nun 2000) to form in countries such as America or Britain – in such a society, people are defined by work positively or negatively, depending on their success or failure in securing the status of worker. Employed or unemployed – work remains the defining feature.

As for Offe's contention that we have more free time; leaving aside increased work hours, unpaid overtime, and widespread failure to take full holiday entitlements, various analyses suggest that work's tentacles extend into most of an individual's waking hours (and for some, no doubt, into their non-waking hours). De Grazia and Marcuse have received attention elsewhere, and both Cleaver and Bunting suggest that in contemporary society, time 'off the job' is spent recuperating from work, as well as doing 'work that could not be done during the previous five days, washing work clothes, grocery shopping...' (Cleaver 1989: 121). For those who choose to Do It Yourself, leisure time even more explicitly takes on many of the characteristics of work.[3] Although reports by market research companies such as Mintel suggest that most people are happy with the amount of free time they have, their surveys are often far from conclusive. State sponsored social research has most recently found that people spend the majority of their time sleeping, working, and watching television, in that order (Office for National Statistics 2006a). This hardly indicates that society has moved away from work at the experiential or temporal level, unless one wishes to propose sleep as the key sociological category.

Offe, of course, was writing in a different decade, and a different socio-political context than that which informs the present analysis. He could not predict, for

---

3   Adorno calls this 'pseudo activity' (Adorno 1998: 173).

example, that it would be Britain, a country which during the 1980s was known in Europe for its high rates of industrial strife and spiralling unemployment, which would become the European paragon of the work based society. It is possible that he was referring to Britain when Offe wrote of the futility of remoralising work, something associated both with the neoliberal economic and ideological restructuring of the Thatcher years, and later with the neoliberal economic and ideological restructuring of New Labour. The latter, while not quite claiming that work sets us free (*The Observer* 1998, March 22), have assertively implemented social policies designed to 'make work pay', through welfare reforms designed to get as many people as possible into work, regardless of trivialities such as looking after one's own children. Little did Offe know, in 1983, that such attempts at remoralisation would produce Europe's highest rates of employment.

In continental Europe, German and French politicians look to the Anglo American model. France, the country that seemed to be confirming Offe's theses, with government restrictions on working hours, and generous welfare benefits, is in the midst of just such a remoralisation of work. Increasingly, political figures claim that in the context of global capitalism, high levels of unemployment coupled with high levels of welfare provision are unsustainable, so back to work the French must go. On the presidential campaign trail in early 2007, French President Nicolas Sarkozy promised to turn France 'from a nation that "regards work as the enemy", into one in which people want to work more to earn more'. Speaking to business leaders, he continued '"The France I love is the France that works...the France that does not count its hours or its efforts, the France that gets up early"' (*The Sunday Times* 2007, January 21).

Offe seems to have believed that in Western Europe, workers had ceased to be motivated by work, and looked instead to intrinsic rewards. They had, in Offe's analysis, reached 'saturation' point with regards to consumer goods (Offe 1985: 144). There is no such thing as saturation as far as consumerism is concerned. The consumer is never satisfied. Offe himself tentatively raises (but then dismisses) the possibility that the reduction of income may have 'a disciplining effect on workers' dispositions' (Offe 1985: 145). Politicians such as Blair and Sarkozy are well aware that if a balance can be found between restrictions on income (both in the form of real term wages and welfare payments), and an ever increasing pressure to consume, just such a disciplining effect can be achieved, and work can be effectively imposed.

A note on Bauman and the work ethic

Although we will discuss the issue of the shift from production to consumption later on, we pause to note the contribution made by Zygmunt Bauman in 1982, and reprised nearly twenty years later. In his book *Memories of Class* (Bauman 1982) Bauman interpreted the inner city riots that shook Britain in the early 1980s as evidence not only of high levels of poverty and unemployment, but of a shift from work to consumption as the basis of identity. Bauman, like Offe, seems to detect a dissolution of the traditional work ethic (Bauman 1982: 180), which he characterises as a kind of Dionysian 'de-civilising process' (Bauman 1982: 180). The 1980s, according to Bauman, witnessed the birth of the first generation for whom status was to be defined by consumption alone (Bauman 1982: 179). Bauman's analysis of urban social breakdown may have seemed hyperbolic in the early 80s, but it is interesting to note the extent to which current opinion on crime, for instance, echoes his words. Often, urban violent crime is viewed as a result of escalating pressure to be seen to be conspicuously consuming (in the conventional rather than then Veblenian sense), whilst being excluded from the job market, and thus the means to earn and consume legitimately.

Bauman's later (1998) suggestion that the poor are seen as lacking consumer skill, as 'flawed consumers' (Bauman 1998: 48), may well come to be the case. At present, however, both government policy and public opinion cling to the supposedly outdated ideas of deserving and undeserving poor, definitions resting on the continued ideological strength of the work ethic. Bauman suggests that in the past, the underclass was seen as a reserve army of labour, but a decline in the necessity to work in the society of consumption has rendered this definition obsolete. The fact that Britain has had to import low skilled labour from abroad in recent years rather contradicts the idea of there being no work for the underclass to do, although the importation of labour is a more complicated issue, and may have as much to do with employers' preference for low wages as underclass indolence. Bauman seems to be arguing that the poor are seen as 'slothful and wicked' (Bauman 1998: 91), presumably because they fail to adhere to the work ethic, yet at the same time, little effort is made to 'make everyone a producer'. This certainly highlights the ideological nature of the work ethic, and in a sense, Bauman is correct. There is not enough useful work on offer to make it necessary for everyone to work conventional full time hours. However, capitalism does not thrive on production for need – that is, useful work, and as we saw in Chapters 6 and 7, the direction of social policy seems to be to maximise employment, however peripheral. The aim is not to make everyone a producer, making them a worker is the primary goal.

The end of the industrial community?

Returning to our discussion of Offe; he is on safer ground, it would seem, in suggesting that the decline of work based milieu has seen the days of 'coal is our life' and the like disappear. Although it is surely true that the number of occupationally based communities has declined along with the mining, steel, pottery, shipbuilding and docking installations around which they orbited, such communities still exist in Britain and elsewhere. The denizens of these communities may find themselves in the position of a cultural minority, but sociology should, and in many other cases does, know better than to marginalise a cultural group because it represents a minority. Incidentally, the same could be said of workers in manufacturing industry in general. Although manufacturing in Britain, for example, has undoubtedly declined, the sector still employs 12% of the working population, or around three million people (Office for National Statistics 2006b). Even when the industry around which these communities are based is removed, the occupational categories, work groups and institutions associated with it seem to have something of an afterlife, according to recent research (MacKenzie et al 2006, Strangleman 2007). Whilst understanding that the workplace may have become less central to traditional industrial communities, and taking into account Offe's argument that work tends nowadays to be purely instrumental, it can still be argued that although work's place in the community may be dissolving, community still has a place at work. As Gilles Dauvé suggests, it is true that 'contemporary work does not socialize well because it tends to become a pure means of earning a living...[but] that socialization does not vanish'. He cites a former Moulinex worker, laid off in 2001, for whom 'the hardest thing now is to be alone' (Dauvé 2002: 23).

Habermas: work and rationality in the administered society

Alastair Macintyre, in *After Virtue* wrote that '[r]eason is calculative; it can assess truths of fact and mathematical relations but nothing more. In the realm of practice it can speak only of means. About ends it must be silent' (Macintire 1981: 54). Habermas, as an inheritor of the Frankfurt project of emancipatory critical theory, in a body of work that takes in a vast array of theories, writers, and indeed disciplines,[4] sets out to re-establish the theoretical grounds upon which ends can be spoken of. Simplifying for the sake of brevity, we might say that this task of normatively underpinning social critique takes place, self consciously, in the context of a modern society in which the supposed traditional separation of state and economy, indeed, of state and society, has broken down. In concert with writers such as Marcuse, Gorz, Negri, and certainly with Offe, Habermas characterises society in the late twentieth century as one that has moved decisively beyond the phase of industrial capitalism, into a form of administered, postindustrial monopoly capitalism. Whereas in the past, society and economy operated largely independently of the state, they are now administered by a technocratic 'system': this system is informed by an ideological melding of knowledge/science with the very objectives of the administration. That is, science, including the human

---

4   Poster suggests that Habermas has 'ransacked the theoretical attic' (464: 1981). This is rather harsh. Certainly, Habermas' tendency to draw on fields as diverse as Piaget's developmental psychology and the philosophy of language means that reading his work is an almost unparalleled challenge for the social scientist, but this tendency can be seen as part of an effort to widen the critical debate on rationality beyond 'traditional' Marxist spheres. For Habermas, the work of the original Frankfurt generation seems almost to have become encompassed in this sphere, in terms of Habermas's theoretical purposes at least.

sciences, comes to resemble nothing more than the legitimating framework for the administration of advanced capitalist societies. So far so Frankfurt School. How then, does Habermas criticise the neo Weberian post-Marxism of his Frankfurt School predecessors, and what relevance does this have to the end of work?

For Habermas, Critical Theory has remained wedded to the paradigm of production, and like Offe, Habermas suggests that work has had its day as the key sociological category. As we shall see, Habermas shares with Baudrillard the sense that the Marxism of Marcuse and the Frankfurt School, not to mention Marx himself, is circumscribed in its emancipatory potential because it remains trapped within a paradigm (of production, labour, the labour theory of value – work) that offers little to modern subjects seeking an escape from the existential dead end of monopoly capitalism. Habermas proposes that the paradigm of production has little or no normative content (1987b: 79), and needs to be replaced by one that emphasises interaction, and more specifically, communicative interaction. It should be said that we will not be evaluating Habermas's proposals for a universal discourse ethics in any great detail. We will generally restrict ourselves to his contention that in theoretical terms, critical social theory must go beyond work.

We have seen how Marx, as well as later writers such as Gorz and Negri, saw production, that is, work, evolving to such a degree that it becomes a sort of scientific exercise. At this stage, work should be transformed into self directed activity by the associated producers. In this sense then, 'the forces of production appear to enter a new constellation with the relations of production' (Habermas 1987a: 84, and see Poster 1981: 461). It is clear to Habermas that, despite society having entered this technoscientific stage, societies remain alienated from themselves: unjust, unequal, unemancipated. The 'associated producers', have not spontaneously liberated themselves from the fetters of capitalism once production moved onto the scientific level. There are two primary reasons for this. Firstly, rationality in production does not necessarily lead to rationality in thought, Habermas would contend (Poster 1981: 461). Secondly, and more specifically, Habermas proposes that production and science/technology are now symbiotically fused. Today, in contrast to the past, when technical knowledge was institutionally separated from theoretical knowledge – the traditional university system, for example – today;

> research processes are coupled with technical conversion and economic exploitation and production and administration in the industrial system of labor generate feedback for science. The application of science in technology and the feedback of technical progress to research have become the substance of the world of work (Habermas 1987a: 55).

This means that production, like science (although by this stage the two are indissoluble, in Habermasian terms) is now part of the 'basis of legitimation' (Habermas 1987a: 84), rather than a self actualising activity for postindustrial 'citizen-producers'. In theory, as in practice, labour and science are fused and share the same conservative function. Thus; 'Marx could not offer an "alternative to existing technology" because his theory of labour was itself scientistic and technical" (Poster 1981: 461). In a technocratic[5] society, the lack of an Archimedian point from which to evaluate the role, vis-à-vis human purposes, of technology is a fundamental flaw in the Marxist analysis. Habermas suggests that we should look to the realm of symbolic interaction, to communication, as the sphere in which the societal drift towards technoculture can be properly critiqued.

The component of Habermas's attack on the 'production paradigm' which we have discussed immediately above is of course open to criticism. It is possible to argue, and indeed, the present work does, that Marxist social theory, although apparently based around the labour theory of value, is not as restricted to the realm of production as Habermas would assert. By 1985, 16 years after the German publication of *Towards a Rational Society*, Habermas was ready to revisit the paradigm of production once more and indeed, to offer a response to this particular criticism. Habermas outlines first Heller's, and then Markus's attempts to show how the concept of production can encompass the totality of social life. Having provided the reader with a summary of her position, Heller is dismissed by Habermas because the paradigm of objectification/production that she provides is unable to give us a normative guide to social activity. Heller speaks of artists and scientists as 'the model for a creative break with the routines of everyday alienated life' (Habermas 1987b: 79). What is wrong with that, one might ask? Presumably, for Habermas, the examples of the artist and the scientist are not suitable for our rationalised society, since art and science are integrated into the system as legitimating factors. Perhaps the use of models, exemplars, in this fashion is simply not transcendental enough.

In terms of what the paradigm of production can encompass, Habermas is scathing about Heller's attempts to situate institutions and linguistic forms of expression (communication) as "'Objectifications proper to the species'" (1987b: 79). This, for Habermas, is simply not saying anything. Markus fares little better in his attempt to show how social life in general can be analysed from the perspective of production. Markus suggests that commodities have a structuring relation to the lifeworld not only in terms of their production, but also in terms of the needs to which they are related. Habermas suggests that Markus sees the sphere of production as connected with the sphere of interaction through a system of social norms and conventions that governs the 'feedback' between the two spheres. He is then ready to deliver the coup de grâce, showing that in fact, by framing his theory within the context of a duel system, Markus separates out the 'technical' sphere, the sphere of production, from the 'social' sphere. The goal, for Markus is to relegate production to its proper place – as a rational, material interchange with nature, rather than something which, through a process of reification, comes to dominate the entirety of social life. Because the forces and relations of production continue,

---

5   If we may use the term as short hand for a society based on advanced technical production and dominated by the systematic application of technology, rather than in the sense of the technocracy movement of the Depression era USA.

conceptually, to 'mutually determine' one another in Markus's theory (Habermas 1987b: 81) it is rather difficult to see how social consciousness can develop in this emancipatory direction, without providing it with a route out of this conceptual cul-de-sac by, in good conceptual faith, separating out the technical/work and interactional/communicative spheres and concentrating on the norm – establishing potential of the latter. This, of course, is Habermas's great contribution to critical social theory.

Social change, system integration and the obsolescence of work

In his 1981 book *The Theory of Communicative Action*, Habermas was at least ready to acknowledge that the labour theory of value served to supply Marx with a means of analysing the linkages between the ontological position of the individual in society (the lifeworld, as Habermas would have it (1989: 337)), and the character and dynamics of the 'system'. But, like Markus, Marx is criticised for supposing that 'theoretical critique has only to lift the spell cast by abstract labour', and workers in technically advanced large industries will become 'critically enlivened' (Habermas 1989: 340). Without advances in the sphere of communication and rational discourse, Habermas suggests that this is unlikely to happen.

On a more empirical basis, Habermas criticises the Marxist paradigm of production for not keeping pace with social and historical change. Although prepared to acknowledge, in the context of high industrialism, that Marx's labour theory provides a way of conceptualising the link between the individual and the system, Habermas contends that changing social conditions have rendered this obsolete both at the analytical and empirical level. Whereas in the past the social subject was integrated into the system through connections with the workplace, that is to say institutions (Unions) and parties, communities, trades, occupational and class identity, system integration today is far more complicated and more dominated by the ideological/symbolic level (1989: 335).

In the past, social conflict took place in a society where the vicissitudes of the market place masked the ideological nature of industrial capitalism; that is, where exploitation and domination could be seen as a feature of the invisible hand of the market. In advanced capitalism[6] on the other hand, the market and the state constitute an administrative structure, and thus '[e]very social battle would now have to be justified administratively, by the state' (Poster 1981: 463). Conflict thus shifts from the sphere of work to the sphere of ideological legitimation. For Habermas, 'Marxian orthodoxy has a hard time explaining government interventionism, mass democracy and the welfare state' (1989: 343). Marx himself, of course, had asserted that modern government amounted to a committee for organising the affairs of the bourgeoisie, which rather suggests that he was at least

---

6   It seems to be the case that the capitalist system of which Habermas writes is very much in the Northern European mould.

aware of the co-ordinating role of the state in relation to the market. Leaving this point to one side, let us consider Habermas's perspective on the welfare state. Here, the critique of the paradigm of production and the critique of theories of class conflict begin rather to conflate. Habermas's contention is that class conflict and work were interconnected at the level of the lifeworld. That is, one assumes, interconnected through shared cultural spaces, localities, industrial identity and so on. Class conflict took place at the coal face, quite literally. Now however, society is coordinated by the system (the state) and the welfare state is a key institutional element of this coordination. This is a sphere of tax credits, benefit cheats, national insurance, waiting lists, hospital closures, and so on. This is the sphere in which social conflict takes place, and since the state is reasonably effective at coordinating it, allowing all classes to live in at least tolerable conditions, regardless of status or ability to utilise labour power, conflict is effectively ameliorated. There will be civil unrest, riots and violence, but Habermas sees conflict at this level as increasingly the province of marginalised groups – immigrants, youth, students.

Habermas is right to assert that class conflict in the traditional sense is effectively a thing of the past. However, it is not clear that the development and expansion of the welfare state must entail the downgrading of the ontological, cultural or indeed sociological significance of work. Most significantly, in terms of the validity of Habermas's argument, it can be seen that the welfare state tends to operate with work and employment as a sort of defining feature. Government policy, in Britain at least, and certainly in the United States, continually refers to paid employment as the normatively positive state to which citizens should aspire. Ever more draconian pronouncements emerge on both sides of the Atlantic; single parents (mothers) should be encouraged to return to work, the unemployed will have their benefits cut if they do not agree to return to work within a particular time period, young people should be encouraged, through a combination of state sponsored incentive and state/media vilification[7] to either stay in education (ever more oriented on career development) or take up employment. As we saw in our discussion of Offe, and our brief excursus on Bauman, the ideology of work remains at the very centre of modern welfare.

How could it not? It is worth remembering how the welfare state is funded. Not through some sort of communicative agreement, but through contributions from workers. Habermas, amongst others, is right to argue that social conflicts in the sphere of state coordination of welfare are more likely to be manifested in the form of policy discussions, media debates, interest group lobbying (by Trade Unions, even?), than tool downing and walkouts, but the former are the ideological and cultural manifestations of the continued centrality of work, rather than evidence for its irrelevance. Our argument here, as in this book as a whole, is that an ever more complex ideological negotiation of work is not evidence of its demise.

---

7   The figure of the dangerous street corner youth continues its ideological career, from gang member, to 'hoodie' and putative knifeman.

Continuing with the theme of social change, Habermas contends that work itself has been transformed. No longer a realm of Dickensian toil, 'the burdens resulting from the character of heteronomously determined work are made at least subjectively bearable – if not through "humanising" the work place, through providing monetary rewards and legally guaranteed securities...' (1989: 349). Clearly, working conditions have improved for many in the West, but it is far from clear that working conditions have improved for all. For some, as we have seen earlier, work in the 'postindustrial' society is characterised by longer hours and greater work intensity, it could be argued (see for example Green 2006, cited in Glyn 2006: 114). In terms of monetary rewards, real wages have stagnated since 1979: 'real wages have grown very slowly in OECD countries since 1979, an extraordinary turn around from the 3–5% growth rates of the 1960s' (Glyn 2006: 116). And what of 'legally guaranteed securities'? Despite what commentators such as Fevre (2007) might argue, the years since Habermas published the German edition of *The Theory of Communicative Action* in 1981 have seen an erosion of job security.

Here perhaps, we might pause to reflect on the issue of historical specificity. Just as Mallet and Gorz predicted the emergence of a class of self actualising scientific workers in the context of a self consciously modernising, newly affluent France, so Habermas can be forgiven, perhaps, for extrapolating from conditions in the pre eminent European economy of the 1980s – West Germany. Just as Habermas criticised Marx for failing to foresee the integration of state and market and the advent of the welfare state (Habermas 1989: 339) so Habermas apparently failed to see that the generous Rhinish welfare model would prove to be the exception, rather than the rule, as the advanced economies moved from the twentieth century and into the twenty first.

Ultimately, Habermas resorts to the generalisation that work is no longer the key sociological category, referencing Offe's eponymous essay as he does so. The paradigm of production, according to Habermas, 'loses its plausibility with the historically foreseeable end of a society based upon labour. Claus Offe opened a recent conference of German sociologists with this question' (1987b: 79). As we saw with Offe, and as we shall see when we examine the cultural turn in sociology, this position is hard to maintain.

The sociological shift

We have explicitly examined Offe and Habermas as key sociological theorists who have argued that the focus of social thought should move away from the sphere of work. In the context of academic sociology in Britain, and America, Offe was right to claim that sociology *has* moved away from work. His analysis holds now as it did in 1983, and if anything is more accurate:

...policy oriented social research in industrial capitalist societies appears to be predominantly concerned with social structures and spheres of activity which lie at the margins, or completely outside the realm of work – domains such as the family, sex roles, health, "deviant" behaviour, the interaction between state administration and its clients and so on (Offe 1983: 134).

Although the sociology of work (and sociology that recognises the importance of work) continues to exist, it is far from the prominent position it held in the 1970s, as recent commentators have noted (Strangleman 2005). This situation is bound up at a fairly fundamental level with the debate over the significance of class. Part of this debate concerned a supposed shift from class to lifestyle as the defining feature of identity. Often, and particularly since the 1990s, lifestyle has been understood either in terms of sexual or perhaps ethnic orientation, or the aesthetics of consumption. Offe has surprisingly little to say about consumption, and while ethnic and gender issues are too important to be contained within the remit of the present discussion, it will now move on to examine the supposed shift from production to consumption in more detail. As with our treatment of Offe, the following debate constitutes a critical examination of a particular point in the development of sociology and should not be considered an exercise in demolishing straw men. Although sociology has (just about) retained an understanding of the value of structural and overarching social thought, relative to what is essentially sociologically unaware literary theory, some of the excesses of the turn to consumption and the critique of work as a sociological category still haunt the discipline, and are worth revisiting.

From production to consumption

Somewhat ironically, it was Critical Theorists such as Adorno, Marcuse, and Lowenthal, whose main concern was in fact the liberation of humanity *from* the consumer society, who helped open the way for critiques of the privileging of work in the social sciences, and the turn to (or celebration of) consumption with which these critiques are often associated. It should be noted that Marcuse himself was writing in a particular intellectual and historical context. During the 1950s and 60s , theories of the 'postindustrial', 'affluent' or 'technological' society were influential; this was the case both in the USA, and in France, where writers such as Touraine and Ellul produced accounts that paralleled those of Bell and Galbraith. The move to the centring of consumption can be seen as closely connected with discussions of the affluent society. These commentaries tended to include predictions of both the declining importance of work in society, and the objective possibility of a decrease in necessary working time.

Interestingly, as early as 1944, Critical Theory was engaging very explicitly with an apparent shift from production to consumption. There is a crucial difference, however, in the conclusions reached by Lowenthal, for example, and those of the writers who will be examined below. We shall return to this in the conclusion.

Often, the diagnostic social theory of writers such as Bell or Touraine was combined with Marxist critiques – as was the case in both Marcuse and Gorz (the latter being considerably influenced by the former). By the May events of 1968, critical analyses of everyday life by writers such as Henri Lefebvre were also gaining in prominence, particularly in France. One writer who, like Guy Debord and the Situationists,[8] was influenced both by the radical critiques of everyday life that so inspired the students of Nanterre, and by the (similarly influential) Marxian analyses of Marcuse and the Critical Theorists, was Jean Baudrillard.

Baudrillard: Shattering the Mirror of Production

The parallels between Marcuse and Baudrillard, during the early 1970s at least, are fairly clear. Wernick suggests that:

> The guiding assumptions are identical: that the masscultural instance has become crucial to social reproduction, that it represents indeed a strategic built-in mechanism for ensuring the social order's real stasis through all the incipient upheavals it continues to induce, and that this is why the Revolution (if the term retains any meaning) has perhaps permanently missed the historical boat (Wernick 1984: 17).

In *The Consumer Society* (1970), Baudrillard's logic does indeed follow that of Marcuse; mass consumer culture exists as a reflection of the alienated world of capitalist labour. Needs for the goods consumerism offers are artificially created by the giant combines which control both production and reproduction, where superfluous consumption predominates. Consumerism offers compensation, to the underlying population, for the stultifying nullity of work in bureaucratic capitalism. The consumer, however, enters into something of a Faustian bargain, since they must continue to sell their labour in an ever more intensive and competitive fashion, in order to keep up with the inexorably rising levels of conventionally expected consumption. Thus, satisfactions are always transitory and economically dependent; satiety is held forever beyond our grasp. While capitalism robs us of our true individuality and independence so that we can be inserted into the economic complex as a disciplined and productive unit, it sells us back a simulation of human identity in the form of fashion, shopping, holidays, hobbies, entertainments.

> Thus, a deep logical collusion links the mega-corporation and the micro consumer, the monopoly structure of production and the "individualistic" structure of

---

8   For an account of the relationship between Baudrillard and the Situationists see Plant 1992.

consumption, since the "consumed" difference in which the individual revels is also one of the key sectors of generalised production (Baudrillard 2000: 110).

A veneer of contentment is created, and any discontent surfaces either as the plaintive cry of the intellectual, the artist, and the dropout, or as outbursts of violence and degradation; the massacre, the gang rape, the riot. The former is easily absorbed as proof that different opinions exist in our democratic society, the latter is absorbed by the prison industrial complex.

Marcuse was not averse to making observations on the concrete ways in which consumption is experienced in everyday life, but Baudrillard, in *The Consumer Society* provides a richer and more detailed dissection of the arrayed elements of consumer culture, taking in kitsch, silent films, and cellulite, along the way. Although the focus is clearly on consumption, Baudrillard still views consumer society in relation to the system of production (Kellner 1989b: 14). Consumerism and leisure, asserts Baudrillard, are subject to the same reality principle as work;

> the obsession with getting a tan, that bewildered whirl in which tourists "do" Italy, Spain and all the art galleries, the gymnastics and nudity which are *de rigueur* under any obligatory sun and, most important of all, the smiles and unfailing *joie de vivre* all attest to the fact that the holiday-maker conforms in every detail to the principles of duty, sacrifice and asceticism (Baudrillard 2000: 155–156).

By the time he wrote *The Mirror of Production* in 1975, Baudrillard had begun to see Marxist social theory itself in a similar way; that is, trapped within the very bourgeois, productivist ideology from which it sought to escape.

Baudrillard acknowledges that Marcuse and Marx are not to be seen as *enthusiasts* of work; rather, they envision a realm beyond labour and political economy, a realm of play, of creativity and humanity. However:

> The sphere of play is defined as the fulfilment of human rationality, the dialectical culmination of man's activity of incessant objectification of nature and control of his exchanges with it. It presupposes the full development of productive forces (Baudrillard 1975: 40).

Baudrillard asserts that Marxian critiques maintain the concept of a realm of freedom beyond necessity as an ideal sphere of transcendence – but one that can only be reached through that from which transcendence is sought – *the productive process*. The very framework of Marxist thought prevents any effective conceptual opposition – critical social theory remains trapped within the confines of productivist discourse, which is not only non-oppositional, but is unable to effectively criticise and oppose a society that has moved *beyond* domination through commodity production, and into domination by images, information and knowledge; by the 'sign'.

Critical social theory should recognise, according to Baudrillard, that domination is no longer the domination of capital and commodities, the consumer is no longer merely a recuperating labourer. In our society of consumed images, domination is the domination of 'the code', which operates through the 'super-ideology of the sign...' (Baudrillard 1975: 122). As in Baudrillard's earlier work, consumption functions as a mechanism of social control, but rather than linking domination to the *production* of commodities, it is now seen in terms of the *reproduction* of the code. Social theory then, should abandon its obsession with production,[9] and move instead to an analysis of the world of consumption, since it is through the consumption of 'signs' (cultural products) that we are enmeshed by the code.

What though, is 'the code'? This is never made clear (Kellner 1989b: 50). In fact, despite Baudrillard's attempts to extricate critical theory from the bourgeois metaphysics of political economy, he continues to use concepts such as 'capitalist' and 'monopolistic'. This may well indicate that social theory remains trapped within the framework of economic thought, which is Baudrillard's very point, but it hardly supports his claim to have discovered a set of categories (such as the code) with which to move beyond conventional critical analyses.

Baudrillard attacks a 'straw man' Marx, apparently ignoring the passages where 'Marx presents his goal as achieving a "realm of freedom" beyond labour ... [where] social activity would supplant labour and production as the organizing principle of society' (Kellner 1989b: 41). A similar accusation could be made of Baudrillard's critique of Marcuse. It is difficult to see how Marcuse, particularly the later, more avowedly utopian Marcuse could be accused of theoretical confinement within the categories of bourgeois political economy. Productivism, under the aegis of the performance principle, is Marcuse's target in *Eros and Civilization,* and *One Dimensional Man* contains critiques of social science that remains under its spell. Marcuse's social philosophy is not based on acceptance of economic principles; play is not, as Baudrillard asserts, seen by Marcuse merely as the 'fulfilment of human rationality' (Baudrillard 1975: 40), but as something connected to the transcendence of this rationality, and the development of a alternative one. Contrary to what Baudrillard asserts, escaping the dialectic of freedom and necessity, both empirically and discursively, is exactly what Marcuse aims at. Of course his writing must retain certain economic categories, in order to prevent it degenerating into some kind of avant-garde poetry, and it is true

---

9   Confusingly, Baudrillard himself writes that an emphasis on the semiotics of consumption 'does not mean that our society is not firstly, objectively and decisively a society of production, an order of production, and therefore the site of an economic and political strategy. But it means that there is entangled with that an order of consumption, which is an order of the manipulation of signs' (Baudrillard, cited in Edwards 2000: 176). As Edwards notes, Baudrillard's style is wilfully ambiguous. Baudrillard's point as stated above is open to interpretation (Edwards 2000: 176), and he did later abandon this viewpoint in favour of a notion of seduction. The treatment offered here then, in fitting post-modern style, can only claim to be one interpretation of Baudrillard's writing.

that Marcuse also continues to take the economic substructure into account, since unlike Baudrillard, he prefers to base his analysis on a social *reality* where (for now), the economic holds sway over people's lives.

Since Marcuse considered that classic Marxist economic category, the traditional working class, as having been integrated quite thoroughly into the capitalist system, he suggested that outsider groups might be more likely handmaidens of revolutionary change. Tellingly, Baudrillard's new revolutionary groups are almost identical to those proposed by Marcuse; 'students, youth who are disqualified in advance, voluntarily or not, as well as all types of social groups, of regional communities, ethnic or linguistic…' (Baudrillard 1975: 134). But just what are these groups disqualified from, if not from participation in the economy as producers? Baudrillard even suggests that these groups end up fighting for their place 'in the circuit of work and of productivity' (Baudrillard 1975: 132), but extricates himself from the charge of productivism by suggesting that labour is now nothing more than 'playing the game', a 'ritual engagement of the worker in the circulation of values of the society' (Dant 2003: 57). The fact that much of what passes for labour in contemporary societies is non productive or service work adds some credence to this line of argument, but we must then consider the question of whether service workers are any less exploited, less subject to the logic of capitalism, than those in primary or secondary industries. Their work may appear as a game, but when one is forced to play, this is hardly the case.

The problem with theories like those expounded by Baudrillard in *The Mirror of Production*, is that they appear to sacrifice the traditional sociological strategy of basing analysis on social reality, to the tactic of creating a sense that they are unprecedentedly radical. Once again though, Baudrillard is off the hook, effectively arguing that even though he describes a society that may not exist, his social theory is still valid.

> The objection that our society is still largely dominated by the logic of commodities is irrelevant. When Marx set out to analyze capital, capitalist industrial production was still largely a minority phenomenon…The theoretical decision is never made at the quantitative level, but at the level of a structural critique (Baudrillard 1975: 121).

New Times and cultural studies: Consumption as resistance

Baudrillard remained fairly pessimistic about society's chances of escaping from the domination of the code, and consumer culture was viewed as an integral part of this domination; certainly it offered little opportunity for resistance to it. For Baudrillard, possible methods of resistance included subverting the system of exchange through spontaneous gift giving; others appeared to parallel Marcuse's notion of a great refusal, conceived of as a total refusal to play by the rules of the code. With the development of what came to be known as cultural studies in the 1980s and 90s, a new understanding of the relationship between consumption and resistance began to emerge. Writers within this sub-discipline of sociology retained a focus on the detail of everyday life, and appeared to heed Baudrillard's call for social thought to privilege the cultural sphere.

We have suggested that the Critical Theorists, and to some extent, even the early Baudrillard were writing in the context of the so called affluent society; post-war America and Western Europe. The production regime associated with this period is often referred to as Fordism. Fordism, it is suggested, was more than merely a regime of production; it also represented a system of social relations, and structured patterns of life outside work. While Fordism is a system of mass production, it can also be seen as a system of mass consumption of standardised products. During the 1970s and 80s, writers from what came to be known as the regulation school such as Lipietz, Piore and Sabel, argued that Fordism had begun to be superseded as a system of production and social relations. This had happened, in broad terms, for two reasons (see Edgell 2006: 81). Firstly, the dehumanising conditions of Fordist production had produced alienated workers prone to the revolt against work discussed in Chapter 6. Secondly, consumers increasingly demanded a multiplicity of pseudo-individualised products, for which short production runs, rapid retooling, and increased research and development are required. Capital responded, again in broad terms, by intensifying attempts to increase productivity through the more extensive and intensive use of fixed capital – thus eliminating as many troublesome workers as possible – and restructuring corporations to make them less monolithic, more flexible, and more responsive to market demand. This usually involved an increase in sub-contracting, and decreases in unit size, as exemplified by the industrial districts of the Third Italy (Kumar 1997: 37), where small, interconnected workshops were able to achieve a high level of 'flexible specialisation' and deliver skilfully produced items to an increasingly choosy and 'individualist' consumer. One result of the corporate restructuring associated with post-Fordism was a rise in unemployment, sanctioned, in Britain at least, by a neoliberal state.

Such was the academic, and arguably the social context in which a group of writers, most of them academics in the field of sociology, cultural studies, or social policy, and associated with the radical journal *Marxism Today*, published a special edition of the journal in October 1988. This special edition was later reprinted in book form in 1989 and 1990. The so called New Times writers were explicit in their acknowledgement of the post-Fordist paradigm. In a society where the giant factories of mass production had all but disappeared, and where the mass worker who had toiled within had been replaced by an individualised consumer, critical analyses of contemporary society and culture clearly had to change. The New Times group were also writing in a period where work and workers were under attack politically, a period of high unemployment, and an apparently unprecedented phenomenon; members of the working class buying into and celebrating the capitalist ethos of conspicuous consumption (in the conventional sense). In terms of those still in work, there are certain parallels between the

New Times characterisation, and that associated with both post-Fordism and some theories of the information society; there will be a growth in the number of individuals working in the service sector, often in highly skilled professions (Hall et al 1990: 33). Unlike some prophets of the information society, The New Times writers do also recognise that there will be a concomitant growth in the low skilled, low paid service sector as well (Hall et al 1990: 33). The service industries are dominated more by aesthetic concerns, and issues such as the aesthetics of the body, adornment, and style have, coincidentally, come to be more important for the individual. The possibility that the need of capital to continually seek out new areas to commodify, and the burgeoning interest in bodies and adornment might somehow be linked is not extensively explored.

Postmodernism is a second key influence on the New Times writers. Baudrillard and Foucault seem particularly influential. The former's influence can be seen in Hebdige's essay 'After the Masses', where he outlines Baudrillard's critique of the Marxist theory of value (Hebdige 1990: 82), and suggests that we might learn to be suspicious of 'rational solutions' (Hebdige 1990: 90) or the 'economy of truth' (Hebdige 1990: 83). This is to be an era of play and potlatch, not objectivity and universality. Hall (Hall 1990: 130) suggests that the Left (which seems to mean primarily the academic left) should no longer peripheralise the politics of the subject, the politics 'of health, of food, of sexuality and the body'. When Hall talks of 'a network of strategies and powers and their articulations' (Hall 1990: 130), the influence of Foucault is clear.

Cultural studies in New Times: A critique of consumption as resistance

Strangely, since Marcuse and the other Frankfurt School writers were instrumental in highlighting the importance of the super-structural level to social theory, they began to be criticised for depicting the consumer as dupe, for overstating both the power of the culture industries to mystify the population, and the susceptibility of the population to this mystification. Mica Nava,[10] in an article from 1991 which deals with the issue of consumption as resistance fairly explicitly, singles out Marcuse for his 'lack of respect for the mentality of ordinary people, exemplified by the view that they are easily duped by advertisers and politically pacified by the buying of useless objects' (Nava 1991: 162). Nava then surveys how cultural studies should, as it moves away from the oppressive primacy of the economic, 'seek to examine what is rewarding, rational and indeed sometimes liberating about popular culture' (Nava 1991: 164). There are, for instance, 'progressive

---

10   While Nava (like Fiske) was not technically part of the New Times group, her article was written during the same period, and reflects a similar reading of the zeitgeist. The article references various of the New Times writers (Nava 1991: 158) and comes to some similar conclusions. Nava acknowledges the 'major' role of Hall in 'setting the critical agenda' (Nava 1991: 164).

elements' in TV soaps and romantic fiction, which offer 'ambiguous pleasures'. Advertisements, far from being some kind of sinister mass hypnosis, are but another element for the consumer, as *bricoleur*, to use for the construction of their individual identity, often in opposition to the messages intended by their producers. Fiske, for example, illustrates this with an anecdote about a group of young people jeering the slogan from an underwear advert at a female student in a short skirt. These kids, according to Fiske, 'were using the ad for their own cheeky resistive subcultural purposes: they were far from the helpless victims of any subliminal consumerism, but were able to turn even an advertising text into their popular culture' (Fiske 1989: 31).

It is not only in the context of the media that consumption offers possibilities for resistance, elsewhere we learn that humorous bumper stickers (Slater 2004 [on Fiske]: 168–169) or torn jeans (Fiske 2000: 284) are other possible 'tactics of resistance'. Nava refers to one writer in whose analysis stockings 'operate as a form of protest and confrontation in a dreary and routinized existence...' (Nava 1991: 165). An extended quote from Frank Mort, one of the New Times group, reveals a perception of the consumer as active and quite possibly resistive, not just at the level of underwear and adverts, but even in the spheres of shopping and make-up;

> what people *do* when they go shopping may be quite different from the official script. Commodities and their images are multi-accented, they can be pushed and pulled into the service of resistant demands and dreams. High-tech in the hands of young blacks or girls making-up are not simply forms of buying into the system. They can be very effectively hijacked for cultures of resistance, reappearing as street-style cred or assertive femininity (Mort 1990: 166).

Analyses such as the ones sketched here are influenced by the work of Michel de Certeau (Edwards 2000: 94 101), who in turn was influenced by the better known French theorist of everyday life, Henri Lefebvre.[11] De Certeau extends the concept of factory workers (de Certeau 1988: 25) 'doing a foreigner'[12] – that is, using the factory or workshop's tools to make things for themselves – into social life and consumption in general. The African immigrant living in a Paris tower block, for instance, uses similar subversive tactics to 'insinuate into the system' elements of his own culture (de Certeau 1988: 30). This is the 'art of being in between' according to de Certeau. There are problems, however, with this analysis.[13]

---

11   For a useful treatment of Lefebvre in the current context, see Dant 2003: 72–75.

12   de Certeau uses the term *la perruque*, which literally translates as 'the wig'. Participant observation by the present author confirms that the equivalent term for English workers is 'doing a foreigner'.

13   For an interesting, if necessarily brief discussion of the resistive potential of the popular media, see Bird 2005.

It is not certain that the 'art of making do' can be considered resistive, even in the more specific context of the workplace. Anyone who has ever worked in a factory or workshop will know that the objects sometimes constructed in time snatched from work are hardly symbols of resistance. Children's bikes are built with off-cuts of steel tubing, and guitars are made with spare plywood,[14] but it is not clear how such activity is resistive. Things are usually built in the worker's own time, sometimes over a long period. Management is often aware of these activities, and workers are sometimes given permission to use works tools for jobs that would otherwise be expensive, but all this is scant compensation for the low wages and poor working conditions that still pertain. The factory worker may be 'sly as a fox and twice as quick' (de Certeau 1988: 25), but he or she is still a factory worker, and the objects they make have a similar status to the Perspex aeroplanes crafted by inmates of Second World War P.O.W camps.

In the world outside work, the idea of making do in the interstices of society may appear to offer some solace for those concerned about the disadvantaged, but it cannot escape from the fact that modern capitalist societies remain unequal, hierarchical societies. As Edwards notes, some people have to do more 'making do' than others (Edwards 2000: 101).

Interestingly, de Certeau conceptualises consumption as poeisis, or a form of production (de Certeau 1988: xii). According to him, the consumer, faced with the systematised products of mass society – television, planned cityscapes, and the like, is able to 'make' or 'do' things with these products. By 'producing' a different meaning from the one intended, the consumer is making 'innumerable and infinitesimal transformations of and within the dominant cultural economy in order to adapt it to their own interests and their own rules' (de Certeau 1988: xiv). These arts of making and doing, supposedly hold out the possibility of composing a 'network of antidiscipline…' (de Certeau 1988: xv). Firstly, we might consider de Certeau's notion of consumption as production as an example of concept stretching. Surely, modification would be a better term? Secondly, de Certeau's analysis is fine as far as cultural anthropology goes, but he, like Fiske, fails to say exactly how the practices he describes are resistive of a particular discipline – presumably, the discipline of consumer capitalism in the context of an unequal society. Surely the truly resistive strategy, or even tactic, would be to attack consumer capitalism *tout court*, rather than relying on infinitesimal (and essentially futile) adjustments *within the dominant economy*. Domination, one might argue, is to be attacked as a whole, rather than endured from within. Sleight of hand, slang, low cunning, and dumb insolence are the resistances most commonly associated with the prison house or the schoolroom, and rarely do they lead to escape.

Elsewhere in the present chapter, the notion of consumption as *re*production is discussed, but it is interesting to note an alternative theory to de Certeau's

---

14   These observations are based on research conducted in 2001 by the author in a medium sized manufacturing installation in the north west of England, employing mostly skilled workers. The factory is now closed – a victim of deindustrialisation.

that also characterises consumption as production.[15] Although the following theoretical arrangement is almost as open to the charge of concept stretching as de Certeau's, it is still interesting. Could not the consumer be seen as taking on the role of producer whilst consuming advertising, which after all constitutes the bulk of imagery in the consumer society? The commercial TV, radio, internet or other media organisation effectively sells the audience's time to the advertiser, and therefore by watching their adverts, this audience is producing value, or 'working' for both the media outfit and the advertising agency. And as a worker in a capitalist system, the audience member is subject to the kind of money trick associated with wage labour, since she herself is paying for the adverts by way of the cost the manufacturer has added to the product to pay for them. This point holds however successful consumers are at tactically or playfully subverting the intended message.

It will have become clear by now that the present chapter is concerned not just with work as a sociological category, but with its position in the categories of critical sociology in particular. Although Offe can not really be characterised as radical, the New Times writers at least had radical intent, and sought a critical viewpoint on contemporary capitalist society. It seems reasonable to judge theories that propose a shift from production to consumption as the critical fulcrum, in terms of their critical or emancipatory potential. Their intention is to move to a new level of radicalism by treating the masses with the respect they deserve, and not patronising them with analysis steeped in cultural snobbery. Consumption-as-resistance writers reject the division of needs into true and false; the basis of neo-Marxist critiques by writers like Marcuse and Gorz. Consumption certainly appears to be a real need for the consumers themselves, just as it appears rational and affords them feelings of happiness. Marcuse's defence against such criticisms is disarmingly straightforward – he admits that judgments on needs *are* effectively quasi personal value judgments on the part of the commentator, but that 'twas ever thus, from Plato to Hegel:

> To be sure, this is still the dictum of the philosopher... He subjects experience to his critical judgment, and this contains a value judgment – namely, that freedom from toil is preferable to toil, and an intelligent life is preferable to a stupid life. It so happened that philosophy was born with these values (Marcuse 1986: 126).

The notion that freedom from toil is preferable to toil is particularly pertinent, since it points to a crucial lacunae in the analyses of Nava, Fiske et al. These analyses fail to take into account the continued importance of work and production in postindustrial society, let alone successfully challenge the observation that rising levels of consumption appear to necessitate the intensification, rather than the elimination, of work.

---

15   For a further discussion see Smythe 1977: 1–29.

The charge that simplistic analyses of consumption as resistance ignore consumption's interconnection with more structural social relations (class or income, for example), is based largely on the fact that consumption is premised, and dependent on production. Leisure options and consumer identity are dependent to a large degree on income and position within the occupational hierarchy. Put simply, If you don't have the money, or the cultural capital (that comes with class and money), your consumption choices are limited (McGuigan 2000: 298). McRobbie has also pointed out how theories of consumer pleasure often, or predominantly, fail to take into account the fact that 'most, if not all, consumerism takes place not so much in the sphere of pure leisure as in the sphere of necessary production' (McRobbie 1994: 32). This point has been mentioned briefly before, but is worth reiterating. As McRobbie notes, reproduction is a useful concept for understanding the way in which consumerism mediates between leisure and work, endowing the former with pleasurable qualities (McRobbie 1994: 32). This analysis has much in common with those of the Critical Theorists, partly because it recognises that consumption may have an ideological role in maintaining a system in which production is acknowledged as at least equally central, and secondly because it recognises that one must look beyond, or behind, the superficial, and understand the hidden connections between the ideological and the material, between production and consumption, between pleasure and control. Thus swimming, as both expression and maintenance of the body beautiful, is not only a pleasurable leisure activity, but may also intersect with the needs of the state for healthy and productive workers (McRobbie 1994: 33).

Arguably then, analyses that privilege consumption as resistance fail to link consumption not only with the prosaic but persistent phenomenon of work, but with the reproduction of a more general, yet less obvious structural level of domination. Nava, for example, professes laudable aims such as better working conditions, rights for immigrant labour, union recognition, environmental improvements, women's rights, and so on (Nava 1991: 168–171). It is true that consumer action, or pressure, can achieve certain goals; in the sphere of the environment, for example. It has not generally been the case, however, that issues around working conditions and union recognition have been contested in the sphere of consumption. Rather, these issues continue to be settled in the sphere of work itself, through striking or working to rule, for example. Clearly issues around work are still important for the thousands of workers who have been involved in labour disputes in Britain in recent years.

Liberatory aims also appear in analyses that see the consumer as a politically pacified dupe, but at least here the fact that such aims remain unfulfilled can be explained. If the population of countries such as Britain or the United States is not pacified by consumerism, why do they tolerate the persistence of mass poverty in the midst of affluence, environmental degradation, low pay, political corruption, racial conflict, and an apparently permanent and costly state of low level warfare? Further, consumerism is linked to the *perpetuation* of such negative phenomena, which are embedded in the global structure of neoliberal capitalism. If we accept that consumption (of oil, bauxite, copper, coltan, cotton, rubber) is the very fuel on which this system depends, it is hard to see how this consumption, much as it may appear momentarily liberating at the checkout or in the nightclub, can take place without running counter to the interests of liberation for all peoples of the globe.

Conclusion: Consumer society and one dimensional thought

The examples of the consumption as resistance approach discussed here are perhaps rather easy targets, as is sometimes the case for ephemeral viewpoints with radical pretensions. Much the same could be said of the present treatment of Baudrillard. If anything, this discussion serves the purpose of illustrating, in terms of contemporary social theory, exactly what is meant by one dimensional thinking.

One of the supposed contributions of cultural studies has been its recognition of the importance of identity. We must always ask, however, whether the idea of identity as constituted through consumption is adequate for the purposes of critical social thought. Contrary to what some might think, there is no commitment to the opposing view – of work as the source of identity in the writings of Marx, or indeed Marcuse, and hence no need to develop critiques of this stance. In industrial society, people may have been categorised by, or identified themselves with, their position in the division of labour which we might more explicitly call class, but this is precisely what Marx criticised, contrasting it with a society in which people's real identity could be expressed, free from the domination of the economic structure. Likewise in postindustrial society, Marcuse was equally critical of consumption as the basis of identity, even though he accepted that for many people, it is through consumption that a simulacrum of identity is created. Baudrillard attacked the notion that there was any true humanity or human essence, although his prescriptions for resisting the code somewhat undermine this argument. At least he understood the position of critical theorists such as Marx and Marcuse, which is that there *is* something more than that which *appears* as real, that there *is* a more authentic dimension to human identity.

Marcuse appears to pre-empt consumerism-as-liberation theories in an answer to an interview question in 1969, and poses superficially similar hypotheses to them. His comment is worth reviewing at length:

> The political economy of advanced capitalism is also a "psychological economy": it produces and administers the needs demanded by the system – even the instinctive needs. It is this introjection of domination combined with the increasing satisfaction of needs that casts doubt on concepts like alienation, reification, and exploitation (Marcuse 1969c: 371).

Marcuse is here accepting that on one level, the consumer is not to be seen as an alienated, exploited dupe, since, at the subjective (even the instinctive) level, the individual appears satisfied. Is this satisfaction not genuine? 'Is the beneficiary of the "affluent society" not in fact "fulfilling" himself in his alienated being? Does he not, in fact, find himself again in his gadgets, his car and his television set?' (Marcuse 1969c: 371). But, asks Marcuse, 'does false subjectivity dispose of the objective state of affairs?' (Marcuse 1969c: 371). In other words, does the fact that it is the oligopolistic system of advanced capitalism which has persuaded the individual to satisfy, define and express themselves through consumption mean that this satisfaction and identity are anything other than authentic? The fact that Marcuse refers to 'false subjectivity' rather suggests an answer in the positive. Of course, this is on one level a circular argument, since we are back to the issue of whether consumers are 'administered' or duped in the first place. Even theorists of New Times would probably have accepted that consumerism in advanced capitalism is coordinated by sophisticated marketing techniques – it seems unlikely that advertising has no effect at all, since billions of dollars are spent on it daily. The issue then becomes the extent to which this administration and coordination are resisted, and while Critical Theorists are able to show how consumption is linked to the perpetuation of capitalist production, with its associated social and existential injustices, theories of resistance through consumption appear at best, as suggesting ways of making the best of a bad lot, and at worst as suggesting that if you can't beat them join them. While Critical Theory, like Marx, posits a radical alternative, the alternative viewpoint discussed here works within the confines of what it views as reality.

Identifying *what seems to be* (consumer pleasure, resistance through shopping) as what actually *is*, is not only not radical, it is not sociological, since it fails to see that the reality of consumerism is also part of a global *system* of capitalist production and domination, replete with global and national inequalities, oppression and war. Of course, the language of systems, like the language of structures, has little place in such discourse.

Writers like Marcuse and Gorz, as critical theorists, seek an escape from the rule of the economic, but at the same time they show an understanding that in order to move towards this, theorists can't pretend that the world of economic structures and imperatives somehow doesn't exist. Effective critical theory has the advantage of acknowledging the importance of both production and consumption, but refusing to accept that either humanity, or social thought, should remain trapped within the confines of either. Marcuse's Frankfurt School colleague Theodore Adorno placed so much importance on the idea that sociologists should recognise the interconnectedness of the realms of consumption and production that he criticised not only consumer society itself, but one of its most important and original critical observers, Thorstein Veblen. Veblen is criticised not only for his commitment to the work instinct, but for his alleged failure to see that industrial capital and the conspicuous consumption associated with pecuniary capital are part of the same system (Kellner 1989a: 149).

Hall, in the New Times volume, criticises the Left for traditionally tending to look for impersonal structures, for processes happening 'behind the backs' of individuals (Hall 1990: 120). At this point, it could be pointed out that much of the New Times thesis, and indeed Offe's as well, is predicated on a narrative of what is surely structural economic change. What is post-Fordism, for example, if not a change in the structural relations of production? Of course, as was noted earlier, post-Fordism can be seen to have been encouraged partly by consumer demand for more varied and individualised products, but this thesis can be criticised on the basis that the consumer has always had access to a veritable cornucopia of trinkets and amusements; that the extent to which the consumer is today offered anything more than pseudo individualised products is highly questionable, and that the move to consumer differentiation was engineered by the producers themselves.

In 1944, Leo Lowenthal published a content analysis of the biographies printed in American popular magazines. Originally entitled 'Biographies in Popular Magazines', but retitled with the somewhat more intriguing 'Triumph of the Mass Idols' when published as a book chapter (in Lowenthal 1961), this study records, between 1901 and 1941 a 'considerable decrease of people from the serious and important professions and a corresponding increase of entertainers' (Lowenthal 1961: 111). By serious and important professions, Lowenthal means those connected with production and politics; engineers, industrialists, politicians, and to a lesser extent, 'serious' artists. In the period when the 'idols of production' predominated, American society, according to Lowenthal, actually wanted to know something about the key figures in the most decisive sectors. By 1941, the American public was being presented, in place of substantive biographical information, with a diet of celebrity tittle tattle, involving models, gamblers, and restaurateurs. Lowenthal states: 'We called the heroes of the past "idols of production": we feel entitled to call the present day magazine heroes "idols of consumption"' (Lowenthal 1961: 115). Rather than seeking to understand the narratives of social production, the biographies now seem to ignore this realm, or assume that it is 'tacitly understood' (Lowenthal 1961: 115). Pre-empting the sociological turn to consumption by about forty years, Lowenthal observes that it now leisure time that is to be extensively studied, by celebrity magazines, at least.

The world where 'Idols of Consumption' dominate the consciousness of the population, is a world of acceptance, not a world of action, let alone resistance.

> These new heroes represent a craving for having and taking things for granted. They seem to stand for a phantasmagoria of world-wide social security; for an attitude which asks no more than to be served with the things needed for reproduction and recreation; for an attitude which has lost any primary interest in how to invent, shape, or apply the tools leading to such purposes of mass satisfaction (Lowenthal 1961: 123).

Such is the attitude that allows work to drift out of analyses of capitalist society. In the analysis of Lowenthal, and indeed other Critical Theorists such as Adorno and Marcuse, consumption is an almost sensible means of escape, rather than resistance, since the 'gap between what an average individual may do and the forces and powers that determine his life has become so unbridgeable' (Lowenthal 1961: 135) that one may as well concentrate on the things one can choose (and which pose no threat to the status quo, and are easily co-opted if they do); fashion, music, style. It is not indicative of snobbery to propose that while this strategy may seem rational for those who capitalism robs of ontological and intellectual possibilities, it should not do for those who profess to be analysts of society. As Lowenthal asserts, the job of the social scientist is to clarify the 'hidden processes and inter-connections of social phenomena' (Lowenthal 1961: 134). Reality may be hidden, but sociologists cannot, or should not, choose to ignore it.

Chapter 9
Travail sans frontières:
Globalisation and the End of Work

Introduction

Globalisation as a sociological theme develops alongside postmodernism, in temporal terms at least, although as a concept, it has never succeeded in becoming fashionable within mainstream sociology in quite the same way postmodernism did. This is perhaps because the concept of globalisation remains hard to place in disciplinary terms; does it really belong first and foremost in geography or economics rather than sociology? Or perhaps it is because the concept of globalisation, almost by definition, retains a commitment to the big idea, the longue durée, to discussion at the most structural of levels; global society itself. In this sense, discourses of globalisation are rather like those of the end of work.

We have seen how the end of work, as a discourse, consists of a framework of shared socio-philosophical positions, with a commitment to taking account of the realities of social change. We have sought to characterise the end of work as an idea that can be used as a strand of critical social theory capable of absorbing and even utilising the contradictions of post Cold War consumer capitalism. Although it is certainly not the case that all commentators on globalisation use the concept for this same purpose, capitalism is usually seen as the dynamic 'underlying' globalisation. Like capitalism and the end of work, capitalism and globalisation seem to be locked in something of a dialectical embrace. Within this dialectical relationship, if such a construction may be permitted, work retains a central position. Work, after all, is the foundation on which capitalism rests – the fate of work, globalisation, and capitalism are intimately connected. We shall see that this is acknowledged both by academic commentators and researchers writing on behalf of capital itself.

Globalisation in perspective

It is with Marx, as the social theorist of capitalist development whose analysis continues strongly to colour the debate over globalisation (and as we know, the end of work) that we begin. Writing in 1848, Marx observed that the 'need of a constantly expanding market for its products chases the bourgeoisie over the entire surface of the globe. It must nestle everywhere, settle everywhere, establish connections everywhere' (Marx 1959b: 324). Clearly, Marx is describing a process, one integral to the nature of modern capitalism that today is known as globalisation. Anyone with an elementary knowledge of world history will know that the concept of transnational trade flows is nothing new, but what Marx describes, and what we now know as globalisation, differs from the empires of earlier epochs in that it is driven not by the expansionist desires of a particular ethnic, national or religious group, or by a desire for plunder in the traditional sense, but by the technical imperatives of a specific system of production. We will see later how globalisation in the twenty first century is seen as having a dire effect on industrial workers in the West. In Marx's time, however, the opposite was the case, and industrialisation in the West was seen as exporting jobs from the East: '…the English cotton machinery produced an acute effect in India. The Governor General reported 1834–35: "The misery hardly finds a parallel in the history of commerce. The bones of the cotton-weavers are bleaching the plains of India"' (Marx 1959c: 13).

By Marx's time, the concept of empire had begun to be adapted to serve the technical imperatives of industrial capitalism. As Marx observed, a constantly expanding market, not to mention a constantly expanding workforce, is for capital a need, rather than a desire. Thus the twentieth century saw not only mass intercontinental (continued) migration to America, and northern Europe from those areas of the world where capitalism remained underdeveloped, amounting to a *global* movement of labour, but also numerous Cold, and not so Cold war battles for political, ideological and market economic control of post colonial nations in Africa and IndoChina.

Defining globalisation

We might note that we have not yet paused to define globalisation. In terms of the traditional scholarly aim of clearly defining one's terms, this is to some extent a vain hope. As noted by the World Bank, '*there does not appear to be any precise, widely agreed definition*. Indeed the breadth of meanings attached to it seems to be increasing rather than narrowing over time'. The World Bank's definition of economic globalisation is certainly not overcomplicated; '*the observation that in recent years a quickly rising share of economic activity in the world seems to be taking place between people who live in different countries*' (World Bank a: 1 [their emphasis]). Contrary to what the World Bank's researchers might claim, there is in fact a widely agreed way to define globalisation; capitalism.

The International Monetary Fund (IMF) defines globalisation as 'The increasing integration of economies around the world, particularly through trade and financial flows. The term sometimes also refers to the movement of people (labour) and knowledge (technology) across international borders'. Even more explicitly: 'It refers to an extension beyond national borders of the same market forces that have operated for centuries at all levels of human activity village markets, urban industries, or financial centers' (IMF 2008: 2). Globalisation then, is the expansion of capitalism, the spread of capitalist imperatives across the globe. This is the creation by capitalism of 'a world after its own image' (Marx 1959b: 325). It seems on this point at least, however, the IMF and the World Bank differ, with the latter body critical of the conflation of terms. For the World Bank, capitalism and globalisation are distinct, if related phenomena (World Bank a).

For Immanuel Wallerstein, any distinction between globalisation and capitalism seems structurally, not to mention historically naïve: 'we are in a capitalist system only when the system gives priority to the endless accumulation of capital. Using such a definition, only the modern world system has been a capitalist system' (Wallerstein 2004: 24). Imperial formations of the past rose and fell for a myriad of reasons on which there is a vast historical literature; the only world system that has proved sustainable is the capitalist world system. For Wallerstein, a central feature of the capitalist world system is its ability to utilise inequalities between countries to construct a global division of labour.

It is important not to ignore the role played by technology in globalisation. Although we would open ourselves up to charges of determinism if we were to assert a causal role for technology, globalisation could not succeed without developments in communications, both in the sense of advanced telegraphy and later virtuality, and in the sense of the transportation of goods and populations around the world. While technology should be seen as an essential facilitating factor, it seems clear that the impetus for globalisation, like the development of technology itself, we could argue, comes primarily from the need of the expanding capitalist system to maximise profit.

Capital, labour, globalisation

For the purposes of relating globalisation to the end of work, global movements of labour and production are clearly highly relevant. In Chapter 6 we briefly discussed the possibility that the economic recession of the 1970s was a reaction to the strengthening hand of labour. Similarly, globalisation can be seen as a reaction by capital to the social conflicts of the late 60s and early 70s, as well as the pressures put on profitability by the rising wage demands of the 'affluent workers' of the late 20th century. It can be argued that these social pressures on capital, combined with international political conflicts around natural resources, prompted a reconsideration of the global structure of capitalism.

Frederick Gluck, erstwhile Director of McKinsey and Company, wrote in 1982 that 'Following a decade of economic turmoil, the climate for international business in the 1980s should be more favourable due to changes in the oil, currency, and labor markets' (Gluck 1982: 22). In an unintentional echo of the British Conservative Party's election campaign slogan of 1996/7, Gluck suggests that the 'dislocations' of the 1970s (industrial conflict signalling the effective defeat of organised labour, the return of mass unemployment, social and infrastructural decay in many areas of the advanced economies civil war and the rise of extremism in the periphery, resource wars) had served as a period of transition to a new era of a deregulated global free market. Yes it hurt, but, from capital's perspective at least, yes it worked: 'Before, there had been an elaborate international network of regulations and cartels. Now, there are global free markets for energy, currency, labour, and other vital business skills' (Gluck 1982: 22).

Focusing, as we should, on labour, the advantage for capital is clear; 'access to a lowwage labour pool is open to anyone'. Gluck was writing before global capitalism found it necessary to adopt a public relations strategy to explain the humanitarian benefits of companies locating their routine production installations in poorer countries with weaker labour laws and more impoverished workers. Thus he was able to be admirably uncomplicated with his example of 'Hewlett Packard's manufacturing chain which reaches halfway around the globe, from well paid, skilled engineers in California to low wage assembly workers in Malaysia' (Gluck 1982: 8).

There are two essential dimensions to this process in terms of the end of work, the first relating to workers in the economies from which routine production and remotely based service work (telephony and so on) are exported, the second relating to the countries belatedly, but inexorably drawn into the capitalist orbit.

The white heat of neoliberalism; globalisation and the West

When reading analyses of the effects of globalisation on employment, one is reminded of Marx's portrayal of a capitalism which has '*drawn from under the feet of industry the national ground on which it stood. All old-established national industries have been destroyed or are daily being destroyed*' (Marx 1959b: 325). In simplistic terms, globalisation has exported jobs, that is, work, from the richer, more capitalistically advanced societies (Europe, North America, Australia, Japan) to poorer, less capitalistically advanced societies. Jobs are exported to poor countries because workers there will work for lower wages, thus increasing profits. The export of jobs will lead to unemployment in the exporting countries. Commentators are divided, however, on the accuracy of this analysis. In fact, it seems almost impossible to find scholarly observers who see globalisation as leading to unemployment in the advanced economies in absolute terms. The furthest anyone seems prepared to go is to acknowledge that the export of jobs is likely to lead to unemployment amongst certain sectors of the population. Usually, the workers seen as affected are those working in manufacturing, particularly manufacturing that requires large amounts of unskilled labour.

In a research paper entitled 'Does Globalization Lower Wages and Export Jobs', Slaughter and Swagel couch their analysis in terms of globalisation producing 'winners and losers' (1997: 12). The losers in this case are low skilled workers in deindustrialising nations such as Britain and the USA. After appearing to argue that in fact, technological advance is a more likely cause of unemployment than globalisation, the authors do acknowledge that there will be groups of workers who are 'displaced by import competition'. Their advice to policymakers is to 'keep in mind potential dislocations and ensure that those who are displaced do not become marginalized' (Slaughter and Swagel 1997: 12). Similarly, the World Bank asserts that unemployment caused by trade liberalisation is 'in most cases, temporary', but recognises that 'adjustment costs' – that is, jobless workers – can be a serious issue because these costs are often concentrated in a particular industrial sector, or in a geographical area (World Bank b: 8).

The argument that globalisation does not lead to unemployment, but that jobs are being eliminated by technology in any case is, in fact, plausible.[1] Indeed, one of the key arguments we have examined in the course of this book is the notion that technology eliminates labour. However, it is clearly the case that when large manufacturing installations or industrial sectors are effectively closed down and shipped overseas, jobs will be lost in the 'exporting' countries. Jobs in the mature industrialised countries may be created by global trade, as well as being destroyed. For example, machine tools requiring high technology precision manufacture are a key export from developed countries to those undergoing the process of industrialisation – China, for example. Andrew Glyn notes, however, that 'for every job in high skill manufactures created by additional exports to the South there are as many as six jobs displaced by the same money value of low-tech manufactured imports from the South' (Glyn 2006: 110). Combined with the advance towards the 'informatization' of the economy (Hardt and Negri 2000: 286), the export of low skilled manufacturing jobs to less industrially advanced economies does indeed signal the end of work in the West, for the unskilled industrial worker at least. An exaggeration perhaps, but the while the demise of the low skilled manufacturing worker has been predicted for decades, we are surely now witnessing its final stages.

Exporting jobs, individualising risk

Commentators such as Slaughter and Swagel acknowledge that there will be 'losers' in the game of globalisation, but that long term gains make these impacts worthwhile. The loss of jobs for individuals and communities, is merely a 'short term adjustment' cost (1997: 12). An adjustment cost for the economy as a whole, perhaps, but at best a severe setback, and at worst, a tragedy for the individuals and communities rendered more or less suddenly obsolete and workless. How are such human costs to be mitigated? The World Bank calls for a 'carefully designed social-safety net and educational or retraining programs to help the most vulnerable affected groups' (World Bank b: 4). Very carefully designed, apparently, since in the same document series, it is claimed that 'Safety nets based on cushioning

---

1   It also seems to be the case that in times of global economic crisis, unemployment (temporary, it is assumed) can rise in postindustrial, high wage economies, and industrialising, low wage economies simultaneously.

workers during temporary periods and a return to the same job are becoming increasingly outdated' (World Bank c: 11).

Globalisation has coincided with, or more accurately, is intrinsically linked with, not only the deregulation of international capital markets, but labour itself. There is an internal consistency to this state of affairs; companies are liberated from the shackles of regulation and become footloose, whilst the same principles of deregulation are applied to the domestic welfare system. The World Bank advises policymakers to look to 'portable' pensions and healthcare (World Bank c: 11) as part of a strategy to minimise the impacts of globalisation on the vulnerable. 'Portable' means the responsibility of the individual. Thus, the supposed long term economic gains can be shared out amongst society's winners – capital, and an elite of highly skilled workers, supposedly – whilst the losses can be borne by (who else?) the losers.

Ultimately, of course, society as a whole can be seen to gain, in economistic terms at least, from the export of low skilled manufacture/extraction jobs, once affected sectors of the population have taken advantage of 'educational opportunities' to 'upgrade their skills' (Slaughter and Swagel 1997: 21), having been 'empowered to adapt to constant economic change' (World Bank c: 10). However, it is not simply the case that *old-established national industries have been destroyed or are daily being destroyed* (Marx 1959b: 325) by globalisation; industries often support entire communities, and when they are exported, myriad human lives are thrown into turmoil. Capitalist society may gain (have cheaper consumer goods, be more competitive[2]) in the long run, but unemployment brings with it hopelessness and despair, frustration and illness, costs not only for individuals and communities but for society as a whole in terms of health and policing costs, not to mention the intrinsic effects of a more unequal and atomised society.

Communities that rely on a small number of industries may be particularly hard hit by globalisation. In 2007 *The Economist* visited Galax in Virginia, USA, a town that previously relied heavily on the textile and furniture industries. When these moved to China and Mexico, three 'big factories closed their doors within months. More than 1000 people, around one-sixth of the town's workforce, lost their jobs', prompting the author to observe that 'in the neat world of economics text-books the downside of globalisation looks much like Galax' (*The Economist* 2007b: 29).

In an explicit acknowledgment that globalisation leads to unemployment, federal funds are available for those displaced by global trade, and an 'Economic Crisis Strike Force' is on hand to lead unemployed textile workers through the bureaucracy involved in accessing them. Unemployed citizens in the world's richest society can also rely upon 'food banks run by private charities' (*The Economist* 2007b: 29), so for globalisation's losers starvation, at least, can be averted. Health care is often funded by the employer in the USA, but those

---

2   Competitive in the sense of having lower paid workers who are easy to dismiss and do not indirectly require a high tax burden.

displaced by global trade also have at their disposal 'temporary subsidies to help pay medical insurance'.

As part of this carefully designed social safety net, some of Galax's residents have been helped to retrain and have become radiologists or picture framers, but clearly, declining Appalachian mountain towns only need so many picture framers, and for some, a bleak future with no healthcare beckons. Fifty nine year old Paul Rotan, for example, is 'terrified' of what will happen when his temporarily subsidised health insurance runs out in 5 months time (*The Economist* 2007b: 29). In the USA, unemployment is traditionally low, although in times of global economic recession things may be rather different. During the 1980s and 90s, 35% of displaced manufacturing workers were able to find work after two years, but most took a pay cut, a quarter of them losing 30% of their previous salary. For our losers, not the end of work then, merely a hop down one or two rungs on the ladder of social dignity. In the UK, 'less than 60% of workers in the same situation had found a new job, but only 7% saw their pay fall more than 30%' (*The Economist* 2007b: 29).

Unfortunately, tragically perhaps, the situation in Galax is repeated across the advanced economies; in Detroit, in Glasgow, in Stoke-on-Trent. Despite the best efforts of crisis management teams or local redevelopment agencies, training programmes and adult education drop in centres, many former unskilled factory workers are not equipped with the social and cultural capital to become website designers or tanning salon entrepreneurs.

Deregulate and punish: work under neoliberal globalisation

It is the case that for perhaps millions of people in the West, globalisation has indeed meant the end of work. Unskilled work, however, persists:

> Some analysts of advanced societies believe that there will be good jobs for individuals with complex skills in fast-growing sectors like information technology or biotechnology; and bad jobs making fast food and the like for the least well-endowed by education, family, and the brute luck of genes (Berger 1999: 2).

Large numbers of low skilled workers are essential to both the (now numerically dominant) service sector, and to those units of production that can not be relocated abroad; food processing, for example, or in installations located close to target markets in order to dodge tariffs.

During the economic boom which, in Britain, America and much of Europe lasted from the late 1990s to 2008, companies relying on low paid labour found the indigenous population of countries like Britain and Ireland less than willing to toil in bad conditions for low pay, although vast numbers of British workers have continued to do so. In September 2007 *The Guardian* newspaper ran a two page spread highlighting the plight of Britain's 'underpaid, easy to sack...second class workforce' of immigrant labour, many of them from the newly integrated EU nations. This is a world of gangmasters, zero hour contracts, the minimum wage, and virtually no employment rights. Thanks to the globalisation of labour, companies located in nations where the indigenous working class has wrested more civilised levels of pay and conditions from capital can circumvent this obstacle by importing low wage workers from poorer countries. Far from leading to the end of work, globalisation can be seen here as a means by which work can be flexibilised and mobilised, the better to increase its intensity and productivity.

> In the conventional framework, labour market regulation of recruitment and dismissals has been considered as the most important hindrance at the enterprise level, and as having the largest adverse impact on enterprise performance and employment (Vivarelli: 2).

It is a matter of neoliberal orthodoxy that a deregulated and flexible labour market is the key to keeping unemployment low. In the strange logic of hypercapitalism, unemployment is to be minimised by making it easier to make people unemployed. In a boom, this allows companies to adapt quickly to fluctuations in demand. This makes companies more competitive and profitable, and, so the logic goes, creates a kind of virtuous circle where workers laid off from a company with a temporarily empty order book are quickly taken on by a firm which finds itself with a glut in production, or a company that has recently set up in a country, possibly attracted by its flexible labour laws.

Given the febrile tempo of globalised capitalism, enterprises want to be sure that in slack periods, workers can be dismissed without too much difficulty. Our hypothetical companies become, in financial terms, more successful, and eventually the firm that was originally laying off will be taking on once more. Again, the theory goes that only if businesses are assured of their ability to shed labour will they employ it in the first place. Economies such as the USA, Britain and the Netherlands are seen as dynamic and adaptable, and thus able to produce low rates of unemployment. Countries like France or Greece, having less deregulated labour markets, have been seen as sclerotic and uncompetitive, hence their higher rates of worklessness. In a globalised world, footloose companies are free to locate in whatever country is most attractive, and these are likely to be those with deregulated labour markets.

As Vivarelli notes, however, 'From an empirical point of view, the impact of deregulation in terms of employment performance is quite doubtful' (Vivarelli: 5). They point out that countries such as Spain and Italy which have experienced significant deregulation, in relative terms at least, continue to experience high rates of unemployment. It could be, they concede, that although Spain and Italy have deregulated in relative terms, they lag behind countries like New Zealand and Ireland in absolute terms.

When boom turns to bust, the flexibility that was seen to make countries such as Britain and Spain (which by 2009 had achieved a significant degree of deregulation) more competitive is exercised to the full. Hundreds of thousands, and ultimately millions of people are made unemployed. It is hard to see deregulation as really reducing unemployment in the context of a deregulated global system which continues in capitalism's traditional cyclical pattern. Taken over the long term, it may be that it makes little difference whether a country has a deregulated labour market or not. In good times, deregulated economies may enjoy lower unemployment rates, but in bad times, these skyrocket. More regulated economies, by contrast, maintain a relatively stable level of unemployment. Indeed, it may be the case that by making it easy to fire employees, deregulation leads to a permanent loss of industrial skills. Come the upturn, this may leave countries with a more stable employment market at an advantage.

Little did *The Guardian* know that the BMW agency workers in Oxford whose inferior pay and conditions the newspaper lamented in 2007 (*Guardian* 2007b: 20) would be summarily dismissed en masse in early 2009. Unemployment persisted during the boom. When recession starts to bite however, the spectre of mass unemployment not so much stalks the land as drives around it in a TVR, and as unemployment levels rise, public anxiety increases. In every recession, the bursting of the consumer bubble prompts a realignment of the collective consciousness away from work and consumption for their own sake and towards more humane, preferably ecologically sound priorities. As we noted in our discussion of Offe, however, this is not a unidimensional ontological movement, and it is also the case that in times of rising unemployment, fear and anxiety about losing one's job lend work a particular significance for those with a job to lose, and make finding work a priority for those victims of Wall Street's hangover.

As the world becomes increasingly globally interlinked, deregulation in the Anglo Saxon model increasingly becomes the touchstone for national economic strategy. This is particularly the case where regional trading blocs such as the European Union coalesce. In this case, nations with formerly highly regulated labour markets are encouraged, as part of the process of full integration, to move to a more deregulated model. In the global context, laissez faire economics holds that although the late industrial countries will never be able to compete with the likes of China or Mexico, they must do everything possible, within their specific social and cultural context, to emulate the 'light touch' approach to labour regulation evidenced in most of the industrialising nations – the better to compete with other mature democracies. Globalisation then, goes hand in hand with deregulation.

We have already discussed deregulation in relation to unemployment, but it is also the case that as global competition intensified during the 1980s and 1990s as previously closed economies entered the marketplace for capitalist production, work itself tended to become more flexible, more contingent, less regulated, and at the same time, the benefits system came under increased pressure. As Vivarelli, amongst many others has noted, higher unemployment benefits can cause unemployment to lose it role as a 'discipline device'. In the same piece,

Vivarelli lists temporary contracts and part time working as other key elements of deregulation. Temporary contracts might also have a disciplining function, since employees could see good behaviour as making the renewal of their contract more likely. Part time working means that typically, parents and students are able to continue to participate in the world of capitalist work, avoiding the possibility of them drifting off into the autonomous spheres of self (or perhaps family) directed time. On the other hand, both temporary and part time contracts can be seen as giving individuals, as well as companies, a measure of flexibility. It is perhaps a rather dubious supposition, however, that people would not prefer to have a measure of certainty as to their financial and social circumstances in at least the near future. Similarly, it is not clear that part time workers would not prefer to be paid the same, per quantum of work done, and have the same employment rights as full time workers; both of which tend not to be the case.

If globalisation means less traditional industrial work for the populations of the West, then the work that remains must be maximised in its intensity and its potential as a disciplinary ideology. This, at least, is the analysis of Hardt and Negri's *Empire* (2000: 256), and is echoed by writers such as Glyn (2006: 114) and Fraser (2003). We have already examined Hardt and Negri's analysis of the way capital, faced with cultural and social change, tends to become intensified and extended *within* the advanced societies. At the same time, the cultural formations that challenged capital in the 60s and 70s become co-opted by it. Production shifts from the industrial to the immaterial. The working class in the industrialised world, in this analysis, had succeeded, through solidarity and struggle, in achieving rising wages, better living standards and working conditions in the sphere of industrial production. At the same time, young people began to rebel against the still intrinsic horrors of work in industry. Whether or not improvements in global communications came about as a result of the former phenomenon is not clear, and rather doubtful, but certainly, just as labour appeared to be fighting capital to a standstill, it became feasible to stage a tactical withdrawal and begin to relocate production in countries or regions without a politically developed proletariat. As Pietro Basso would have it, expansion of production in the Third World is used to 'cudgel the "guarantees" of industrial workers back in the West, bludgeoning them into accepting the fact that the "good old days" are gone forever' (2003: 214).

The possibility of a return of manufacturing to the deindustrialising regions of the advanced economies is held open – once their previously militant working class has been politically crushed and socially impoverished. Such has been the pattern for motor vehicle manufacture in the UK since the 1980s for example.

The new cultural values of the post 1968 generation fitted in well with the economic structure that is left once low wage, low skill manufacturing could be exported. Market research, the media, computing, military technology, research and development functions for the global combines; all these could best be served by the increasingly well educated and apparently creatively minded post war generation.

For Fraser, as for Hardt and Negri, it seems that capital began to understand that the disciplinary regime of Fordism could not be maintained under these conditions. Indeed, the late 1960s and 1970s had proved, in countries such as America, Italy, France and Britain, that it was too prone to challenge. Part of the Fordist settlement had been the provision of welfare and workers' rights, in return for disciplined work. According to Fraser, drawing on Foucault's accounts of the disciplinary society, Fordist disciplinarity was anchored by a *national* state apparatus, and diffused through the capillaries of the education system, medicine, child psychology, and so on (Fraser 2003: 164). After the decline of the Fordist mode, and in the era of globalisation, however, 'the ordering of social relations is undergoing a major shift in scale, equivalent to *denationalization* and *transnationalization*' (Fraser 2003: 165).

We suggested earlier that global competition encourages the deregulation of work, and the concomitant downgrading or privatisation of welfare in an effort to minimise both wage costs and taxes, thus attracting investment. This process, according to Fraser, represents globalization generating a 'new landscape of social regulation' (Fraser 2003: 166). Pensions and healthcare become portable and privatised. Prisons, hospitals and schools are marketised, and with QUANGOs and 'community partnerships' taking over functions previously held by the state, social reproduction is increasingly subject to economic rationality. The welfare state existed as a kind of buffer or intermediary between the individual and the market. In Fraser's analysis, the market so invades the realms previously administered by the state – the most intimate and meaningful aspects of life, childbirth, childhood, access to water – that the individual faces the economic sphere directly; a client or stakeholder, rather than a patient or student.

Across the postindustrial world, as we have seen, societies are segmented into a productive, well educated, adaptable population, well suited to the brave new world of global capitalism, and a 'marginal sector of excluded low-achievers' (Fraser 2003: 169). This latter group consists, to a large extent, of the traditional workers rendered irrelevant by globalisation. By handing over welfare to private (often global) companies and making it the ultimate responsibility of the individual, the flotsam and jetsam of high industrialism can be cut loose, their role at the bottom of productive society taken instead by a plentiful supply of desperate immigrants; the immigrants' own countries having been rendered narcomaniacal bedlams by the laissez faire policies imposed on them by the IMF or the World Bank, or yet another war for the mineral resources needed to fuel global consumerism.

The traditional working class developed a culture replete with certain expectations of work – including the expectation that it provide enough money to live on, so the most exploitative forms of capitalist work must become the domain of a shadow population without cultural memory of such historical curiosities as 'the family wage' or the eight hour day. The global South can be relocated to the North. In the largest European and American cities, day labourers wait at dawn to be offered illegal work. In some cases, whole production facilities are staffed by vulnerable illegal immigrants.[3]

The new respectable classes live in an atmosphere of high anxiety, an anomic world of constant organizational restructuring, short term contracts, and uncertainty. By now even the well educated service sector worker with a portfolio of flexible skills knows that the vicissitudes of the global economy mean that they are never too far away from the next crash; from redundancy, foreclosure, indignity. Even at the height of the early twenty first century boom, there was no collapse in work discipline, no questioning of the ideology of work, no cultural shockwaves. Not that this was ultimately enough to save millions from the dole queue.

Conclusion: work in the global South

Although globalisation can be seen to be eliminating work in particular sectors in the developed West, we have seen that there is little evidence that unemployment overall is increased by globalisation itself (as opposed to technological advance), and capitalist societies continue to rely on work as an ideological and cultural legitimating factor. In global terms, work in the capitalist sense of work for a wage, expands. 'In 2005, the world's labor force ages 15 and older – comprising those in work and people seeking jobs – topped 3 billion, up almost 17 percent from 1995' (Schmidt 2006: 1). As in the analysis of Wallerstein, the pervasiveness of wage labour can be seen as the defining characteristic of capitalism (Wallerstein 2000: 58) the spread of capitalism is part of the same process as the global expansion of work; the two are, in fact, inseparable. Once again, we see echoes of Marx, who argued that capitalism:

> compels all nations, on pain of extinction, to adopt the bourgeois mode of production; it compels them to introduce what it calls civilization into their midst, i.e., to become bourgeois themselves. In one word, it creates a world after its own image (Marx 1959b: 325).

We saw in Chapter 2 how work in the West developed both as a cultural artefact and as social practice. It is possible to argue that the process of acculturation to industrial work is taking place in the developing world as we speak. Indeed, when factories relocate to underdeveloped countries, working conditions for the putative working class can be reminiscent of those in nineteenth century Britain, although

---

3   The case of TNS Knitwear being the most prominent recent example. In this case, a textile factory near the heart of Manchester, one of Britain's largest cities, was alleged after a BBC investigation to be employing hundreds of illegal workers, including asylum seekers from Afghanistan, working in squalid conditions, and being paid well below the national minimum wage (BBC 2009).

a new global language of zones, chains and subcontracting has replaced that of mills and Methodism.

Export Processing Zones (EPZs) have been a characteristic organisational form of the globalisation of production since they were introduced by the UN, IMF and World Bank, along with the governments of developing nations, in the 1960s and 70s (Hurley and Miller 2005: 36). Poor working conditions and repression of trade unions are key features of work in EPZs. In Namibia, for example, Malaysian textile concern Ramatex located in Windhoek municipality, attracted, one assumes, by a 99 year tax exemption and the absence of a minimum wage. This latter (alongside abject poverty, one supposes) made it possible to pay workers 12 UK pence per hour. The attraction for the Namibian government was the creation of jobs – that is the creation of work in the capitalist form. Far from work ending, work in the developing world seems to be undergoing a similar process of development as it did in the West, except that now, the international financial network means that the creation of jobs can seen in the context of an already existing capitalist structure. Increasing the amount of work taking place in the capitalist circuit means Third World nations are taking steps towards improving their economic status as defined by the governance arms of global capital – the IMF, World Bank, and so on. Success is defined as being able to plug into the framework of global capitalism, and only having a society dominated by capitalist work can facilitate this.

Worker resistance, just as it was in 19th century Britain, is far from absent, however, as evidenced by our Namibian example. When Filipino workers[4] down tools and petition their embassy to inspect their poor working conditions, one has to assume that working conditions are very poor indeed (Hurley and Miller 2005: 36).

The labour intensive textile industry came to characterise the industrial revolution in Britain, for schoolroom historians at least; British workers working with Indian raw materials. Today, areas such as the Indian subcontinent are a key link in the global supply chain for the garment industry. Production can take place in EPZs from Namibia to Sri Lanka. In the latter, the abuse of workers is reminiscent of the worst excesses of nineteenth century British industry – that is, widespread and gratuitous (see Hale 2005: 47 for example).

Global capitalism takes place in a context where even in the developing world; companies can be informed by changes in the modes of production thrown up by the development of capitalism in the advanced societies. As Fordism in the West gives way to a more 'flexible' system of subcontracting production, 'cottage industry' is alive and well in the developing world. Thirty miles north of Colombo, Sri Lanka, 'self employed' (meaning, amongst other things, ineligible for welfare benefits which might accrue to an employee) workers embroider beaded letters onto T Shirts at US$0.001 per T Shirt (Hurley 2005: 103).

---

4   Brought to Namibia by Ramatex. One wonders why. Could it be that these workers are better 'broken in' to industrial work than their Namibian counterparts, their presence serving to set an example of how to work with the *correct attitude and behaviour*?

If cost effective, Third World working conditions can be imported into the West, as we saw with the case of TNS Knitwear, but many more, less sensational cases exist. All over countries such as Britain, Italy and Spain, home workers, often (but far from always) themselves immigrants from the developing world, work for poverty wages either in a shadow world of illegal production facilities, or in the even more socially opaque domestic sphere (Warren 2005: 151). In what used to be called declining, (but may be more accurately described as declined) industrial areas like Oldham, Rochdale, and Bury, King Cotton has gone underground, but even low paid work in the shadow economy is ultimately threatened by low cost production in, for example, the Far East. In terms of subcontracting of course, it is not always accurate to suggest that producers in developing countries have been informed by developments in the West. Cottage industry has always existed in the developing world. In the era of global capitalism, however, it can be integrated into a production chain which might include 'flexible specialisation' in Turin or Munich, as well as 'just in time' production in a village in rural Bangladesh.

In many areas of the Third World, poverty is enough to encourage people to work for a wage, whatever it might be. As commentators such as Sklair have noted, however, consumerism as a value system is well suited to the transition to capitalist modernity (Sklair 1991: 129). Production of cheap consumer goods makes even more economic sense if they can be sold to internal populations once the external market is satisfied. Once, the burgeoning 'middle' and more affluent working classes in North America and Europe coveted, and could, with hard and disciplined work eventually afford to buy, a model T Ford or a Volkswagen Beetle. Today, India's rising salariat are presented with their own version of motoring for the masses, the Tata Nano. Much of the same technology that allows international trade to function (satellites, fibre optics etc.) can also be utilised to facilitate global media flows, with the media overwhelmingly oriented towards the expansion of consumerism.

Chapter 10
Conclusion:
The End of Work as Critical Social Theory

I hope to have shown in the course of this book that theories of the end of work offer a promising line of analysis within critical social theory, one that has indeed escaped proper notice. Having explored how modern understandings of work, and the modern ideology of work, were established in Chapter 2, we began to see in Chapter 3 the way that the end of work was conceptualised by utopian thinkers. It seems to have been the case that the advances in production technology that were linked with the new ideology of work held a counter tendency within them. Nineteenth and early twentieth century thinkers were inspired to think beyond existing social relations not only by the obvious possibilities of developing technologies, but by the fact that rapid social change appeared to open up spaces for new and radical social transformations beyond the confines of existing social structures. Industrialisation had seen whole populations transposed into new settings, and indeed whole classes coalesce and expand, or conversely, decline. Changes in work and production were correctly seen as being behind many of these social changes. Utopians such as Fourier, Etzler, Bellamy, and Morris all placed work at the centre of their social critique, since they firmly grasped the fact that work is the key social, if not sociological category. They also observed that as capitalist work's hold over society became ever more total, the content of work itself seemed to become increasingly degraded. Degraded work, it was observed, led to the degradation of people, something which utopians opposed. The most radical way to oppose degrading work was to oppose capitalist work as a whole.

I have characterised Marx as an end of work theorist also. I cannot claim to be an expert on Marx, as are some of the writers to whom I have referred throughout this book. However, it seems to me that he conducts critical social theory at the heart of which is the end of work. This element of Marxism is rarely emphasised, although Marx's writings on the degradation of work are fairly well known. Not only did Marx propose a politics of time, he attempted to posit free time as central to the establishment a new form of value that was better suited to measuring human freedom – itself the most valuable commodity of all. It can be seen as particularly radical to propose freedom from work at a historical and social juncture where the ideology of work, and indeed working hours themselves, were reaching new heights. Marx himself noted the reluctance of industrialists to reduce working hours, fearing financial collapse; this rationale endures, and gains credence from government policies to reverse curtailments on working hours, as is happening in France at present. In the context of global capitalism of course, restrictions on working hours are indeed harmful in terms of competitiveness. The argument for an end of work must, therefore, also call for a change in the economic system as a whole.

Marx's theories are theories of social development, and the end of work is posited as the next stage of social development beyond advanced capitalism. Even with mechanisation and automation at what would now be considered a low level, Marx extrapolated from the most advanced sectors of the industrial economies to present a compelling analysis of the way the internal logic of capitalism tends to eradicate human labour. It is the case that Marx's totalising analysis of social, economic and industrial change, laid much of the foundation for social thought since, and the overwhelming majority of the subsequent end of work theories draw on Marx to a considerable extent.

Critical Theorists such as Marcuse, for instance, shared Marx's faith in technology, despite Critical Theory sometimes being seen as anti-technological. Using theories of the end of work to unmask the irrationality of prevailing social and ideological conditions became even more pertinent in the post Second World War period. Clearly, technology had advanced phenomenally since Marx's time. The Second World War had been won, arguably, on the basis of advances in production technology and systems, and the products of the world's most advanced industries had begun to show their potential – primarily to eliminate millions of human beings, if not humanity entirely. Far from technology liberating people from toil and poverty, the dominant tendency in the post-war period seemed to be the rise of consumerism, itself making use of advances in technology and mass production. Consumerism, like the capitalist mode of production, is increasingly a truly global phenomenon. Not only did writers of the Frankfurt School such as Marcuse criticise work in the context of the society where it is perhaps held in the highest esteem, the United States, they attacked consumerism under the same conditions. The link between needs and work had been made by More, and indeed is not hard to grasp. In critiquing work, theories of the end of work are forced to include the realm of consumption in their analysis. This is an example of the way in which theories of the end of work, as critical social theories, must consider the totality of social relations. Increasingly, the totality of social relations is understood to encompass the global dimension, and in a world of work and consumption that is increasingly globally interlinked, this is just as well.

Even mainstream commentators and futurologists predicted a decline in the domination of work, as we saw in Chapter 6. It is interesting to observe the extent to which Marxist and non-Marxist thinkers make similar diagnoses of the internal tendencies of capitalism as a system of production, and capitalist society. Once again technology has a role to play, and the 1960s and 1970s were periods of rapid technological change. Actually, although we could argue over this point, it seems that rapid technological and social change have become a permanent state of affairs in most of the world. At times when this becomes particularly obvious, perhaps because of a new invention, or a new government policy that will help lead to social rupture, commentators tend to speculate on where social change is heading. We saw in Chapter 6 that although many writers on the future of work predicted a decline in the importance of work, this was often associated with a decline in social coherence and a rise in polarisation. It can be argued that they were correct more in the second instance (social incoherence and polarisation) than in the first. It seems to have been the case that many writers on the future of work confused temporarym but admittedly, possibly tendential imbalances in the structure of employment (mass unemployment in the 1980s, for example) with permanent changes in the status of work.

Many analyses on the future of work can be considered as critical social theory to the extent that they highlight the possibility of a more equitable, better organised, and less antagonistic society in the future, with this possibility opened up by new ideas about how to transform work and enlarge the sphere of self enhancing activities. Most future of work theorists failed to understand the central and specific role that work plays in capitalism however, and they therefore underestimated the system's ability to maintain an emphasis on work, even with prevailing social conditions (unemployment, deindustrialisation, computerisation) suggesting a different developmental path.

Gorz's analysis is particularly effective as critical social theory because he combines Critical Theory's totalising critique of capitalism, including its cultural dynamics, with an understanding of changes in the world of work in the postindustrial period. Gorz shows how changes in the world of work are shaping the social structure, for instance, and shares with some of the future of work writers a sense of social polarisation. As with writers such as Marcuse or Robertson, there are some elements in his analysis that may be rather overstated, such as the influence of the immaterial worker, in Gorz's case. However, as Kumar notes (Kumar 1995: viii), overstatement is not always a hindrance in terms of criticality, since some of the most insightful critical theory sometimes picks out tendencies that while not quantitatively dominant, represent an important underlying dynamic. It is the responsibility of writers *on* theory to approach all theories, including the end of work, critically. Conversely, Gorz's work may be an advance over previous writers such as Marcuse, and certainly Fourier, in understanding the limitations of the end of work, without accepting that work should ever be exploitative or degrading. Gorz also effectively avoids the trap of proposing some kind of return to nature in a world without factories. He accepts, sensibly, I would argue, the need for large scale impersonal structures to continue to exist, but points out that these structures are capable of being organised for the benefit of society as a whole, rather than a particular group. In the future, perhaps, we will not need copper wire or iron ore, and advances in small scale production may mean profound changes in how sociologists understand industrial life.

Theories such as Gorz's and Negri's are clearly an attempt, like those of the original Critical Theorists, to pursue Marxist critical social theory in the light of profound social change – particularly the supposed deindustrialisation of much of the West. This application of Marxism is motivated not only by the political background of these theorists, but by the fact that it continues to offer insights into the way capitalist societies develop. Theories of the end of work continue to place work at the centre of human existence, and while they emphasise the interconnectedness of society, point out that fundamental changes in the sphere of work have unique liberatory potential. Although some theorists of a consumer society argue that work is no longer the key sociological category, they profoundly underestimate the extent to which production dominates existence under capitalism. The debate over true and false needs may never be settled, but as environmental degradation and financial turmoil threaten all manner of calamities, theories of the end of work have the virtue of emphasising the possibilities of consumption as a conscious process, integrated with the needs (environmental and ontological) of society as a whole.

Critical Theorists such as Adorno, Horkheimer and Marcuse suggested that the realm of consumption and leisure come increasingly to resemble the sphere of work. Contemporary end of work writers such as Gorz and Negri go further, and suggest that even social reproduction is becoming subsumed under economic rationality – as work. Again, there is perhaps some over-statement, but it is hard to deny, in the face of ubiquitous communications technology (allowing people to work at home, on holiday, at weekends…), the vocationalisation of education, and the rise[1] in personal services, that the realm outside of work, and therefore the economic logic of capital, is diminishing. If the whole of life is becoming work, as writers such as Gorz and Negri suggest, with characteristic hyperbole, then a critique of work is necessarily a critique of life itself, that is, life under existing social conditions – it is therefore totalising critique.

Currently the work ethic – the ideology of work occupies an unassailable position in politics, policy, and popular discourse, with the exception of a few well to do idlers – the usual 'cultural commentators', artists and sensualists. It is a deeply established feature of life in modernity. In some ways, even from the standpoint of theories of the end of work, this is to be celebrated. Although an ideology that promotes work, however un-enriching and destructive, is clearly flawed, the work ethic could not have come to be as dominant as it is, if it did not reflect a human need for production; that is, for creative activity by which people can build personal and social lives, and move society forward in the process (whilst determining what 'forward' will mean). End of work theories, as this book has hopefully shown, are far from an invitation to idleness; rather, they are analyses that suggest a rational approach to organising work and society, rather than allowing structures of domination (the market, ideology, state policy) to determine human life activity. A vision of a world without work is a utopian vision, certainly, but utopias have a powerful critical function within social thought. By pointing to the radical possibilities for transforming work, end of work theories highlight the possibilities for radical transformation of society as a whole, and through demanding the seemingly impossible, they suggest that the

---

1   Perhaps we should say resurgence, since the existence of a servant class is nothing new, as already noted.

rationale for such transformation, as well as the technical means of achieving it, are entirely realistic.

References

Abrams, F. (2002), *Below the Breadline* (London: Profile).

Adorno, T. (1998[1969]), 'Free Time', in T. Adorno, *Critical Models*, trans. H. W. Pickford. pp. 167–175 (New York: Columbia University Press).

Agger, B. (1992), *The Discourse of Domination* (Evanston Ill: Northwestern University Press).

Agger, B. (1998), *Critical Social Theories* (Oxford: Westview Press).

Agger, D. et al. [letter – 30 signatories] (1964), 'Triple Revolution', URL (consulted September 2007): http://www.educationanddemocracy.org/FSCfiles/C_CC2a_TripleRevolution.htm.

Andrew, E. (1970), 'Work and Freedom in Marcuse and Marx', *Canadian Journal of Political Science* 3(2): 241–256.

Anonymous. (2005), '"Must Try Harder!": Towards a Critique of Autonomist Marxism', *Aufheben* 13: 18–36.

Anonymous. (2006), 'Keep on Smiling: Questions on Immaterial Labour', *Aufheben* 14: 23–44.

Anthony, P. D. (1977), *The Ideology of Work* (London: Tavistock).

Applebaum, H. (1992), *The Concept of Work* (New York: SUNY Press).

Arendt, H. (1958), *The Human Condition* (Chicago: University of Chicago Press).

Aronowitz, S. (1974), *False Promises* (New York: McGraw Hill).

Aronowitz, S. and W. DiFazio (1994), *The Jobless Future* (Minneapolis: University of Minnesota Press).

Arthur, C. J. (1986), *Dialectics of Labour* (London: Basil Blackwell).

Avineri, S. (1976), *The Social and Political Thought of Karl Marx* (Cambridge: CUP).

Axelos, K. (1976), *Alienation, Praxis, and Techne in the Thought of Karl Marx* (Austin: University of Texas Press).

Basso, P. (2003), *Modern Times, Ancient Hours*, trans. G. Donis (London: Verso).

Baudrillard, J. (1975), *The Mirror of Production*, trans. M. Poster (St Louis: Telos).

Baudrillard, J. (2000 [1970]), *The Consumer Society: Myths and Structures*, trans. C. Turner (London: Sage).

Bauman, Z. (1982), *Memories of Class* (London: RKP).

Bauman, Z. (1998), *Work, Consumerism and the New Poor* (Buckingham: Open University Press).

BBC (2009) 'Inside the TNS Knitwear Factory', URL (consulted March 2009): http://news.bbc.co.uk/1/hi/uk/7824774.stm.

Beck, U. (2000), *The Brave New World of Work*, trans. P. Camiler (Cambridge: Polity).

Beder, S. (2000), *Selling the Work Ethic* (London: Zed Books).

Bell, D. (1956), *Work and its Discontents* (Boston: Beacon Press).

Bell, D. (1974), *The Coming of Post-industrial Society* (London: Heinemann).

Bellamy, E. (1986[1888]), *Looking Backward 2000 – 1887* (London: Penguin).

Bellini, J. (1982), *Rule Britannia* (London: Abacus).

Benhabib, S. (1986), *Critique, Norm and Utopia* (New York: Columbia).

Berger, S. (1999), 'Globalization and the Future of Work', presentation prepared for the *Volkswagen Foundation Symposium on The Future Role of Work in Lives and Societies*, Hanover, Germany, January 22, 1999, URL (consulted March 2009): http://web.mit.edu/polisci/research/berger/Future_of_Work1.pdf.

Berki, R. N. (1979), 'On the Nature and Origins of Marx's Concept of Labour', *Political Theory* 7(1): 35–56.

Bird, E. (2005), Book Review: K Glynn, 'Tabloid Culture: Trash Taste, Popular Power and the Transformation of American Television', *Cultural Studies* 19(1): 127–132.

Bix, A. (2000), *Inventing Ourselves out of Jobs?* (London: Johns Hopkins University Press).

Black, B. (1996), 'The Abolition of Work', URL (consulted August 2007): http://www.inspiracy.com/black/abolition/abolitionofwork.html

Blackburn, R. and A. Cockburn (eds.) (1969), *Student Power* (Harmansworth: Penguin).

Blakely, G. and V. Bryson (eds.) (2005), *Marx and Other Four Letter Words* (London: Pluto).

Blauner, R. (1964), *Alienation and Freedom* (London: University of Chicago Press).

Booth, W. (1989), 'Gone Fishing: Making Sense of Marx's Concept of Communism', *Political Theory* 17(2): 205–222.

Booth, W. (1991), 'Economies of Time: On the Idea of Time in Marx's Political Economy', *Political Theory* 19(1): 7–27.

Bowring, F. (1996), 'Misreading Gorz', *New Left Review* (217): 102–122.

Bowring, F. (2000), *Andre Gorz and the Sartrean Legacy: Arguments for a Person–Centered Social Theory* (Basingstoke: Macmillan).

Bowring, F. (2002), 'Post-Fordism and the End of Work', *Futures* 34(2): 159–172.

Bronner, S. E. (1988), 'Between Art and Utopia: Reconsidering the Aesthetic Theory of Herbert Marcuse', in R. Pippin, A. Feenberg, and C. Webel (eds.) *Marcuse: Critical Theory & the Promise of Utopia*, pp. 107–142 (New York: Bergin and Garvey).

Bunting, M. (2004), *Willing Slaves* (London: HarperCollins).

Burnett, J. (1974), *Useful Toil* (London: Allen Lane).

Butt, J. (1977), 'Introduction', in R. Owen, *A New View of Society and Other Writings* (London: Dent).

Caffentzis, C. G. (1998), 'The End of Work or the Renaissance of Slavery: A Critique of Rifkin and Negri', URL (consulted August 2007): http://multitudes. samizdat.net/The-End-of-Work-or-the-Renaissance.html

Caffentzis, C. G. (1997), 'Why Machines Cannot Create Value; or, Marx's Theory of Machines', in J. Davis, T. Hirschl and M. Stack (eds.) *Cutting Edge*, pp. 29–56 (London: Verso).

Carlyle, T. (1843), *Past and Present*, URL (consulted August 2007): http://www. online-literature.com/thomas-carlyle/past-and-present/34/

Casey, C. (1995), *Work, Self and Society* (London: Routledge).

Chytry, J. (1989), *The Aesthetic State* (Berkeley: University of California Press).

Clarke, J. (2000), 'Dupes and Guerrillas: The Dialectics of Cultural Consumption', in M. Lee (ed.) *The Consumer Society Reader*, pp. 288–294 (Malden: Blackwell).

Cleaver, H. (1989), 'Work, Value and Domination: On the Continuing Relevance of the Marxian Labour Theory of Value in the Crisis of the Keynsian Planner State', URL (consulted April 2006): http://www.eco.utexas.edu/~hmcleave/ offenegri.html.

Cleaver, H. (2002), 'Work is *Still* the Central Issue! New Words for New Worlds', in A.C. Dinerstein, M. Neary (eds.) *The Labour Debate*, pp. 135–148 (Aldershot: Ashgate).

Coats, D. (2005), 'An Agenda for Work: The Work Foundation's Challenge to Policy Makers, Provocation Paper', Series 1 Number 2, URL (consulted June 2007): http://www.theworkfoundation.com/products/publications/azpublications/ anagendaforworktheworkfoundationschallengetopolicymakers.aspx.

Cohen, G. A. (1977), 'Labour, Leisure and a Distinctive Contradiction of Advanced Capitalism', in G. Dworkin (ed.) *Markets and Morals*, pp. 107–36 (New York: John Wiley).

Cohen, G. A. (1988), *History, Labour and Freedom* (Oxford: Clarendon).

Conly, C. (1978), 'Alienation, Sociality, and the Division of Labour: Contradictions in Marx's Idea of "Social Man"', *Ethics* 89(1): 82–94.

Cooke, M. (2004), 'Redeeming Redemption: The Utopian Dimension of Critical Social Theory', *Philosophy and Social Criticism* 30 (4): 413–429.

Dant, T. (2003), *Critical Social Theory* (London: Sage).

Dauvé, G. (2002), 'To Work or Not to Work? Is that the Question?' *Troploin* 3, URL (consulted January 2007): http://troploin0.free.fr/biblio/lovlabuk/lovlabuk.pdf.

Davis, J., T. Hirschl and M. Stack (eds.) (1997), *Cutting Edge* (London: Verso).

De Certeau, M. (1984), *The Practice of Everyday Life* (Berkeley: University of California Press).

De Grazia, S. (1964), *Of Time, Work, and Leisure* (Garden City: Anchor).

Dinerstein, A. C. and M. Neary (eds.) (2002), *The Labour Debate* (Aldershot: Ashgate).

Donovan, T. W. (2004), *Modernity's Unfinished Project: Labor, Meaning and Reconciliation* (Unpublished Ph.D., Riverside: University of California).

Dyer Witheford, N. (2004), 'Autonomist Marxism', URL (consulted March 2007): http://ledland.pollon.com.au/Treason/Pamphlets/AutonomistMarxism_consecutive.pdf.

Edgell, S. (2006), *The Sociology of Work* (London: Sage).

Edgell, S. (2007), 'Non Standard Work in Contemporary Britain', in S. Renshaw (ed.) *Prime*, pp. 12–17 (Liverpool: Prime).

Edwards, T. (2000), *Contradictions of Consumption* (Buckingham: Open University Press).

Elster, J. (1986), 'Self Realization in Work and Politics: The Marxist Conception of the Good Life', *Social Philosophy and Policy* 3(2): 97–126.

Engels, F. (1999[1845]), extract from 'The Condition of the Working Class in England', in K. Thomas (ed.) *The Oxford Book of Work*, p. 516 (Oxford: OUP).

Etzler, J. A. (1842), *The Paradise Within the Reach of All Men, Without Labour, by Powers of Nature and Machinery: An Address to All Intelligent Men* (London: J Cleave).

Ewen, S. (1977), *Captains of Consciousness* (McGraw Hill, New York).

Feenberg, A., R. Pippin and C. Webel (1988), *Marcuse: Critical Theory and the Promise of Utopia* (South Hadley, MA, USA: Bergin and Garvey).

Feenberg, A. (2005), *Heidegger and Marcuse* (London: Taylor and Francis).

Fevre, R (2007), 'Employment Insecurity and Social Theory: The Power of Nightmares', *Work Employment and Society* 21(3): 517–535.

Fiske, J. (1989), *Understanding Popular Culture* (London: Unwin Hyman).

Fiske, J. (2000[1989]), 'The Commodities of Culture', in M. Lee (ed.) *The Consumer Society Reader*, pp. 282–287 (Malden, MA: Blackwell).

Fourier, C. (1972), *The Utopian Vision of Charles Fourier*, trans. J. Beecher, and R. Bienvenu (London: Jonathan Cape).

Franklin, J. (1901), *Selections from the Works of Fourier* (London: Swan Sonnenschein).

Fraser, N. (2003), 'From Discipline to Flexibilization? Rereading Foucault in the Shadow of Globalization', *Constellations* 10(2): 160–171.

Freud, S. (1975[1930]), *Civilization and its Discontents* (London: The Hogarth Press).

Fry, T. F. (1975), *Computer Appreciation* (London: Newnes–Butterworth).

Galbraith, J. K. (1958), *The Affluent Society* (London: Hamish Hamilton).

Gantman, E. (2005), *Capitalism, Social Privilege and Managerial Ideologies* (Aldershot: Ashgate).

Gershuny, J. (1978), *After Industrial Society?* (London: Macmillan).

Gluck, F. W. (1982), 'Meeting the Challenge of Global Competition', *McKinsey Quarterly* 3: 2–12.

Glyn, A. (2006), *Capitalism Unleashed: Finance, Globalization and Welfare* (Oxford: Oxford University Press).

Godelier, M. (1980), 'Work and its Representations: A Research Proposal', *History Workshop Journal* (10): 164–174.

Gorz, A. (1964), *Stratégie ouvrière et néocapitalisme* [Strategy for Labour] (Paris: Seuil).

Gorz, A. (1967), *Strategy for Labor*, trans. M. A. Nicolaus and V. Ortiz (Boston: Beacon Press).

Gorz, A. (1975), *Socialism and Revolution*, trans. N. Denny (London: Allen Lane).

Gorz, A. (1980), *Adieux au proletariat: au–dela du socialisme* [Farewell to the Working Class] (Paris: Galilée).

Gorz, A. (1982), *Farewell to the Working Class*, trans. M. Sonenscher (London: Pluto).

Gorz, A. (1983), *Ecology as Politics*, trans. P. Vigderman and J. Cloud (London: Pluto).

Gorz, A. (1985), *Paths to Paradise*, trans. M. Imrie (London: Pluto).

Gorz, A. (1986), 'The Socialism of Tomorrow', *Telos* 67: 199–206.

Gorz, A. (1986–87), with R. Maischein and M. Jander, 'Alienation, Freedom, and Utopia: Interview with André Gorz', *Telos* 70: 137–154.

Gorz, A. (1989), *Critique of Economic Reason*, trans. G. Handyside and C. Turner (London: Verso).

Gorz, A. (1999), *Reclaiming Work*, trans. C. Turner (Cambridge: Polity).

Gorz, A. (2003), *L'immatériel. Connaissance, valeur et capital* (Paris: Galilée).

Green, F. (2001), 'It's Been a Hard Day's Night: The Concentration and Intensification of Work in Late Twentieth Century Britain', *British Journal of Industrial Relations* 39(1): 53–80.

Greenberg, D. (1990), 'Energy, Power and Perceptions of Social Change in the Early Nineteenth Century', *The American Historical Review*, 95(3): 693–714.

Grint, K. (1990), *The Sociology of Work* (Oxford: Polity).

Gusinde, M. (1961[1931]), *The Yamana* (New Haven: Human Relations Area Files).

Habermas, J. (1987a[1969]), *Towards a Rational Society* (Cambridge: Polity).

Habermas, J. (1987b[1985]), *The Philosophical Discourse of Modernity* (Cambridge: M.I.T Press).

Habermas, J. (1989), *The Theory of Communicative Action, Volume Two: The Critique of Functionalist Reason* (Cambridge: Polity).

Hale, A. (2005) 'Organising and Networking in Support of Garment Workers: Why we Researched Subcontracting Chains' in A. Hale and J. Wills, *Threads of Labour*, pp. 40–69 (London: Blackwell).

Hall, S. and M. Jacques (eds.) (1990), *New Times* (London: Lawrence and Wishart).

Hall, S. (1990), 'The Meaning of New Times' in S. Hall and M. Jacques (eds.) *New Times*, pp.116–133 (London: Lawrence and Wishart).

Handy, C. (1984), *The Future of Work* (Oxford: Blackwell).

Hardt, M. and A. Negri (1994), *Labor of Dionysus* (London: University of Minnesota Press).

Hardt, M. and A. Negri (2000), *Empire* (Harvard: Harvard University Press).

Harris, A. L. (1950), 'Utopian Elements in Marx's Thought', *Ethics* 60(2): 79–99.

Harvie, C., G. Martin and A. Scharf (1970), (eds.) *Industrialisation and Culture, 1830–1914* (London: Macmillan for the Open University Press).

Hebdige, D. (1990), 'After the Masses', in S. Hall and M. Jacques (eds.) *New Times*, pp. 76–93 (London: Lawrence and Wishart).

Hegedus, A., A. Heller, M. Markus and M. Vadja (eds.) (1976), *The Humanisation of Socialism* (London: Allison and Busby).

Heller, A. (1974), *The Theory of Need in Marx* (London: Allison and Busby).

Hirsch, A. (1982), *The French New Left* (Montreal: Black Rose).

Hodgkinson, T. (2004), *How to be Idle* (London: Hamish Hamilton).

Horkheimer, M. (1972[1937]), 'Traditional and Critical Theory', in M. Horkheimer, *Critical Theory*, pp. 188–244 (New York: Seabury Press).

Hundert, E. J. (1972), 'The Making of Homo Faber: John Locke Between Ideology and History', *Journal of the History of Ideas* 33(1): pp. 3–22.

Hunnicutt, B. K. (1988), *Work Without End* (Philadelphia: Temple University Press).

Hurley, J. (2005), 'Unravelling the Web: Supply Chains and Workers' Lives in the Garment Industry' in A. Hale and J. Wills, *Threads of Labour*, pp. 95–133 (London: Blackwell).

Hurley, J. and D. Miller (2005), 'The Changing Face of the Global Garment Industry', in A. Hale and J. Wills, *Threads of Labour*, pp. 16–40 (London: Blackwell).

International Monetary Fund [IMF] (2008) 'Globalization: A Brief Overview', URL (consulted March 2009): http://www.imf.org/external/np/exr/ib/2008/pdf/053008.pdf.

James, O. (2007), *Affluenza* (London: Vermillion).

Jenkins, C. and B. Sherman (1979), *The Collapse of Work* (London: Methuen).

Jones, B. (1982), *Sleepers, Wake!* (Oxford: OUP).

Joyce, P. (ed.) (1987), *The Historical Meanings of Work* (Cambridge: CUP).

Kahn, H. and A. J. Wiener (1967), *The Year 2000* (New York: Macmillan).

Kane, P. (2004), *The Play Ethic* (London: Macmillan).

Katz, B. (1982), *Herbert Marcuse and the Art of Liberation* (London: Verso).

Kellner, D. (1984), *Herbert Marcuse and the Crisis of Marxism* (London: Macmillan).

Kellner, D. (1989a), *Critical Theory, Marxism and Modernity* (Cambridge: Polity).

Kellner, D. (1989b), *Jean Baudrillard: From Marxism to Postmodernism and Beyond* (Cambridge: Polity).

Kellner, D. (ed.) (1998), *Technology, War and Fascism: Collected Papers of Herbert Marcuse Volume 1* (London: Routledge).

Kellner, D. (ed.) (2005), *Herbert Marcuse, the New Left and the 1960s* (London: Routledge).

Keynes, J. M. (1932), *Essays in Persuasion* (New York: Harcourt Brace).

Krell, D. (ed.) (1993), *Heidegger, Basic Writings* (London: Routledge).

Kumar, K. (1978), *Prophecy and Progress* (Harmondsworth: Penguin).

Kumar, K. (1987), *Utopia and Anti–Utopia in Modern Times* (Oxford: Blackwell).

Kumar, K. (1988), *The Rise of Modern Society* (London: Basil Blackwell).

Kumar, K. (1997), *From Post-Industrial to Post-Modern Society* (Oxford: Blackwell.

Lafargue, P. (1883), *The Right to be Lazy*, URL (consulted September 2007): http://www.marxists.org/archive/lafargue/1883/lazy/index.htm

Lantos, B. (1943), 'Work and the Instincts', *International Journal of Psychoanalysis* 24: 114–119.

Lechner, F. J and J. Boli (eds.) (2000) *The Globalization Reader* (Oxford: Blackwell).

Lee, M. (ed.) (2000), *The Consumer Society Reader* (Malden: Blackwell).

Lefkowitz, B. (1979), *Breaktime* (New York: Hawthorn Books).

Lerner, S. (1994), 'The Future of Work in North America', *Futures* 26(2): 185–196.

Levitas, R. (1990), *The Concept of Utopia* (London: Philip Allan).

Lodziak, C. and J. Tatman (1997), *André Gorz: a Critical Introduction* (Chicago, Ill: Pluto Press).

Lowenthal, L. (1961), *Literature, Popular Culture and Society* (Englewood Cliffs: Prentice–Hall).

Lowy, M. (1980), 'Marcuse and Benjamin: The Romantic Dimension' *Telos* 44: 25–33.

Lynes, R. (1958), 'Time on our hands', in E. Larrabee and R. Meyersohn (eds.) *Mass Leisure*, pp. 345–353 (Glencoe: Free Press).

Macey, D. (2000), *The Penguin Dictionary of Critical Theory* (London: Penguin).

MacIntire, A. (1981), *After Virtue* (Duckworth: London).

Mallet, S. (1969), *The New Working Class*, trans. A. Shepherd and R. D. Shepherd (Nottingham: Spokesman).

Mann, K. (1992), *The Making of an English Underclass* (Milton Keynes: Open University Press).

Manuel, F. and F. P. Manuel (1979), *Utopian Thought in the Western World* (Oxford: Blackwell).

Marcuse, H. (1964), *One Dimensional Man* (London: RKP).

Marcuse, H. (1967), 'The Obsolescence of Marxism?', in N. Lobkowicz (ed.) *Marxism and the Western World*, pp. 409–417 (Notre Dame: University of Notre Dame Press).

Marcuse, H. (1969a[1941]), *Reason and Revolution* (London: RKP).

Marcuse, H. (1969b), 'The Realm of Freedom and the Realm of Necessity: A Reconsideration', *Praxis* 5(1–2): 20–5.

Marcuse, H. (1969c), 'On Revolution' in R. Blackburn and A. Cockburn (eds.) *Student Power*, pp. 367–372 (Penguin: Harmondsworth).

Marcuse, H. (1970), 'The End of Utopia', in H. Marcuse, *Five Lectures*, pp. 62–82 (Boston: Beacon).

Marcuse, H. (1972a), *An Essay on Liberation* (London: Penguin).

Marcuse, H. (1972b[1945]), 'The Foundations of Historical Materialism', in J. De Bres, *Studies in Critical Philosophy*, pp. 3–48 (London: New Left).

Marcuse, H. (1972c[1936]), 'On the Concept of Essence', in H. Marcuse, *Negations*, pp. 43–87 (London: Penguin).

Marcuse, H. (1972d[1938]), 'On Hedonism', in H. Marcuse, *Negations*, pp. 159–200 (London: Penguin).

Marcuse, H. (1972e[1964]), 'Industrialism and Capitalism in the Work of Max Weber', in H. Marcuse, *Negations*, pp. 201–226 (London: Penguin).

Marcuse, H. (1972f [1967]), 'Aggressiveness in Advanced Industrial Society', in H. Marcuse, *Negations*, pp. 248–268 (London: Penguin).

Marcuse, H. (1973[1933]), 'On the Philosophical Foundation of the Concept of Labor in Economics', trans. D. Kellner, *Telos* 16: 9–37.

Marcuse, H. (1986[1964]), *One Dimensional Man* (London: Ark).

Marcuse, H. (1987[1955]), *Eros and Civilization* (London: Ark).

Marcuse, H. (1998[1941]), 'Some Social implications of Modern Technology', in D. Kellner (ed.) *Technology, War and Fascism: Collected Papers of Herbert Marcuse Volume 1*, pp. 39–65 (London: Routledge).

Marcuse, H. (2005a[1974]), 'A Conversation with Herbert Marcuse', in D. Kellner, D. (ed.) *Herbert Marcuse, the New Left and the 1960s*, pp. 154–164 (London: Routledge).

Marcuse, H. (2005b[1968]), 'Marcuse Defines his New Left Line', in D. Kellner (ed.) *Herbert Marcuse, the New Left and the 1960s*, pp. 100–118 (London: Routledge).

Marcuse, H. (2005c[1974]), 'Marxism and Feminism', in D. Kellner (ed.) *Herbert Marcuse, the New Left and the 1960s*, pp. 165–172 (London: Routledge).

Marglin, S. (1982), 'What Do the Bosses Do? The Origins and Functions of Hierarchy in Capitalist Production', in A. Giddens and D. Held (eds.), *Classes, Power, and Conflict*, pp. 285–298 (Basingstoke: Macmillan).

Marramao, G. (1975), 'Political Economy and Critical Theory', *Telos* 24: 56–80.

Marx, K. (1959a[1845]), 'The German Ideology', in M. Eastman (ed.) *Capital, the Communist Manifesto and Other Writings*, pp. 1–2 (New York: The Modern Library).

Marx, K. (1959b[1848]), 'The Communist Manifesto', in M. Eastman (ed.) *Capital, the Communist Manifesto and Other Writings*, pp. 315–355 (New York: The Modern Library).

Marx, K. (1959c[1867]), 'Capital', in M. Eastman (ed.) *Capital, the Communist Manifesto and Other Writings*, pp. 11–302 (New York: The Modern Library).

Marx, K. (1967), *Writings of the Young Marx on Philosophy and Society*, trans. and eds. L. D. Easton and K. H Guddat (Garden City: Doubleday).

Marx, K. (1972a[1857–8]), *Grundrisse* (London: Macmillan).

Marx, K. (1972b[1875]), *Critique of the Gotha Programme* (Peking: Foreign Languages Press).

Marx, K. (1974[1867]), *Capital* (Dent: London).

Marx, K. (1975a[1843]), 'Franco – German Yearbooks', in L. Colletti (ed.) *Early Writings*, pp. 199–210 (London: Penguin).

Marx, K. (1975b[1844]), 'Economical and Philosophical Manuscripts', in L. Colletti (ed.) *Early Writings*, pp. 279–400 (London: Penguin).

Marx, K. (1975c[1844]), 'Excerpts from James Mill's Elements of Political Economy', in L. Colletti (ed.) *Early Writings*, pp. 259–278 (London: Penguin).

Marx, K. (1976[1845]), 'The German Ideology', in K. Marx and F. Engels, *Collected Works Vol. 5.* pp. 19–539 (London: Lawrence and Wishart).

Marx, K. (1977[1894]), *Capital Vol. III* (London: Lawrence and Wishart).

Marx, K. (1993 [1857–8]), *Grundrisse* (London: Penguin).

Marx, K. and F. Engels (1996[1848]), *The Communist Manifesto* (London: Phoenix).

McClelland, K. (1987), 'Time to Work, Time to Live', in P. Joyce (ed.) *The Historical Meanings of Work*, pp. 181–209 (Cambridge: CUP).

McGuigan, J. (2000), 'Sovereign Consumption', in M. Lee (ed.) *The Consumer Society Reader*, pp. 294–299 (Malden: Blackwell).

McRobbie, A. (1994), *Postmodernism and Popular Culture* (London: Routledge).

Montano, M. (1992[1975]), 'Notes on the International Crisis', in Midnight Notes Collective (eds.) *Midnight Oil: Work, Energy, War, 1973–1992*, pp. 115–142 (Autonomedia: Brooklyn).

More, T. (1962[1516]), *Utopia* (London: Dent).

Morris, W. (1915[1885]), 'Useful Work Versus Useless Toil', in W. Morris, *Signs of Change; Lectures on Socialism*, pp. 98–120 (London: Longmans).

Morris, W. (1889), 'Bellamy's *"Looking Backward"*', *in Commonweal*, URL (consulted July 2007): http://www.marxists.org/archive/morris/works/1889/backward.htm.

Morris, W. (1979a[1890]), *News From Nowhere or an Epoch of Rest* (London: RKP).

Morris, W. (1979b[1885]), 'Useful Work Versus Useless Toil', in W. Morris, *Political Writings of William Morris*, pp. 86–108 (London: Lawrence and Wishart).

Mort, F. (1990), 'The Politics of Consumption', in S. Hall and M. Jacques (eds.) *New Times*, pp. 160–72 (London: Lawrence and Wishart).

Mumford, L. (1955[1934]), *Technics and Civilization* (London: RKP).

Nava, M. (1991), 'Consumerism Reconsidered: Buying and Power', *Cultural Studies* 5(2): 157–73.

Negri, A. (1988), *Revolution Retrieved* (London: Red Notes).

Negri, A. (1989), *The Politics of Subversion* (Cambridge: Polity).

Negri, A. (2005), *Time for Revolution*, trans. M. Mandarini (London: Continuum).

Nicholson, L. W. (1996), 'Work is Becoming Obsolete', *The Northwest Technocrat* 342, URL (consulted June 2007): http://www.technocracy.org/Archives/Work%20Is%20Becoming%20Obsolete–r.htm.

Nisbet, R. (1970), *The Sociological Tradition* (London: Heinemann).

Nun, J. (2000), 'The End of Work and the "Marginal Mass" Thesis', *Latin American Perspectives* 27(1): 6–32.

Ochs, P. (1964), 'Automation Song', on *All the News that's Fit to Sing* (Album), Elektra Records.

Offe, C. (1985), 'Work: The Key Sociological Category?', in Claus Offe, *Disorganized Capitalism*, pp. 129–150 (Cambridge: Polity).

Offe, C. (1985), *Disorganized Capitalism* (Cambridge: Polity).

Office for National Statistics (2006a), '2000 and 2005 Time Use Survey', URL (consulted March 2007): http://www.statistics.gov.uk/CCI/nugget.asp?ID=7&Pos=1&ColRank=1&Rank=374.

Office for National Statistics (2006b), 'Labour Market Review 2006', URL (consulted March 2007): http://www.statistics.gov.uk/CCI/nugget.asp?ID=1424&Pos=1&ColRank=2&Rank=224.

Office of the Deputy Prime Minister (2005), 'Introduction to Slivers of Time', URL (consulted June 2007): http://www.sliversoftime.com.

Ollman, B. (1976), *Alienation: Marx's Conception of Man in Capitalist Society* (Cambridge: CUP).

Overton, M. (1986), 'Agricultural Revolution?: England, 1540–1850', *ReFRESH* 3, URL (consulted July 2007): http://www.ehs.org.uk/society/pdfs/Overton%203a.pdf.

Owen, R. (1977), *A New View of Society and Other Writings* (London: Dent).

Paden, R. (2002), 'Marx's Critique of the Utopian Socialists', *Utopian Studies* 13(2): 67–87.

Plant, S. (1992), *The Most Radical Gesture* (London: Routledge).

Poster, M. (1975), *Existential Marxism in Post-War France* (Princeton: Princeton University Press).

Poster, M. (1979), 'Semiology and Critical Theory: From Marx to Baudrillard', *Boundary 2* 8(2): 275–288.

Poster, M. (1981), 'Technology and Culture in Habermas and Baudrillard' *Contemporary Literature* 22(4): 456–476.

Postone, M. (1993), *Time, Labor, and Social Domination* (Cambridge: CUP).

Rachleff, P. (1977), 'Answer to Reeve's Article', *Fifth Estate*, URL (consulted June 2007): http://www.geocities.com/CapitolHill/Lobby/2379/row.htm.

Rachlis, C. (1978), 'Marcuse and the Problem of Happiness' *Canadian Journal of Political and Social Theory* 2(1): 63–89.

Ransome, P. (1996), *The Work Paradigm* (Aldershot: Avebury).

Ransome, P. (1999), *Sociology and the Future of Work* (Aldershot: Ashgate).

Ransome, P. (2005), *Work, Consumption and Culture* (London: Sage).

Reeve, C. (1976), 'The "Revolt Against Work", or Fight for the Right to be Lazy', *Fifth Estate,* URL (consulted June 2007): http://www.geocities.com/CapitolHill/Lobby/2379/row.htm.

Riasanovsky, N. (1969), *The Teaching of Charles Fourier* (Berkeley: University of California Press).

Riesman, D. (1958), 'Leisure and Work in Post-industrial Society', in E. Larrabee and R. Meyersohn (eds.) *Mass Leisure*, pp. 363–385 (Glencoe, Ill: Free Press).

Rifkin, J. (1995), *The End of Work* (New York: G.P. Putnam).

Robertson, J. (1985), *Future Work* (London: Gower/Maurice Temple Smith).

Rose, M. (1985), *Re-Working the Work Ethic* (London: Batsford).

Rosenberg, S. (1993), 'More Work for Some, Less Work for Others: Working Hours in the USA', *Futures* 25(5): 551–560.

Rule, J. G. (1991), 'Labour in a Changing Economy, 1700–1850', *ReFRESH* 12: 5–8.

Richards, V. (ed.) (1990), *Why Work?* (London: Freedom Press).

Russell, B. (1990[1932]), 'In Praise of Idleness', in V. Richards (ed.) *Why Work?* pp. 25–34 (London: Freedom Press).

Sahlins, M. (1972), *Stone Age Economics* (New York: Aldine de Gruyter).

Sayers, S. (1998), *Marxism and Human Nature* (London: Routledge).

Sayers, S. (2003), 'Creative Activity and Alienation in Hegel and Marx', *Historical Materialism* 11(1): 107–128.

Shaw, C. (1974[1903]), 'An Old Potter', in J. Burnett, *Useful Toil*, pp. 287–304 (London: Allen Lane).

Schiller, F. (2004[1759]), *On the Aesthetic Education of Man*, trans. R. Snell (Mineola, N.Y: Dover).

Schmidt, D. (2006), 'Globalization at Work', *Finance and Development* 43 (1): 1–7, URL (consulted March 2009): http://web.nps.navy.mil/~relooney/00_New_434.pdf.

Schoolman, M. (1973), 'Further Reflections on Work, Alienation, and Freedom in Marcuse and Marx', *Canadian Journal of Political Science* 6(2): 295–302.

Schor, J. (1993), *The Overworked American: The Unexpected Decline of Leisure* (New York: Basic Books).

Segal, H. P. (1985), *Technological Utopianism in American Society* (Chicago: University of Chicago Press).

Sibley, M. Q. (1973), 'Utopian Thought and Technology', *American Journal of Political Science* 17(2): 255–281.

Simpson, I. H. (1999), 'Historical Patterns of Workplace Organization: From Mechanical to Electronic Control and Beyond', *Current Sociology* 47(2): 47–75.

Sklair, L. (1995), *Sociology of the Global System* (London: Prentice Hall).

Slater, D. (2004), *Consumer Culture and Modernity* (Cambridge: Polity).

Slaughter, M. J. and P. Swagel (1997), 'Does Globalization Lower Wages and Export Jobs' (Washington D.C: IMF).

Smith, T. V. (1924), 'Work as an Ethical Concept', *The Journal of Philosophy* 21(20): 543–554.

Smythe, D. (1977), 'Communications: Blindspot of Western Marxism', *Canadian Journal of Political and Social Theory* 1(3): 1–29.

Snell, R. (2004), 'Introduction', in F. Schiller, *On the Aesthetic Education of Man*, trans. R. Snell (Mineola, N.Y.: Dover).

Strangleman, T. (2005), 'Sociological Futures and the Sociology of Work', *Sociological Research Online* 10(4), URL (consulted September 2007): http://www.socresonline.org.uk/10/4/strangleman.html.

Strangleman, T. (2007), 'The Nostalgia for Permanence at Work? The End of Work and its Commentators', The *Sociological Review* 55(1): 81–103.

Stuart, R. M., C. Forde, I. Greenwood, J. Gardiner and R. Perret (2006), '"All that is Solid?" Class, Identity and the Maintenance of a Collective Orientation amongst Redundant Steelworkers', *Sociology* 40(5): 833–852.

Suedfeld, P. and L. M. Ward (1976), 'Dark Trends: Psychology, Science Fiction, and the Ominous Consensus', *Futures* 8(1): 22–39.

Sünker, H. (2007), 'Foundations of Critical Theory: On the History of the Frankfurt School', *International Sociology Review of Books* 22(2): 129–37.

Tawney, R. H. (1961), *Religion and the Rise of Capitalism* (London: Penguin).

The Economist (2007a), 'Globalisation and the Rise of Inequality: Rich Man, Poor Man', January 18.

The Economist (2007b), 'In the Shadow of Prosperity', January 18.

The Guardian (2007a), 'Today Second Life, Tomorrow the World', May 17.

The Guardian (2007b), 'Underpaid, Easy to Sack: UK's Second Class Workforce', September 24.

The New Statesman (1998), 'Dispatches from a Turbulent Decade', October 16.

The Observer (1998), 'Why I Adore Adorno', March 22.

The Observer (2009) 'Review Section Special Edition on Work' (15 March).

The Sunday Times (2004), 'How Leisure Disappears from our Crowded Hours; Cover Story', December 11.

The Sunday Times (2007), 'Softer Sarko Steals Lead Over Sego', January 21.

Therborn, G. (1986), *Why Some People are More Unemployed than Others* (London: Verso).

Theriault, R. (1995), *How to Tell When You're Tired* (New York: Norton).

Thomas, K. (ed.) (1999), *The Oxford Book of Work* (Oxford: OUP).

Thompson, E. P. (1982[1967]), 'Time, Work–Discipline and Industrial Capitalism', in A. Giddens, and D. Held (eds.) *Classes, Power, and Conflict*, pp. 299–309 (London: Macmillan).

Tichi, C. (1986), 'Introduction', in E. Bellamy, *Looking Backward 2000–1887* (London: Penguin).

Tilgher, A. (1930), *Work: What it has Meant to Men Through the Ages* (New York: Harcourt, Brace and Co.).

Tressell, R. (1967[1914]), *The Ragged Trousered Philanthropists* (London: Panther).

Ure, A. (1967[1835]), *The Philosophy of Manufactures* (New York: Augustus M. Kelly).

U.S. Department of Health, Education and Welfare (1973), *Work in America: Report of a Special Task Force to the Secretary of Health, Education, and Welfare* (London: M.I.T. Press).

Vaki, F. (2002), *Marx and Habermas on the Paradigm of Production: Towards a Re-Interpretation of the Normative Foundations of Critical Theory* (Unpublished Ph.D., University of Essex).

Valente, J. (1985), 'Hall of Mirrors: Baudrillard on Marx', *Diacritics* 15(2):54–65.

Veblen, T. (1915[1899]), *The Theory of the Leisure Class* (New York: Macmillan).

Vivarelli, M. [International Labour Organisation] (no date given) 'Unemployment and the labour market', URL (consulted March 2009): http://actrav.itcilo.org/actrav-english/telearn/global/ilo/art/1b.htm.

Wallerstein, I. (2000[1974]), 'The Rise and Future Demise of the Capitalist World System', in F. J. Lechner and J. Boli (eds.) *The Globalization Reader*, pp. 57–62 (Oxford: Blackwell).

Wallerstein, I. (2004) *World Systems Analysis: An Introduction* (Durham and London: Duke University Press).

Warren, C. (2005), 'Coming Undone: The Implications of Garment Industry Subcontracting for UK Workers' in A. Hale and J. Wills, *Threads of Labour*, pp. 133–161 (London: Blackwell).

Weber, M. (1958[1904–05]), *The Protestant Ethic and the Spirit of Capitalism*, trans. T. Parsons (New York: Scribners).

Wernick, A. (1984), 'Sign and Commodity: Aspects of the Cultural Dynamic of Advanced Capitalism', *Canadian Journal of Political and Social Theory* 8(1–2): 17–35.

Wesley, J. (1877), *A Collection of Hymns for the Use of People Called Methodists* (London: Wesleyan Conference Office).

Wessel, L. P. (Jr.) (1978), 'The Aesthetics of Living Form in Schiller and Marx', *The Journal of Aesthetics and Art Criticism* 37(2): 189–202.

Whipp, R. (1987), '"A Time to Every Purpose": An Essay on Time and Work', in P. Joyce (ed.) *The Historical Meanings of Work*, pp. 210–236 (Cambridge: CUP).

Wilson, S. (2004), *The Struggle Over Work* (London: Routledge).

World Bank (a – no date given), 'Assessing Globalisation: What is Globalisation, Briefing Paper 1', URL (consulted March 2009): http://www1.worldbank.org/economicpolicy/globalization/documents/AssessingGlobalizationP1.pdf.

World Bank (b – no date given), 'Does More International Trade Openness Increase World Poverty?', URL (consulted March 2009): http://www1.worldbank.org/economicpolicy/globalization/documents/AssessingGlobalizationP2.pdf.

World Bank (c – no date given), 'Does More International Trade Openness Increase Inequality?', URL (consulted March 2009): http://www1.worldbank. org/economicpolicy/globalization/documents/AssessingGlobalizationP3.pdf.

Wright, S. (2005), *'Reality Check: Are We Living In An Immaterial World?'*, *Mute*, URL (consulted November 2005): http://www.metamute.org/en/node/5594.

Wright, S. (2002), *Storming Heaven* (London: Pluto Press).

Zerzan, J. (1974), 'Organized Labor Versus "The Revolt Against Work"', URL (consulted November 2006): http://www.insurgentdesire.org.uk/ organisedlabour.htm.

Zerzan. J, and P. Zerzan. (1977), 'Answer to C. Reeve's Article', *Fifth Estate,* URL (consulted June 2007): http://www.geocities.com/CapitolHill/Lobby/2379/ row.htm.

Index